Berlioz, Verdi, Wagner, Britten
Great Shakespeareans
Volume XI

Great Shakespeareans

Each volume in the series provides a critical account and analysis of those figures who have had the greatest influence on the interpretation, understanding and cultural reception of Shakespeare, both nationally and around the world.

General Series Editors:

Peter Holland, University of Notre Dame, USA
Adrian Poole, Trinity College Cambridge, UK

Editorial Advisory Board:

David Bevington (University of Chicago, USA), Michael Cordner (University of York, UK), Michael Dobson (Birkbeck College, University of London, UK), Dominique Goy-Blanquet (University of Picardy, France), Barbara Hodgdon (University of Michigan, USA), Andreas Höfele (University of Munich, Germany), Tetsuo Kishi (Kyoto University, Japan), Russ McDonald (Goldsmith's College, University of London, UK), Ruth Morse (University of Paris 7, Denis Diderot, France), Michael Neill (University of Auckland, New Zealand), Stephen Orgel (Stanford University, USA), Carol Rutter (University of Warwick, UK), Ann Thompson (King's College, University of London, UK) and Paul Yachnin (McGill University, Canada).

Great Shakespeareans: Set I

Volume I: *Dryden, Pope, Johnson, Malone*, edited by Claude Rawson
Volume II: *Garrick, Kemble, Siddons, Kean*, edited by Peter Holland
Volume III: *Voltaire, Goethe, Schlegel, Coleridge*, edited by Roger Paulin
Volume IV: *Hazlitt, Keats, the Lambs*, edited by Adrian Poole

Great Shakespeareans: Set II

Volume V: *Scott, Dickens, Eliot, Hardy*, edited by Adrian Poole
Volume VI: *Macready, Booth, Irving, Terry*, edited by Richard Schoch
Volume VII: *Jameson, Cowden Clarke, Kemble, Cushman*, edited by Gail Marshall
Volume VIII: *James, Melville, Emerson, Berryman*, edited by Peter Rawlings
Volume IX: *Bradley, Greg, Folger*, edited by Cary DiPietro

Great Shakespeareans: Set III

Volume X: *Marx and Freud*, Crystal Bartolovich, Jean Howard and David Hillman
Volume XI: *Berlioz, Verdi, Wagner, Britten*, edited by Daniel Albright
Volume XII: *Joyce, T. S. Eliot, Auden, Beckett*, edited by Adrian Poole
Volume XIII: *Empson, Wilson Knight, Barber, Kott*, edited by Hugh Grady

Great Shakespeareans: Set IV

Volume XIV: *Hugo, Pasternak, Brecht, Césaire*, edited by Ruth Morse
Volume XV: *Poel, Granville Barker, Guthrie, Wanamaker*, edited by Cary Mazer
Volume XVI: *Gielgud, Olivier, Ashcroft, Dench*, edited by Russell Jackson
Volume XVII: *Welles, Kozintsev, Kurosawa, Zeffirelli*, Mark Thornton Burnett, Kathy Howlett, Courtney Lehmann and Ramona Wray
Volume XVIII: *Hall, Brook, Ninagawa, Lepage*, edited by Peter Holland

Berlioz, Verdi, Wagner, Britten

Great Shakespeareans
Volume XI

Edited by
Daniel Albright

continuum

Continuum International Publishing Group

The Tower Building   80 Maiden Lane
11 York Road   Suite 704
London SE1 7NX   New York NY 10038

www.continuumbooks.com

© Daniel Albright and Contributors 2012

British Library Cataloguing-in-Publication Data
A catalogue record for this book is available from the British Library.

ISBN: HB: 978–1–4411–7909–8
      Set: 978–1–4411–6011–9

Library of Congress Cataloging-in-Publication Data
Berlioz, Verdi, Wagner, Britten / edited by Daniel Albright.
    p. cm. – (Great Shakespeareans ; v. 11)
  Includes bibliographical references and index.
  ISBN 978–1–4411–7909–8 (hardcover) – ISBN 978–1–4411–2407–4 (pdf)
1. Shakespeare, William, 1564–1616–Appreciation. 2. Shakespeare, William, 1564–1616–Criticism and interpretation. 3. Music and literature. 4. Berlioz, 1803–1869–Criticism and interpretation. 5. Verdi, Giuseppe, 1813–1901–Criticism and interpretation. 6. Wagner, Richard, 1813–1883–Criticism and interpretation. 7. Britten, Benjamin, 1913–1976–Criticism and interpretation. I. Albright, Daniel, 1945-

  PR2976.B417 2012
  822.3'3–dc23

                2011042157

Typeset by Fakenham Prepress Solutions, Fakenham, Norfolk NR21 8NN
Printed and bound in Great Britain

Contents

Series Editors' Preface

What is a 'Great Shakespearean'? Who are the 'Great Shakespeareans'? This series is designed to explore those figures who have had the greatest influence on the interpretation, understanding and reception of Shakespeare, both nationally and internationally. Charting the effect of Shakespeare on cultures local, national and international is a never-ending task, as we continually modulate and understand differently the ways in which each culture is formed and altered. *Great Shakespeareans* uses as its focus individuals whose own cultural impact has been and continues to be powerful. One of its aims is to widen the sense of who constitute the most important figures in our understanding of Shakespeare's afterlives. The list is therefore not restricted to, say, actors and scholars, as if the performance of and commentary on Shakespeare's works were the only means by which his impact is remade or extended. There are actors aplenty (like Garrick, Irving and Olivier) and scholars too (Bradley, Greg and Empson) but our list deliberately includes as many novelists (Dickens, Melville, Joyce), poets (Keats, Eliot, Berryman), playwrights (Brecht, Beckett, Césaire) and composers (Berlioz, Verdi and Britten), as well as thinkers whose work seems impossible without Shakespeare and whose influence on our world has been profound, like Marx and Freud.

Deciding who to include has been less difficult than deciding who to exclude. We have a long list of individuals for whom we would wish to have found a place but whose inclusion would have meant someone else's exclusion. We took long and hard looks at the volumes as they were shaped by our own and our volume editors' perceptions. We have numerous regrets over some outstanding figures who ended up just outside this project. There will, no doubt, be argument on this score. Some may find our choices too Anglophone, insufficiently global. Others may complain of the lack of contemporary scholars and critics. But this is not a project designed to establish a new canon, nor are our volumes intended to be encyclopedic in scope. The series is not entitled 'The Greatest Shakespeareans' nor is it 'Some Great Shakespeareans', but it will, we hope, be seen as negotiating and occupying a space mid-way along the spectrum of inclusivity and arbitrariness.

Our contributors have been asked to describe the double impact of Shakespeare on their particular figure and of their figure on the understanding, interpretation and appreciation of Shakespeare, as well as providing a sketch of their subject's intellectual and professional biography and an account of the wider context within which her/his work might be understood. This 'context' will vary widely from case to case and, at times, a single 'Great Shakespearean' is asked to stand as a way of grasping a large domain. In the case of Britten, for example, he is the window through which other composers and works in the English musical tradition like Vaughan Williams, Walton and Tippett have a place. So, too, Dryden has been the means for considering the beginnings of critical analysis of the plays as well as of the ways in which Shakespeare's plays influenced Dryden's own practice.

To enable our contributors to achieve what we have asked of them, we have taken the unusual step of enabling them to write at length. Our volumes do not contain brief entries of the kind that a Shakespeare Encyclopedia would include nor the standard article length of academic journals and Shakespeare Companions. With no more than four Great Shakespeareans per volume – and as few as two in the case of volume 10 – our contributors have space to present their figures more substantially and, we trust, more engagingly. Each volume has a brief introduction by the volume editor and a section of further reading. We hope the volumes will appeal to those who already know the accomplishment of a particular Great Shakespearean and to those trying to find a way into seeing how Shakespeare has affected a particular poet as well as how that poet has changed forever our appreciation of Shakespeare. Above all, we hope *Great Shakespeareans* will help our readers to think afresh about what Shakespeare has meant to our cultures, and about how and why, in such differing ways across the globe and across the last four centuries and more, they have changed what his writing has meant.

Peter Holland and Adrian Poole

Notes on Contributors

Daniel Albright is the Ernest Bernbaum Professor of Literature at Harvard University. He has written widely on nineteenth- and twentieth-century literature and music; his chief interest as scholar and teacher lies in comparative arts – the interrelations of music, painting and poetry. Among his books are *Musicking Shakespeare, Music Speaks*; *Modernism and Music: An Anthology of Sources* and *Untwisting the Serpent: Modernism in Music, Literature, and the Visual Arts.*

Peter Bloom has written on Schumann, Wagner and Debussy, but is known primarily for his work on Berlioz. He is author of *The Life of Berlioz* (Cambridge, 1998) and editor of five collections of essays on Berlioz and his era, of which the most recent is *Berlioz: Scenes from the Life and Work* (2008). He is editor of volumes 7 (*Lélio ou Le Retour à la vie*) and 24 (*Grand Traité d'instrumentation et d'orchestration modernes*) of the *New Berlioz Edition* and coeditor of Flammarion's *Dictionnaire Berlioz* (2003). He is a member of the editorial board of the *Critique musicale d'Hector Berlioz* and is currently preparing a new supplementary volume of Berlioz's *Correspondance générale* and, with two French colleagues, a new critical edition of *Les Mémoires d'Hector Berlioz*. Bloom is the Grace Jarcho Ross 1933 Professor of Humanities at Smith College, in Northampton, Massachusetts.

Seth Brodsky is Assistant Professor of Music and the Humanities at the University of Chicago. He has published previously on the music of Wolfgang Rihm, Franz Schubert and Kurt Weill, and focuses in particular on how contemporary composers fantasize and shepherd their affiliations with the musical past, both consciously and unconsciously. He is currently completing a book for University of California Press on the music and writings of Ligeti, Berio, Rihm and Lachenmann entitled *Fail Better: Listening for Utopia in European Composition, 1961–2001*. He has been awarded fellowships from Deutsche Akademische Austausch Dienst and the Paul Sacher Foundation, a substantial grant from the Yale Center for Media and Instructional Innovation, and in 2005–6 was one of the Humboldt Foundation's German Chancellor Scholars.

David Trippett is a Lecturer in Music at Cambridge University, and a Junior Research Fellow at Christ's College. His research on nineteenth- and twentieth-century topics has been published in various journals and books, including *19th-Century Music, Journal of Musicology, Musical Quarterly, Musiktheorie*, and *Cambridge Opera Journal*. Additionally, he has served as editor of *Musiktheorie* and *The Wagner Journal*, and has contributed entries to the Grove Dictionary of American Music and the *Cambridge Wagner Encyclopedia*. Currently he is working on a monograph, *Wagner's Melodies*, for Cambridge University Press, and a translation of Carl Stumpf's *Die Anfänge der Musik* for Oxford University Press. He recently received the Alfred Einstein Award of the American Musicological Society, and remains active as a collaborative pianist.

List of Abbreviations

CG   Hector Berlioz, *Correspondance générale*. Edited by Pierre Citron et al., 8 vols. Paris: Flammarion, 1972–2003.

CM   Hector Berlioz, *Critique musicale*. Edited by H. Robert Cohen, Yves Gérard, Anne Bongrain, Marie-Hélène Coudroy-Saghaï et al., 6 vols [of a projected ten]. Paris: Buchet/Chastel, 1996–2007.

CT   *Cosima Wagner's Diaries*. Edited by Martin Gregor-Dellin and Dietrich Mack, English trans. by Geoffrey Skelton, 2 vols. London: Collins, 1978.

ML   Wagner, *My Life*. Edited by Mary Whitall, trans. by Andrew Gray. Cambridge, New York, Melbourne: Cambridge University Press, 1983.

NBE   *New Berlioz Edition*. Edited by Hugh Macdonald et al., 26 vols. Kassel: Bärenreiter, 1967–2004.

PW   *Richard Wagner's Prose Works*, Eng. trans. William Ashton Ellis. Lincoln, NE, and London: University of Nebraska Press, 1995.

SB   *Richard Wagner: Sämtliche Briefe*, ed. Gertrud Strobel and Werner Wolf (vols. 1–5), Hans-Joachim Bauer and Johannes Forner (vols. 6–8), Klaus Burmeister and Johannes Former (vol. 9), Andreas Mielke (vol. 10), Martin Dürrer (vols. 11–13, 16), and Andreas Mielke (vols. 14–15). Leipzig: Deutscher Verlag für Muski 1967–2000 (vols. 1–9); Wiesbaden, Leipzig and Paris: Breitpkopf & Härtel, 2000–(vols. 10–).

SSD   *Richard Wagner: Sämtliche Schriften und Dichtungen*. Edited by Richard Sternfeld, 16 vols. Leipzig: Breitkopf & Härtel, and C. F. W. Siegel, 1911 [vols. 1–12], 1914 [vols. 13–16].

Note on References to Shakespeare

All references to Shakespeare are to *The Riverside Shakespeare*, general edition
Edited by G. Blakemore Evans, 2nd ed. Boston, MA: Houghton Mifflin, 1997.

Introduction

Daniel Albright

Opera has long had a certain reputation for flamboyant bad taste. And of all the great playwrights, the one who had the strongest reputation for flamboyant bad taste was Shakespeare. For example, the eighteenth-century dramatist Voltaire, a refined ironist and a censor of all vulgarity, considered Shakespeare a sublime genius, but so poor in taste that he had ruined English drama; Voltaire used a scene in *Julius Caesar,* where the cobblers crack jokes while Brutus and Cassius make serious talk, as an example of the way in which Shakespeare's tragedies were only (as he called them) 'monstrous farces'. So you would think that Shakespeare was the perfect dramatist for opera. But composers have not always been comfortable in taking Shakespeare's texts as the bases for libretti: it seems that Shakespeare's flamboyant bad taste somehow differs from opera's flamboyant bad taste.

It is not a hard trick to adapt a number of Shakespeare's plays so thoroughly to the conventions of opera that little Shakespeareanness remains. In Antonio Salieri's *Falstaff* (1799), closely modeled after *The Merry Wives of Windsor,* Falstaff's big boastful aria *Nell' impero di Cupido* is built around the standard military tropes of eighteenth-century music; Falstaff doesn't seem fat or clownish, simply a generic soldier, though a cheerful one. In Ambroise Thomas's *Hamlet* (1868), Hamlet's *To be or not to be* soliloquy is reduced to a terse moment of casual despair, while the Hamlet–Ophelia relationship expands until it nearly engulfs the opera; Ophelia's mad scene is one of the longest and most elaborate in all French opera. (Romantic love is such a crucial matter in opera that Rossini managed to provide a subplot of desperate lovers even in the story of Moses's revolt against Egyptians.) Shakespearean and operatic conventions tend to place the accent on quite different moments of the drama; the awesome strangeness of Shakespeare's patterns and dismemberings of patterns, his figures of speech that tilt the universe of discourse – all may vanish into smooth familiar opera.

But other composers, including those discussed in this volume, try to come to terms as best they can with the specific challenges of adapting Shakespeare into music drama. Instead of resisting the non-operatic aspects of the plays, they try to meet him, to some extent, on his own ground.

For example, Giuseppe Verdi (1813–1901), in *Macbeth* (1847), the first of his three Shakespearean operas, pays almost as little attention to the great soliloquies as Thomas does. 'Tomorrow and tomorrow and tomorrow' becomes just a brief exclamation against fate, despite the fact that an actor can easily read Shakespeare's original speech in the manner of an Italian aria, with a quiet first part like a cavatina (the slow lyrical section of an aria) followed, at the words 'Out, out, brief candle', by a loud emphatic part like a cabaletta (the agitated second section of an aria). But this sort of quasi-aria text didn't strike Verdi or his librettist Francesco Piave as a basis for a genuine aria, perhaps because it is addressed to no one in particular and has no real consequence in any of the characters' actions, including Macbeth's own. On the other hand, the music for the sleepwalking scene, one of the high points of the entire Verdi canon, follows the contours of Shakespeare's scene with extreme precision: Verdi fragments the structure of an operatic *scena* into disconnected spasms, thereby creating a derangement of musical form comparable to the movements of Lady Macbeth's disabled brain. It is not much like the traditional mad scene of Italian opera: in *Lucia di Lammermoor* (1835), Gaetano Donizetti provided quotations of tunes heard earlier in the opera, as the soprano recalls the events that drove her to madness; Verdi, however, provides none. So we see that sometimes Verdi listens to the conventions of opera, other times to Shakespearean dramatic rhythms that can't easily be forced into familiar operatic forms.

Of course, when I speak here of Shakespeare, I mean the Shakespeare that Verdi and the nineteenth century knew – a Shakespeare different from the Shakespeare we know in the twenty-first century. To some extent, I think it is fair to say that the nineteenth-century response to Shakespeare's plays was to conceive them as a heap of opportunities for grand gestures. Shakespeare's language was compelling then, as it has been in every age, but even the language was often conceived less as a text than as a pretext for elocutionary gestures – facial grimaces, movements of hands and legs and torsos. The comparative lack of emphasis on language is suggested by the fact that one of the most potent and widely admired actors was Tommaso Salvini, who performed Shakespeare in Italian. In 1890, Edward Tuckerman Mason wrote an entire book called *The Othello of Tommaso Salvini*, going through the play line by line and describing exactly the bodily carriage, the outthrusts and indraws of limbs, the vocal intonation:

Then he seizes the point of the curved sword with his left hand, grasps the blade, just below the hilt, with his right hand, and, leaning backward as he says 'thus' ('così'), he draws it violently across his throat, sawing backward and forward. His head falls back, as if more than half-severed from his body; he drops the sword and staggers backward (his full front to the audience) toward the alcove, but before he can reach the bed, he falls backward, and dies, in strong convulsions of the body and the legs.[1]

Verdi was equally sensitive to gesture, as we see in a letter he wrote while revising *Macbeth* in 1865, concerning another Italian actor, Adelaide Ristori:

we reach the sleepwalking scene, which is always the high point of the opera. Anyone who has seen Ristori knows that it should be done with only the most sparing gestures, even being limited to just about a single gesture, that of wiping out a bloodstain that she thinks she has on her hand. The movements should be slow, and one should not see her taking steps; her feet should drag over the ground as if she were a statue, or ghost, walking.[2]

To find musical equivalents to such gestures was the task of the nineteenth-century operatic composer who confronted Shakespeare. In Lady Macbeth's mad scene, there is a specific theme that Verdi seems to use as a hand-washing motive.

Indeed the whole notion of motivic thinking-in-music can be understood as a response to gesture. Richard Wagner (1813–83) was the most celebrated deviser of *leitmotif* in the whole history of music, and many of his motifs describe something like muscle contraction: in *Der Ring des Nibelungen* there is a motif always called *spear*, because Wagner can scarcely mention the word 'spear' without making it sound in the orchestra, but it might better be 'smiting', since its straight-downward force irresistibly suggests thrusting; similarly the motif called 'sword' might be better called 'brandishing'. Wagner's motifs are verbs, and gerunds might be better names than nouns.

Wagner's only opera based on Shakespeare was *Das Liebesverbot* (The Ban on Love, 1836), based on *Measure for Measure*. It had only one performance in Wagner's lifetime, and Wagner was happy to let it slip unobtrusively out of his canon. But it contains one moment with an intensity at once Shakespearean and Wagnerian: it occurs in the scene where Friedrich (whom Shakespeare called Angelo) confronts Isabella and offers to stay the execution of her brother if she will have sex with him. Isabella vehemently refuses and threatens to go public with this vile blackmail; but Friedrich tells her that no one will believe her, for all the world knows him as a man of immaculate honor. Here Friedrich sings elatedly as he laughs in her face; Wagner's music is a carol of pure triumph, moving up and down the scale in long strides – it is like some of the music for Wotan, the head god in *Der Ring des Nibelungen*. For a moment, the music says, Friedrich is master of the universe. It is through Shakespeare that the young Wagner found a gesture of compelling authority that would figure strongly in his more mature music. And *Measure for Measure*'s rhythm of chastity versus sexual license would inform some of Wagner's operas, especially *Tannhäuser* and *Parsifal*.

Generally the imitation of Shakespeare led composers to reach for bold effects, amplitude and a certain sprawl – a complete performance of *Das Liebesverbot* is very long. But in the case of Hector Berlioz (1803–69), Shakespeare inspired a fierce concentration of affect, a paring-down to the essential. In his dramatic symphony *Roméo et Juliette* (1839), Berlioz transposed most of the drama into symphony – Romeo and Juliet never sing, for they have the orchestra to do their entwining delight and horror for them. The singing characters are Mercutio, who wraps a veil of fantasy around the musical bodies of the lovers, and Friar Lawrence, who defends them, at the end of the piece, before a frenzied chorus of Montagues and Capulets. The symphony is the Shakespearean part, reaching beyond words into the unspeakable frenzies of emotion, just where Shakespeare's words leave off; but the symphony is embedded in an operatic frame, as Berlioz struggled to reconcile Shakespearean theatre with operatic discourse.

In his last opera, *Béatrice et Bénédict* (1862), Berlioz took *Much Ado about Nothing*, removed the subplot, and, with great economy and speed, drew the outline of the action and emotion – a caprice written with the point of a needle, Berlioz called it. Berlioz hoped to find the Shakespearean quintessence, stripped of all the ornaments and tropes and lovely superfluities, as if he could do Shakespeare better than Shakespeare himself could. Berlioz eliminates the chief buffoon, Dogberry, a constable so extremely considerate that he refuses to arrest thieves on the grounds that those who touch pitch will be defiled by it; Dogberry is also the source of commonplace malapropisms ('Is our whole dissembly appeared?'), not particularly rewarding when translated into French. To replace Dogberry, Berlioz invented a comical semi-competent composer and music-master, the donkeyish Somarone – a grotesque, but in his way a witty grotesque. One of his songs goes as follows:

Le vin de Syracuse
Accuse
Une grande chaleur
Au cœur

De notre île
De Sicile.
Vive ce fameux vin
Si fin!

This is silly verse, but the rhymes are carefully controlled, in the manner of Dr. Seuss. And Somarone is better integrated into Berlioz's work than Dogberry is into Shakespeare's; the musical jokes are a smiling acknowledgement that *Béatrice et Bénédict* is an opera, a smiling glance at the artifice of the whole dramatic contrivance.

The thematic prominence of music glances at other aspects of *Much Ado about Nothing*: for example, Benedick exasperates himself as he tries to write a poem to Beatrice, and concludes he has no skill in the art:

Marry, I cannot show it in rhyme; I have tried. I can find out no rhyme to 'lady' but 'baby', an innocent rhyme; for 'scorn', 'horn', a hard rhyme; for 'school', fool', a babbling rhyme: very ominous endings: no, I was not born under a rhyming planet, nor I cannot woo in festival terms. (5.2.36–41)

As an artist, Somarone is more arrogantly incompetent, but, still, *Béatrice et Bénédict* is an opera about music, just as *Much Ado about Nothing* is a play about poetry.

Though Berlioz eliminates the plot contrivance in which Hero's reputation is destroyed (her maid dresses up in her clothes and makes herself conspicuous during a sexual act), he finds ways of including a bit of its emotional tension. Beatrice famously commands Benedick, 'Kill Claudio' (4.1.289), when Claudio repudiates Hero for being a slut; in Berlioz's opera, no one wants anyone killed, but Somarone's grotesque epithalalium begins 'Mourez, tendres époux' (Die, sweet spouses); in the context of *Much Ado about Nothing*, this feels like a displacement of real hatred into miscarried poetical elation.

Berlioz, Verdi and Wagner all wrote about their intimacy with Shakespeare. Verdi grew angry at those who suggested that he had a poor understanding of Shakespeare; Wagner recorded a dream in which he had met Shakespeare and talked with him in the flesh; Berlioz thought that Shakespeare would have loved Berlioz if Shakespeare had had the luck to meet him. But when we enter the twentieth century, and the responses to Shakespeare by Benjamin Britten (1913–76 – he was born exactly 100 years after Verdi and Wagner), we find something cooler, more objective. Britten certainly enjoyed Shakespeare, and, in addition to the opera *A Midsummer Night's Dream*

(1960), talked for many years with John Gielgud over a possible collaboration on *The Tempest*, and considered writing a *King Lear* opera in the 1960s. But Britten was not an effusive man, and didn't seem to treat Shakespeare with much more reverence than the other poets he set to music.

The whole world of Shakespearean reception was transformed by 1960. Instead of the old focus on emotive gesture, the focus came to be on choreographed movement, something like circus. Britten's Puck is athletic, anticipating Peter Brook's famous 1970 production of the play with acrobats and trapezes. Shakespeare's own stagings ended with dancing: in 1599, one Thomas Platter saw *Julius Caesar* and recorded that, after the play's end, two actors in men's clothing and two in women's clothing danced in a manner, as he put it, 'quite exceedingly finely'. To make the total play a kind of dance seemed to be the mission of certain directors in the twentieth century. In the last scene of *A Midsummer Night's Dream* there is a dance called a *bergomask*, and Britten of course provides music for one; but throughout the opera little dances threaten to break out. It is instructive to compare Britten's treatment of the fairy song 'You spotted snakes with double tongue' with Mendelssohn's: Mendelssohn provided lyrical ravishment, while Britten provides abrupt percussion in kinetically strong rhythms.

The nineteenth century emphasized the passion and self-insistence of the characters in Shakespeare's plays; Britten undoes the whole apparatus of characterization. In the music Lysander is almost indistinguishable from Demetrius: the lovers are caught so tightly in an orchestral–vocal web that they can scarcely extricate themselves for a moment. At first the fairies, with their high celestial music, seem to enter the opera in a manner utterly distinct from the entry of the mechanicals, with their low brass; but Britten amuses himself by writing their same music for both, although at opposite ends of orchestral registration. Britten's opera is not about individual characters, but about symmetries that keep dissolving and reforming.

Each essay in this volume has a different approach. Peter Bloom offers a full, detailed and, I think, moving historical account of Berlioz's lifelong engagement with Shakespeare, sometimes a love affair, sometimes a fencing match. David Trippett offers the intellectual context for Wagner's admiration for Shakespeare, a context informed by Dr. Trippett's remarkable knowledge of German music and speculative discourse. Seth Brodsky is a post-structuralist musicologist, and delights in parsing the constructs and deconstructs of Britten's dramatic practice. In my piece on Verdi, I try to suggest the evolution of Verdi's responses to Shakespeare, and to trace the aesthetic that lies behind Verdi's practice.

Give us your hand if we be friends.

Chapter 1

Berlioz

Peter Bloom

Avec son Roméo quand Juliette expire
Évitez Letourneur et son français banal,
Avec Berlioz seul vous comprendrez Shakespeare
Le traducteur est grand comme l'original.

— Joseph Méry[1]

Prologue

Music lovers know Berlioz as the composer of the *Symphonie fantastique*. Shakespeareans among them, if one *Shakespeare Companion* may stand for many, know also that he 'wrote an overture to *King Lear*, and the dramatic symphony *Roméo et Juliette*'.[2] But there is more, much more, because the plays inspired the French artist from the first to the last of his hours upon the stage. As the outstanding composer–critic of his generation, Berlioz found in Shakespeare an immense wealth of invention, an immeasurable fount of wisdom, and surprisingly, for it is here that he exceeds his contemporaries, a privy councilor, a poetic confidant, a kindred spirit, a *dieu personnel*. Of all the great composers – rank them as you wish – none was more smitten by Shakespeare than Berlioz.[3]

In the *Mémoires* he completed in the mid–1860s, a mosaic of writings old and new, Berlioz brings the story of his life to a close with a melancholy account of late love: Estelle Fornier *née* Dubœuf, his final enchantment, had also been his first. 'She loves me not, it is true,' he writes, 'and why would she? But she might have forever remained oblivious of me, and now she is at least aware that I adore her. I must resign myself to the fact that she came to know me too late, just as I must resign myself to not having known Virgil, whom I should have loved, or Gluck, or Beethoven … or Shakespeare … who might have loved *me*.'[4]

Why, in these ultimately disconsolate reflections, does Berlioz single out Shakespeare –'qui m'eût aimé peut-être' – with the almost heart-breaking reserve of the pluperfect subjective? Virgil (Berlioz worked out the Latin during his schooldays in La Côte-Saint-André) would motivate his youthful reveries and his mature French grand opera. Gluck (Berlioz initially read about him in Michaud's *Biographie universelle*) would awaken the provincial boy to the art of music itself. Beethoven (Berlioz heard the works performed after arriving in Paris in 1821) would reveal to him the dramatic intensity of the symphony, and of what he would call the *genre instrumental expressif*.[5] But Shakespeare, whose work on the stage he first encountered in 1827, would become and remain the veritable 'interpreter' of his life.[6]

Berlioz makes explicit announcement of this fact by framing the *Mémoires* with the quintessential expression of despair and disillusionment, 'Life's but a walking shadow.' On a separate page, after the inside title and before the *Préface*, we read: 'La vie n'est qu'une ombre qui passe; un pauvre comédien qui, pendant son heure, se pavane et s'agite sur le théâtre, et qu'après on n'entend plus; c'est un conte récité par un idiot, plein de fracas et de furie, et qui n'a aucun sens.'[7] And on a supplementary sheet – after the table of contents – the legendary quotation in the original language. Here, an error – 'a tale / Told by an idiot, foul [*sic*] of sound and fury' – reminds us of two salient realities: that Berlioz invariably cites from memory, and that he hears English as sound as much as sense.[8] Enclosing the *Mémoires* in the bookends of the same Shakespearean verse – taken by his longtime friend the deeply religious Princess Carolyn von Sayn-Wittgenstein as an announcement of his atheism, and possibly intended as such – echoes the rounded form of the autobiographical narrative as a whole, encircled by the alpha and omega of his love for Estelle.[9]

In 1864, Berlioz wrote to Jean-Jacques Humbert Ferrand, his oldest and dearest friend, with whom he had shared passions for literature and music since the early 1820s, of his still vibrant feelings for the very heroes I have mentioned: Virgil ('who must have been gentle, welcoming, and affable'), Gluck ('superb'), Beethoven ('intolerant and brutal, yet gifted with remarkable sensitivity'), and Shakespeare – 'grandly indifferent, as glacial as a reflective mirror', but a man who must 'have had for everything an immense compassion'.[10] Shakespeare would have 'loved' Berlioz, if I understand what the composer meant by that formulation, because the poet would quite simply have recognized and appreciated the conspicuous uniqueness of the French artist's readings and renderings of his work.

Evidence abounds for the study of Berlioz and Shakespeare, but it is treacherous, for much of it comes from *Mémoires* that, whatever else it may do, paints a premeditated portrait of the artist as he wished to be seen: in the ecstasy of victory and the agony of defeat. In the book, we see the youthful spectator and the elderly master ever delighted by the discovery and rediscovery of the plays. In private correspondence we find the same sentiment. We also find the older reader excited by a critical study of 'De l'amitié des femmes dans Shakespeare', for example, confirming that his appreciation, deepened by a complexity of reflection sometimes absent in the young, grew from the performative to the literary.[11] In the effort to trace that growth, I shall proceed in this essay in a way that is loosely chronological. I shall treat, first, the impact of Shakespeare upon Berlioz's biography as a struggling artist in what Jacques Barzun distinctively called the 'Romantic Century' in France, considering his simultaneous fascination with Shakespeare and infatuation with the Anglo–Irish actress Harriet Smithson; his citations and readings of the plays in letters, articles, and stories; and his activities as a public Shakespearean devoted to the cause of the Bard.[12] Then, after a brief second section that treats the question of Berlioz in English and Shakespeare in French, I shall consider in a third the Shakespearean aspects of Berlioz's musical compositions, from the fledgling *Huit Scènes de Faust*, with their various epigraphs from *Hamlet* and *Romeo and Juliet*, to his two final masterpieces, *Les Troyens*, the French grand opera he baptized 'Virgil Shakespeareanized,' and *Béatrice et Bénédict*, the opéra comique he drew from *Much Ado About Nothing*.

Shakespeare in Berlioz's Words

When Berlioz was inducted into the Académie des Beaux-Arts, the disrespectful critic of the respected *Revue des deux mondes* expressed disappointment: 'We shall not repeat here Figaro's well-known phrase: "A musician was needed, a journalist was chosen."'[13] In fact, the person chosen in June 1856 to occupy the seat in that exalted confraternity lately held by the composer Adolphe Adam was indeed a journalist, a fine one, albeit one whose estimation of his talents was moderate: 'I do not know if the Academy wishes to acknowledge the worth of my work as music critic published in the *Journal des débats* and elsewhere,' Berlioz wrote in an earlier letter of candidacy, 'but I do believe that in performing these dangerous duties I have demonstrated a genuine and devout love of art.'[14] At that moment, Berlioz was the author of over 700 critical articles, of a treatise on orchestration celebrated more for its poetic accounts of the expressive possibilities of the instruments and their combinations than for its technical descriptions of their attributes, of two volumes of travel writings, of five short stories later included in what has been called his 'comic masterpiece,' *Les Soirées de l'orchestre,* and of the draft of an autobiography that has been favourably compared to the *Confessions* of Rousseau and the *Mémoires d'outre-tombe* of Chateaubriand.[15] He was furthermore the author of the libretto of a 'mélologue' or 'monologue', *Le Retour à la vie,* of a good deal of the text of the *Damnation de Faust,* and of what would soon be the completed 'poem', as librettos were called, of *Les Troyens.*[16] In retrospect, a place at the Institut de France – whose members occupied the equivalent of chaired professorships in a great university, and whose academies were designed to inventory the state of mankind's general knowledge – was fitting and proper for a man whose devotion to art was both visceral and intellectual, and whose education was filled with reading and writing both notes and words.

Berlioz's introduction to Shakespeare

It is fair to say, most modern scholars agree, that Berlioz's account of his life is essentially truthful and correct. The *Mémoires,* the autobiographical articles, and even the letters – public and private – are nonetheless *composed.* They are designful reductions of complex psychological realities in necessarily concentrated prose. When you see Berlioz's script, his elegant and confident characters, you understand the word 'designful': his writing seems literally to etch life into the facts. Nothing is more apparently factual than Berlioz's description in Chapter XVIII, set down ex post facto, in 1848, titled 'Apparition de Shakespeare. Miss Smithson. Mortel amour.'

> I come now to the supreme drama of my life. I shall in no way recount all its sad vicissitudes. I will say only this: an English company came to Paris to give performances of the plays of Shakespeare, at that time quite unknown to the French public. I attended the première of *Hamlet* at the Odéon. In the role of Ophelia I saw Harriet Smithson, who five years later became my wife. The impression made on my heart and mind by her extraordinary talent, nay by her dramatic genius, was equaled only by the havoc wrought in me by the poet she so nobly interpreted. That is all I can say.[17]

Berlioz, who should have said 'six years later' rather than 'five' – when it comes to figures we must always check his homework – goes on to describe the havoc: days if not weeks of suffering, rootlessness and insomnia. He slept twice in the fields in the country, he tells us, once in the frozen snow on the banks of the Seine, and once on a table at the café du Cardinal, at the intersection of the boulevard des Italiens and the rue de Richelieu (it is still there), 'where I dozed for five hours, to the great horror of the waiters, who dared not come near me, fearing that I was dead'.

The final detail reminds us that even recounting a quasi-religious awakening, Berlioz can never resist a sardonic smile. But the emotional truth of the account of his dual fixation upon the Bard and his bewitching interpreter is confirmed by a letter contemporary with the event. To Ferdinand Laforest, a friend from the years that Berlioz spent in medical school (1821–4) before rejecting his father's profession and turning by *esprit de contradiction* to music, Berlioz said, 'I hope you never come to know the intolerable agony I have suffered since your departure.' Laforest must have gone off in mid-September 1827. Berlioz's letter, dated 13 October 1827, continues: 'You left Paris just as the explosion was going to occur. I will tell you all about it when you return. For the time being I am simply incapable of describing the events of my sad novel. I have only been able to write since a few days ago. It was certainly not my wish that you ever see me again.'[18]

This letter, which came to light only in the 1980s, is the first we have in which Berlioz alludes, without explanation, to the 'explosion' he experienced on seeing Miss Smithson as Ophelia and Juliet in September of 1827. To Ferrand, he was equally enigmatic. Writing on 29 November 1827, in the wake of the successful performance one week earlier of his own *Messe solennelle*, he said:

> For three months now [it had been just over two] I have been afflicted with incessant and unremitting despair; my abhorrence of this life has gone as far as it can possibly go. Even my recent success has not for a second lifted the heavy burden of grief that weighs upon me, and that now presses even more heavily than before. I cannot give you the key to the enigma; it would take too long. Furthermore, I don't think I could even form the letters to write to you about it. When I see you, I will tell you everything. I close with the words that the ghost of the King of Denmark speaks to his son Hamlet: '*Ferwel ferwel remember my* [*sic*].'[19]

If Daniel Egerton, the English actor who played the Ghost, spoke the words printed in the 1827 edition of the play ('from the acting copy'), he said: 'Adieu, adieu, adieu! Remember me.'[20] Berlioz may be excused for his eccentric recollection, as 'remember' occurs in the play more than a dozen times. Like 'foul' and 'fool', 'ferwel' and 'my' are the Frenchman's phonetic renderings – of little consequence in an age when spelling itself was far from uniform. We may be certain, however, that this is the *first time* in his preserved correspondence that Berlioz quotes from Shakespeare. 'Farewell, remember me', or some version of those words, will find itself frequently in Berlioz's subsequent writings.[21] In 1859, when he fancied himself in love with the renowned contralto Pauline Viardot, he used the quotation suggestively: 'Adieu, adieu, *remember me*', he more accurately wrote, adding, 'Paroles de *Ghost* d'un être qui n'est que trop *body*: H. Berlioz'.[22] He cites the words again, in English, in 1863, to Edward Jerome Hopkins, 'Farewell, farewell, remember me', adding: 'les dernières paroles du *Gost* [*sic*] d'*Hamlet*.'[23]

Surely, in the section of Chapter XVIII of the *Mémoires* quoted above, Berlioz exaggerates the French public's ignorance of the plays. François Guizot's 13-volume revision of Le Tourneur had been available since 1821, and Berlioz (who, by 'Le Tourneur,' presumably meant the Guizot revision) was not alone to explore it.[24] A modicum of public awareness of Shakespeare would have been a sine qua non of the phenomenal success of the English company in Paris in 1827. Still, hearing the works in the original language was for some newly electrifying. Berlioz's own stunning reaction is that of born-again believer: an apostle of the religion of art who has unexpectedly rediscovered God.

It was on 11 September 1827 that William Abbot's English company, with Charles Kemble as Hamlet and Harriet Smithson as Ophelia, offered their reading of Shakespeare's great tragedy. The scene at the première is carefully and sympathetically described by David Cairns, in the chapter of his definitive biography of Berlioz appropriately entitled 'Epiphany at the Odéon': 'The effect of Shakespeare was intoxicating. It was an earthquake that burst the prison gates and set them free.'[25] Let it be said at the outset that what most moved the enlightened spirits to whom Cairns refers – Alexandre Dumas, Alfred de Vigny, Théophile Gautier, Émile Deschamps, Charles-Augustin Sainte-Beuve, Étienne Delécluze, Eugène Delacroix and especially Victor Hugo, whose *Préface de Cromwell* (October 1827),[26] the defining literary manifesto of the age, literally deifies the Shakespearean fusion of the sublime and the grotesque – was Shakespeare not on the page but indeed *on the stage*. In Restoration Paris, in the relative intimacy of the Odéon, whose 1,600 seats were approximately half as many as those of London's theatrical spaces at Drury Lane and Covent Garden, and in the eyes and ears of an unusually attentive French audience, it was the English players' voices and intonations, and especially their movements and gestures – all more physical and free than the artificial stillness of both the Garrick generation and the longstanding French tradition – that fuelled the war against Corneille and Racine.[27] The young romantics reacted to the *performance*, and would have said 'the play's the thing'!

'What is most remarkable', wrote Delécluze of Harriet Smithson's Ophelia, 'is her pantomime: she assumes fantastic postures and employs pungent vocal inflections while remaining entirely natural.'[28] Smithson's language may have sounded ill-bred to certain English aristocrats in Paris – over 14,000 English persons lived there at the time[29] – but to Berlioz, and to the French, it was incantatory. Indeed, it was Harriet's *voice* that Jules Janin so well remembered: 'In that pure, sonorous, and golden voice, the prose and poetry of Shakespeare resonated with triumph, adoration, and eternal vitality. A whole world attended closely to the grace, to the voice, and to the enchantment of that woman.'[30]

The role of Ophelia requires an actress who can sing. Janin's comments, like those of a reviewer for the *Gazette de France* – 'The softness of her words, the tentative modulations of her songs, everything made of this scene a perfect whole'[31] – suggest that Smithson managed the music with aplomb. Charles Moreau said 'she sings without being aware that she is singing'.[32] Berlioz tells us more: mocking the custom of having a professional singer appear downstage to deliver the songs with Italianate roulades, he admits that Smithson 'is not a singer' but admires the novelty of her interpretation: 'she interrupted her sad song with a completely unexpected pantomime; then, kneeling before the black shawl fallen from her head, believing she was weeping upon her father's shroud, she let out sobs more heartbreaking than any conceivable human language or any conceivable action of the art of music itself, and left the stage with the audience trembling, weeping, and applauding (because, unfortunately, in such circumstances there are always some poor devils who find the strength to applaud)'.[33]

Berlioz returned to the Odéon for *Romeo and Juliet* on 15 September. He makes no mention of seeing *Othello* on 18 September,[34] but years later he remembered seeing Harriet enter the theatre for a rehearsal of that play. It is nonetheless one of the oddities of his biography that Berlioz should have seen at the time only *Hamlet* and *Romeo and Juliet*, when, during the three seasons they gave in Paris in 1827–9, the Théâtre-Anglais offered 37 Shakespeare performances. Indeed, never again would Paris experience this sort of *Shakespeare-manie* on the stage. Readers would continue to revel in the plays, but when Shakespeare's principles of *contrastes et oppositions* became embodied in *French* romantic drama, the number of Shakespeare's fans fell off. This is the reason that Harriet Smithson's career went into decline, as Berlioz sensed as early as October 1830, when he actually encountered her close up. She had returned to Paris in March of that year to take the role of Cécilia de Montalban, the English wife of a Frenchman, in an opéra comique by Carafa and Hérold called *L'Auberge d'Auray*. In October (when Harriet's English accent had lately been lampooned), Berlioz reported to Ferrand that he was thinking of 'unhappy Ophelia': 'Oh, how miserable she is! Because of the bankruptcy of the Opéra-Comique, she has lost more than six thousand francs. She is still here; I happened upon her a few days ago; she greeted me with utmost sang-froid.'[35]

Harriet herself, whom Berlioz ultimately married in October 1833, would warn the composer that he might be in love more with the idea of her as a Shakespearean heroine than with the woman she was, just as his father would warn him that that he would hurt her and leave her for another. Both were right.[36] Performing rarely after her marriage, Harriet did appear at the Hôtel Castellane, in March 1836, in the fourth act of *Hamlet*. 'Never was the great tragédienne more nobly inspired', wrote a reviewer for *La Quotidienne*.[37] And yet, after another performance of the mad scene, at the Théâtre des Variétés, on 15 December 1836, Harriet simply vanished from the stage. It would not be long before the matrimonial love she may have enjoyed would likewise fade into thin air.

But the composer would never forget the force of her inspiration. On 6 March 1854, two days after her death, Berlioz wrote of Harriet to his sister: 'she taught me to understand Shakespeare and the lofty dramatic art'.[38] On 4 April 1854, speaking of her death to his uncle Félix Marmion, Berlioz said the same thing: 'She had furthermore revealed Shakespeare to me, and God only knows the impact that that revelation had and still has upon my career. It is incalculable; it is infinite.'[39] And in the last chapter of the *Mémoires*: 'Shakespeare! Where is he? Where are you?' Shakespeare alone, writes the composer of his union with Harriet, could have understood and taken pity upon us: 'two poor artists in love yet tearing each other apart'.

Berlioz's quotation from Shakespeare

It is a not unremarkable fact that Berlioz early on developed the habit of frequent quotation from the works of the English playwright. His writings are laced with citations from the *Aeneid*, in Latin, and from the classic dramatists and poets, notably La Fontaine, in French. But Shakespeare, in both English and French, figures everywhere, something that establishes the composer as an exceptional contributor to the unfolding internationalization and canonization of the poet and his work – for it must be remembered that Berlioz and his cohort did not hold that prior belief in his greatness that colours our own early experience. Many of the lines that Berlioz quotes do seem familiar, of course, and lead us at least to wonder if they come from gatherings of 'famous quotations'. In France there were not as many such gatherings as you might imagine, but there were some. One that Berlioz might have come upon is *Shakespeare proverbs; or, The wise saws of our wisest poet collected into a modern instance,* published in London by Chapman and Hall in 1848, because Mary Cowden Clarke, the compiler, was personally known to him: Mrs Clarke, the daughter of the music publisher Vincent Novello, was an eminent *shakespearienne,* and the English translator, in the 1850s, of Berlioz's treatise on orchestration. Earlier, Berlioz might have come upon one of the illustrated *Galéries de Shakespeare,* such as those published in the 1820s by Audot, with engravings of central scenes accompanied by lengthy excerpts from the plays (in the Guizot translation).[40] Another item he might have seen is *Pensées de Shakspeare* [*sic*], *suivies de quelques scènes de ses tragédies,* published in Paris by the Librairie nationale et étrangère in 1822; the translator was Charles Nodier, librarian at the Arsenal and host there of a celebrated literary salon.[41] In 1839, *The Beauties of Shakspeare,* William Dodd's often reissued selection of quotable passages (in English) went on sale in at least six Parisian bookstores.[42]

Despite *our* familiarity with his quotations from Shakespeare, however, Berlioz's lifelong abhorrence of *arrangements* suggests that books of selections and aphorisms were not his cup of tea. In these *Pensées* and *Beauties,* citations can appear without identification. Berlioz always tells us who is speaking – proof, if proof were needed, that his assimilation of the plays was real. 'To read Shakespeare all the way to the end, without skipping a line', wrote one of his literary heroes, 'is to carry out a pious but painful duty in search of glory and death'. Berlioz might have appreciated Chateaubriand's *bon mot,* but would not have found it funny.[43]

In what follows, in what has had to be something of a catalogue, I record a number of Berlioz's favourite quotations, which reveal him as a close reader of an astounding number of plays. Most come from the one he loved the most: not *Romeo and Juliet,* from which he would draw his greatest symphony, but *Hamlet,* with whose title character he – like everyone from Goethe to Joyce – so obviously identified. I employ the traditional Shakespearean categories rather than a strictly Berliozian timeline because we know often but not always when he first encountered a play that would have an impact on his musical and literary work, or a play to which he would make only passing reference.

The Tragedies

Hamlet

How often did Berlioz see *Hamlet* on the stage? In a letter of 30 November 1844 he says that he has not attended a performance of the play for 14 years.[44] I presume he refers to the performances of 1827–8, 16 years in the past. Three years later, during a concert tour that took him to Riga in May 1847, he wrote to a friend: 'You will be amazed to know that I saw *Hamlet* there, the *real Hamlet* by Shakespeare, surprisingly well acted by an actor named Baumestier whom I had never heard of. As always, I was bowled over by this Shakespearean miracle … .'[45] 'As always' suggests having seen the play on a number of occasions, but correspondence shows that the number was not large. He would see the play again in London, in 1848, in a version likewise notable for its fidelity: 'They deigned on this occasion to give us *Hamlet* as written, almost complete, something very rare in this country, where you find so many people superior to Shakespeare, most of whose plays are corrected and perfected by the likes of Cibber, Dryden, and other clowns who merit a public spanking.'[46]

What *Hamlet* did Berlioz own? I assume that he purchased the separate pocket-sized texts that went on sale in 1827, although Berlioz's letter to Ferrand of 10 October 1832, in which he invites his friend to visit him at home in La Côte-Saint-André, gives pause: 'Bring along with you the volume with *Hamlet* and also the volume with *Othello* and *King Lear* […]; all of that will come in handy.' Perhaps the friends would read aloud from the plays, each with his own copy in hand. Still, purchasing books in the 1830s was not common for those of limited income, lending libraries did not exist and *cabinets de lecture*, which did, may not have stocked Shakespeare. As we shall see, Berlioz was first given a copy of the complete works in 1835.

On 21 August 1829, writing to Ferrand of the recurrence of his anguish over Harriet Smithson, his sets down in English Hamlet's 'the new pangs of my despised love' (3.1.71). 'New' does not appear in the 'to be or not to be' soliloquy, which he cites, and 'despised' rather than 'disprized' indicates that the English he knew was based on the Second Quarto, which prefers 'despiz'd' to the First Folio's now more commonly adopted 'dispriz'd'. He cites the passage in his 1829 biography of Beethoven – the first mention of Shakespeare in his published writings – when suggesting that in order fully to appreciate a work as astonishing as the C-sharp minor Quartet, Op. 131, which flummoxed early hearers, one must know the 'fléaux' – calamities – enumerated by Hamlet, whom he quotes:

The oppressor's wrong, the proud man's contumely,
The pangs of despised love, the laws of delay,
The insolence of office, and the spurns
That patient merit of the unworthy takes.[47]

One wonders why he omits 'the whips and scorns of time'. Did Berlioz take 'time' to mean 'the present', as the Shakespeareans suggest? The Guizot translation has 'les flagellations et les humiliations du présent'. This, we may presume, is what Berlioz understood.

I have mentioned Berlioz's fondness for the final line of the Ghost, 'Farewell, Remember me' (the Second Quarto has 'Adieu, adieu, adieu! remember me' (1.5.91)). In 1839, exasperated by having to write yet another feuilleton – he had been an active music critic for some five years and would continue for 25 more – he cites Marcellus's comment after the ghost's disappearance, and does so in the correct English: 'Tis gone, and will not answer' (1.1.52).[48]

In Rome, in November 1831, as winner of the prize in composition offered by the Académie des Beaux-Arts, Berlioz spent time with Felix Mendelssohn, whom he much admired. In a letter of 3 December 1831, he expresses that admiration via quotation, even giving his source: ' "C'est un homme et véritablement digne de ce nom" (*Hamlet*, Shakespeare acte 1er.)'[49] – Hamlet's ''A was a man, take him for all in all, / I shall not look upon his like again' (1.2.187–8). Elsewhere, speaking of Carl Maria von Weber, Berlioz quotes the lines in both French and in English: '[...] c'était *un homme* (*He was a man, we shall not look upon his like again*) et que nous ne reverrons pas son pareil!'[50] Paraphrase, rather than quotation, is often the more appropriate term. On 22 June 1834, dwelling on so many poor musical performances at the court of Louis-Philippe, for example, he regrets not being able simply to cry out, with Hamlet, 'Des flûtes! holà! qu'on m'envoie des flûtes!' – his recollection of Hamlet's line in the scene with the players, 'Ah, ha! Come, some music! Come the recorders!' (3.2.291–2).[51] Guizot renders the line as: 'Ah! ah! – Allons, un peu de musique! les flageolets!' – which may have resonated with Berlioz because as a boy he played not the recorder (the flûte à bec) but the flageolet, from which he graduated to the transverse flute, becoming, if not a virtuoso, a perfectly competent player.

The scenes with the players (2.2 and 3.2) particularly inspired Berlioz when he revised the sequel to the *Symphonie fantastique*. In a review of a miserable performance of one of the operas he treasured the most, Spontini's *La Vestale*, Berlioz writes that after a few minutes of painful concentration, he was forced to say, with Hamlet, 'ceci est de l'absinthe.'[52] In the midst of 'The Murder of Gonzago', when the Player Queen speaks the line on the horror of remarriage, 'none wed the second but who killed the first', Hamlet recites, aside, 'That's wormwood!' (3.2.180–1). The Guizot translation, apparently based on the First Folio's repetition of the word, has: 'Voilà l'absinthe! voilà l'absinthe!' The Laroche translation, presumably based on the Second Quarto, has the single 'Voilà de l'absinthe.' The expression, which we find again in a letter of 1 December 1865, remained with Berlioz throughout his life.[53]

In June 1843, waiting for the popular librettist Eugène Scribe to complete the text of the opera *La Nonne sanglante*, eventually set not by him but by Gounod, Berlioz suggests in a letter that he might in the meantime bring to fruition something of smaller dimension. He thus quotes Hamlet's reply to Rosencrantz, who asserts that with the support of the King, the Prince will succeed to the throne of Denmark: 'pendant que l'herbe pousse pousse le cheval' – 'while the grass grows', to translate literally, 'so, too, does the steed'.[54] In fact the line reads: 'Ay, sir, but, "While the grass grows – " The proverb is something musty' (3.2.343–4). Hamlet does *not* cite the entire proverb – which is, of course, 'While the grass grows, the steed starves.' Berlioz's citation (I copy the English from the 1827 publication) fits the context of his letter, but turns on its head the sense of the proverb that Hamlet intends.

In his feuilleton of 28 September 1849, Berlioz again seems to rely on this scene, now in order to criticize the indifference of the audience. 'You cite an aphorism of the greatest of poets', he has his narrator say, 'and you repeat with him that "it is better to merit the approbation of a single man of good taste" than it is to solicit by means unworthy of art "the applause of an auditorium filled with common spectators." '[55] It is likely that the 'aphorism' comes from the second scene with the players: 'Now this overdone, or come tardy off, though it make the unskillful laugh, cannot but make the judicious grieve; the censure of the which one must in your allowance o'erweigh a whole theatre of others' (3.2.24–8).[56] The theme is as old as Boileau – 'Craignez-vous pour vos vers la censure publique? / Soyez-vous à vous-même un sévère critique' – whom Berlioz, like all schoolboys of his era, both read and remembered.[57]

This scene with the players was on Berlioz's mind again on 28 April 1859, when he wrote to Ferrand about a passage in *Les Troyens*, recently completed, where the forsaken Didon announces to her people that she will perish ('Je vais mourir'): 'Shakespeare has said it', writes Berlioz (in French), fearing a poor performance of the Queen's final monologue:

'Nothing is more atrocious than passion torn to rags and tatters.'[58] The words paraphrase Hamlet's 'Speak the speech' speech, on the dangers of overacting: 'O, it offends me to the soul to hear a robustious periwig-pated fellow tear a passion to tatters, to very rags...' (3.2.8–10).

One of Berlioz's eternal themes as a critic is the mediocrity of the public's artistic awareness, formalized in the memorable note – 'Le public n'a point d'imagination' – that he affixed to the most daring moment of his most daring composition, the 'tomb scene' of the dramatic symphony *Roméo et Juliette* (which we shall examine below). A by no means uncritical friend of Gounod's, Berlioz had to admire the elegant aria from *Faust*, 'Salut, demeure chaste et pure', to which the reaction of the audience at the première had been only lukewarm. 'De la confiture aux cochons' is what most Frenchmen would have written; 'Caviar to the general' is what Berlioz set down in the review he published on 26 March 1859. A few years later, writing about the nature of beauty itself, he said to his son that one must always remember the words of Hamlet, which he cites in English and in French: 'It is caviar to the general (C'est du caviar pour la foule).'[59]

Berlioz's quotations derive from scenes well beyond those already mentioned. In October 1840, hearing the rumblings of war between England (an ally, with Prussia and Russia, of the Turks) and France (an ally of Egypt, then trying to free itself from Ottoman authority), the composer – whose alertness to political affairs has been underplayed by the commentariat – pointed hopefully to the strength of art as impervious to the threat of violence: 'It is also the case that art is immortal, that art is king, and that for art as for kings, as Shakespeare said [quoting now in English]: "There's such divinity doth hedge a king, / That treason can but peep to what it would, / Acts little of his will"' (4.5.124–6).[60] As an invocation of inviolate authority, these lines, ironically spoken by a usurper, are hardly transparent, but Act 4 of *Hamlet* was the scene of Harriet's greatest triumph and Berlioz would have had time to contemplate the text. Did he fully fathom the meaning of such words as 'hedge' and 'peep' in Claudius's magisterial pronouncement? Guizot's version – 'il y a une magie divine qui entoure les rois d'une telle haie, que la trahison peut à peine regarder à la dérobée ce qu'elle voudrait et met en action peu de sa volonté!' – is more straightforward. I would not be surprised if, to grasp Shakespeare's sense, Berlioz peeped through the hedge of a translation. In 1854, when the English writer James William Davison became irritated by Berlioz's criticism of one of Sophie Cruvelli's performances at the Opéra (Davison was the diva's admirer), Berlioz apologized to his friend – one of the few individuals with whom he used the 'tu' form of address – by asking that he kindly recall the passage where Hamlet tells Laertes that he intended no harm: 'Supposez qu'en décochant une flèche par-dessus le toit d'une maison j'aie blessé mon frère par hasard'[61] – a free translation of Hamlet's 'That I have shot my arrow o'er the house / And hurt my brother' (5.2.243–4).

If Berlioz used quotation from *Hamlet* to lend weight to the matter at hand, he also did so to underline a smirk. On 30 July 1837, mentioning in his column the cancellation of a performance at the Louvre by the Société des Concerts du Conservatoire, the leading orchestra of the capital, and the cancellation of the performance of his own *Requiem* at the Invalides, Berlioz chides the government for its parsimony, quoting from *Hamlet* (in English): 'Thrift! Thrift! Horatio!' (1.2.179) – Hamlet's equally ironic condemnation of his mother's hasty and miserly marriage to her husband's brother. When he is bitter, he evokes Polonius. After Pauline Viardot's great success as Orphée at the Théâtre-Lyrique, in Berlioz's version of Gluck's *Orphée*, the composer wrote to his son: 'The Polonius-types (you have seen in my column that I use the name of this character in *Hamlet* to designate all of those heartless boors and vulgar creatures who understand nothing of what is sublime), the Polonius-types, I say, are now all practically furious.'[62] When he is droll, he evokes Yorick. On 12 September 1861, in the second part of an open letter to the members of the Académie des Beaux-Arts, Berlioz comments on the irony of performing excerpts from his *Requiem* before the pleasure-seeking public at Baden-Baden: 'It was precisely this antithesis that seduced me when drawing up the programme. It seemed to me to be the musical realization of what Hamlet had in mind when holding Yorick's skull: "Allez maintenant dans le boudoir d'une belle dame, dites-lui que, quand elle se mettrait un pouce de fard sur le visage, il faudra qu'elle en vienne à faire cette figure-là. Faites-la rire à cette idée" '[63] – Berlioz's version of 'Now get you to my lady's chamber, and tell her, let her paint an inch thick, to this favour she must come; make her laugh at that' (5.1.192–5).

When he is morose, he evokes Hamlet. To the Princess Wittgenstein, on 2 December 1859, in response to her urging that he do an opera on *Cleopatra*, Berlioz writes: 'Yes, I will do a *Cléopâtre* if I find the time. But you know the words of Hamlet [quoting now in English]: "Had I but time ... death is strict in his arrest" ' (5.2.336–7).[64] In another letter to the Princess, of 30 August 1864, he becomes similarly morbid, citing in English Hamlet's earlier words (again with exactitude): 'O God! O God! / How weary, stale, flat, and unprofitable / Seem to me all the uses of this world' (1.2.132–4).[65]

Hamlet's last words (5.2.357) were for Berlioz something of a mantra. Of the final bars of the slow movement of Beethoven's Seventh Symphony, for example, which he, like so many others, calls Adagio rather than Allegretto, he writes, thinking of the inconclusive second inversion triad at the close: 'et ... le reste est silence'.[66]

'To be or not to be' was already celebrated in 1765, when Samuel Johnson published his great edition of Shakespeare, and it would not be long before it became the most quoted and the most parodied utterance in the English language. In 1861, Berlioz, himself already a parodied parodist, devoted most of a review of a little opéra comique, *Le Jardinier gallant*, by one Ferdinand Poise, to a paraphrase of his own.[67] The composer's 'to be', much indebted to the translation by Benjamin Laroche, is extensive, detailed and too amusing to be excluded here. It appears in Appendix I with a translation that includes as much Shakespeare as possible. Berlioz replaces Ophelia by a singer, physical magnetism by vocal beauty, and the anguish and anger of the Prince by the anxiety and ire of the critic. Unlike Mark Twain's later mutilation of 'to be' in Chapter 21 of *The Adventures of Huckleberry Finn*, where the hodgepodge reveals presumptuous fakery, Berlioz's exploit allows him to associate with a smile an artistic credo with a meditation on life and death.

Romeo and Juliet

In the beginning, after *Hamlet*, there was *Romeo and Juliet*. In fact the drama had a musical impact upon the composer that was more immediate than most scholars have recognized. In his writings, too, quotation from *Romeo* is frequent. In 1839, reviewing Louis Clapisson's one-act opera *La Symphonie*, for example, Berlioz calls the hero 'un homme de cire (*a man of wax*) comme dit Shakespeare'.[68] He presumably refers to Friar Lawrence's line, to Romeo, 'Thy noble shape is but a form of wax' (3.3.126), although he could refer to Theseus's line, to Hermia, in *A Midsummer Night's Dream*, that she is to her father 'but as a form in wax' (1.1.49). In the same article, Berlioz admits that he is 'out of breath' from reviewing so many singers' débuts – another familiar theme – and immediately pokes fun at himself by quoting Juliet to her 'out of breath' Nurse:

'Il te reste assez de soufflé pour me dire que tu es essoufflée, et tu passes plus de temps à t'excuser qu'il ne t'en faudrait pour me satis-faire. Qu'as-tu à m'apprendre? De bonnes ou de mauvaises nouvelles? Réponds, réponds seulement là-dessus! Quand aux détails, j'attendrai.

Voyons, sont-elles mauvaises ou bonnes?'[69] ('How art thou out of breath, when thou hast breath / To say to me that thou art out of breath? / The excuse that thou dost make in this delay / Is longer than the tale thou dost excuse. / Is thy news good, or bad? Answer to that. / Say either, and I'll stay the circumstance. / Let me be satisfied, is't good or bad?' (2.5.31–7)).

The French resembles neither Guizot's nor Laroche's (the passage does not appear in the Mme Vergne edition) and is presumably Berlioz's. For the composer, Juliet's impatience found resonance with his own.

Berlioz uses *Romeo and Juliet* for a similarly humorous purpose in his letter of 3 December 1849 to his much admired friend the violinist Heinrich Wilhelm Ernst, where he jokes, in English, that 'I shall be, tomorrow, as poor Mercutio, a very *grave* man' – citing the mortally wounded Mercutio: 'ask for me to-morrow, and you shall find me a grave man' (3.1.97–8).[70] This, for Berlioz, was wordplay on a comfortable level – as was that of a later scene, in which the objects of Shakespeare's mockery are musicians. Condensing the episode from Act 4, he quotes:

Pierre: 'Et toi, Jacques Colophane, que dis-tu?'
Troisième musicien: 'Ma foi, je ne saurais rien dire.'
Pierre: 'Tu n sais rien dire? Ah! c'est juste! *Tu es le chanteur de la troupe* .... '
Deuxième musicien: 'Descendons; *attendons le convoi funèbre; nous souperons.*'[71]

This is Berlioz's version of 4.5.136–46 – lines so full of wordplay that Le Tourneur and the 1827 translator left them out. Francisque Michel left them in, but added a note: 'This entire passage, full of wordplay and allusions the keys to which are lost, has embarrassed all commentators; it embarrasses even more this translator, who, unlike Le Tourneur, is unable to omit it.'[72] For the first name of Shakespeare's 'James Soundpost', Berlioz uses the conventional 'Jacques'. For 'Soundpost' – the dowel that carries the vibrations between the top and back plates of the violin, often made from pine – the conventional French term 'âme' (soul) would have been ambiguous. Modern translators have given the fellow such names as Charlot Chanterelle (the 'chanterelle' being the E-string of the violin) and Jacques Larchet (the 'archet' being the bow),[73] but Berlioz's choice of 'Colophane' – meaning rosin, which is made from pine – is closer, and cleverer than the rest.

Othello

Othello figures obliquely in Berlioz's musical compositions – an opera on the play, with a libretto by Rouget de Lisle, author of *La Marseillaise*, was a momentary might-have-been[74] – but directly in the formation of his character, for Othello-like suspicion and revenge become elements of his fiction and his behaviour, and battling 'precious villains' a major pursuit.[75] When he finally became engaged to Harriet Smithson, in January 1833, Berlioz told friends that 'like Othello', he had recited to her the vicissitudes of his life.[76] Othello's 'Her father lov'd me' recitation (1.3.128–60) is a telling of the sort we find in the music dramas of Richard Wagner, where retrospection allows the composer to create a symphony of *Leitmotive* for a song of narration. But it was misery, not music drama, that led to Berlioz's identification with the Moor of Venice.

Reviewing a performance of Beethoven's Fifth Symphony, on 27 April 1834, Berlioz links the drama of the first movement to the drama of *Othello*:

> It is possible that Beethoven was not thinking of it while composing this sublime passage, but in fact there could be no more exact musical translation of the famous scene in Shakespeare (*Ha! Ha! False to me? to me?*) [Berlioz quotes in English] in which the unhappy Othello – progressing gradually from rage to tenderness (… *O now, forever, / Farewell the tranquil mind! farewell content! / Farewell the plumed troop, and the big wars, / That make ambition virtue, … […] Farewell! Othello's occupation's gone*), and from sadness to rage (*Villain! be sure thou prove my love a whore; / Be sure of it; give me an ocular proof*), carried away with anger at Iago and then, his voice broken, calling him back with a friendly word (*Nay, stay: – Thou shouldst be honest*) – displays to us the most terrifying, unprobed depths of the human heart.[77]

With one small but significant exception, Berlioz's quotations (from 3.3.333–81) follow with precision the text of Mme Vergne's 1827 edition of the play. Mme Vergne gives what Shakespeare wrote: '*the* ocular proof'. Berlioz thought he had seen '*an* ocular proof'. Be this as it may, the dramatic analogy between Shakespeare's words and Beethoven's notes is surely more effective than grammatical parsing via dominants and tonics. Beethoven himself, asked to explain the D-minor Sonata, Op. 31 No. 2, is reported to have said, 'just read Shakespeare's *Tempest*.'[78] Berlioz, asked to explain the C-minor Symphony, Op. 67, seems here to say, 'read Shakespeare's *Othello*'.

On 1 February 1857, the Princess Wittgenstein told Berlioz that Franz Liszt's much admired student, Hans Bronsart von Schellendorf, wanted to give a concert in Paris – to which Berlioz replied, quoting Iago to Roderigo: 'Prends de l'argent, fournis-toi d'argent, remplis ta bourse !' – 'get money, find money, fill thy purse.'[79] It is Shakespeare's own varied repetition of Iago's 'Put money in thy purse' (1.3.339–58) that leads to Berlioz's three-fold injuction, freighted with cynicism, because *giving* a concert meant *spending* money. On 3 July of that year, in his feuilleton for the *Débats*, speaking in a similar vein of the lack of respect for artists whose labours have been Herculean, Berlioz quotes the last scene of *Othello:* 'They know it, no more of that [5.2.339–40]. (On le sait, n'en parlons plus.)'[80]

In a letter to the Princess of 21 September 1862, announcing that he has set down the last note of music that he will ever compose, Berlioz writes in English: 'No more of that, Othello's occupation's gone.' Here again he conflates Othello's final monologue, 'No more of that' (5.2.340), with what he earlier says to Iago: 'Farewell! Othello's occupation's gone' (3.3.357).[81] Berlioz uses the line again in the Postface of the *Mémoires:* 'ma carrière est finie, *Othello's occupation's gone*'. This speech will find an echo in Didon's moving farewell to her people, near the end of *Les Troyens*, just before she takes her own life.

After a public reading of *Othello* in 1864, Berlioz once more reflected on the play:

> My god, what a devastating revelation of the depths of the human heart! What a sublime angel, this Desdemona, what a wretched yet noble man, this Othello, and what a horrible demon, this Iago! And to think that it is a creature of our species who wrote all of that! […] It would take a very long study to comprehend the author's point of view and to grasp the vast fluttering of the wings of his genius.[82]

King Lear

After *Hamlet, Romeo and Juliet, Othello* and *The Tempest* (which he musicked in 1830), Berlioz next encountered *Lear*. His first reading, in 1831, inspired him to write the overture we shall consider below. As an older man, he began to set down citations from the drama with some frequency. On 26 December 1856 he told the Princess Wittgenstein that he had just re-read *Lear*, and cites a bit from this oft-cited passage:

Lear:	Pray, do not mock me.
	I am a very foolish fond old man,
	Fourscore and upward, not an hour more nor less;
	And, to deal plainly,
	I fear I am not in my perfect mind.
	Methinks I should know you, and know this man;
	Yet I am doubtful; for I am mainly ignorant
	What place this is; and all the skill I have
	Remembers not these garments; nor I know not
	Where I did lodge last night. Do not laugh at me;
	For (as I am a man) I think this lady
	To be my child Cordelia.
Cordelia:	—And so I am! I am! (4.7.58–69)

Berlioz's recollection –'Je ne suis qu'un pauvre vieillard dont la raison s'affaiblit … pourtant je crois … que cette dame … est ma fille Cordélie! … – *And so! I am! I am!* [*sic*]'[83] – is a drastic condensation, but it does underline Cordelia's simple yet ecstatic utterance, which, for one critic, exemplifies Shakespeare's 'unpoetic poetry', whose weight derives not from inherent lyrical quality but rather from context alone.[84] By italicizing the words, which he may have heard intoned by the great actress who was his first wife, Berlioz would recognize their larger than life importance. And yet his exclamation point after 'so' would reveal a smaller than necessary understanding of the sonic life of the line.

In an article on the revival of *Alceste* at the Opéra, Berlioz uses *Lear* to make a larger point about artistic integrity:

> In general, when an outdated masterpiece is revived on the stage after the death of the author, King Lear is no longer king; the theatre becomes the palace of his daughters, Goneril and Regan, and a nest of irreverent servants who treat rudely the officers of the illustrious host, show no respect for him, and always appear ready to say, in response to complaints about their indignant behavior, "Yes, I sent Kent in the stocks; he was giving us orders, and this much displeased us."[85]

Coriolanus

On 5 March 1835, in an article for *Le Rénovateur*, Berlioz proposed a grand musical and dramatic entertainment of the sort that he had carried out on 14 November 1833, when, after scenes from *Hamlet* and from

Alexandre Dumas's *Antony* performed by Harriet and the celebrated French actors Firmin and Mme Dorval, he conducted a concert of his own. Now, again taking advantage of the presence in France of Miss Smithson, Charles Kemble and William Abbot, he imagined a dual enterprise of Beethoven's *Coriolan* Overture and *Eroica* Symphony joined to the tragedy of *Coriolanus*.[86] For Berlioz, the new event, which never materialized, would have been didactic: as he later wrote of the *Coriolan* Overture, 'In order to comprehend the drama of Beethoven, one must know Shakespeare's *Coriolanus*. Obviously, the great majority of the public does not satisfy this requirement.'[87] Such a slight, which Berlioz directs at 'the plebeians', might have been spoken by Shakespeare's Roman hero, who was prepared to make war upon his own people. Indeed, Berlioz's distaste for the crowd – manifest frequently if incoherently during his career, but especially after the Revolution of 1848 – is one he believed he shared with Shakespeare. Had Beethoven not written music for *Coriolanus*, Berlioz would surely have been tempted to do so himself.

On 28 November 1853, in an open letter to the musicographer Johann-Christian Lobe that was destined for publication in Lobe's new *Fliegende Blätter für Musik*, Berlioz suggests that if he were to run for election, he could do no better than emulate Coriolanus: stand in the public forum and display the wounds he received 'pour la défense de la patrie'.[88] Despite his disparagement of the masses, then, Berlioz, like patricians elsewhere, seems to take his own artistic struggle as tantamount to defending the homeland. In the same vein, in a letter to the Princess Wittgenstein of 10 March 1859, Berlioz cites a long passage from the tirade in Act 3, quoting from memory the translation of *Coriolanus* by Benjamin Laroche. He concludes: 'Objets de mon mépris, je tourne le dos à votre ville. Le monde ne finit pas ici'[89] – a rendering of 'Despising, / For you, the city, thus I turn my back; / There is a world elsewhere' (3.3.133–5). To Shakespeare, to Beethoven, and even to Victor Hugo, Berlioz attributed a certain *contemptuousness* of the multitudes. In doing so, it is not especially pleasant to report, he was surely justifying his own.

Macbeth

In October 1848, Berlioz saw *Macbeth* at the Odéon in the verse adaptation by Émile Deschamps.[90] It may have been this reawakening that led him to frame the *Mémoires*, the principal object of his attention in November and December, with the celebrated quotation, 'Life's but a walking shadow', that we have spoken about above.

On 24 March 1857, in a letter to Princess Wittgenstein in which he excoriates composers' intentional use of extended dissonance, Berlioz sets down his disagreement in English: 'Non, *the fair is not foul, the foul is not fair.*'[91] The witches chant the opposite, of course ('fair is foul, and foul is fair'), and they omit (as the Frenchman does not) the definite article. In February 1859, Berlioz's new collection of articles, *Les Grotesques de la musique*, appeared with a chapter on 'Les Athées de l'expression' that was immediately reproduced in the *Revue et Gazette musicale* of 27 February 1859. In this humorous piece, Berlioz gives two versions of the same paradoxical passage: 'Le vrai est le faux, le faux est le vrai! L'horrible est beau, le beau est horrible!'[92] On 21 September 1862, speaking in a letter to Pauline Viardot of the marvels of Molière and Corneille, he writes: 'Quelle poésie! … ah! les sorcières de *Macbeth* ont beau dire, le beau est beau.'[93] This Gertrude Stein-like repetition results from the (for us) difficultly translatable French expression 'avoir beau': 'Despite what the witches say in *Macbeth* [that 'fair is foul'], fair is [in fact] fair.'

Julius Caesar

On 23 March 1855, Berlioz wrote an amusing letter to Franz Liszt that includes some self-deprecatory humour about the importance of art. He includes a paraphrase of the conversation between Cinna the poet and the four plebeians: ' – Tear him to pieces; he's a conspirator. / – I am Cinna the poet, I am Cinna the poet. / – Tear him for his bad verses, tear him for his bad verses' (3.3.28–30). Berlioz writes:

> 'Comment t'appelles-tu? dit le peuple de Rome à un malheureux qu'il venait de saisir après le meurtre de César. – Je m'appelle Cinna. – Cinna! un des assassins du grand César! aux égouts, qu'on le mette en pièces! – Arrêtez! Grâce! je ne suis pas celui que vous croyez, je suis Cinna, Cinna le Poète! – Ah! tu es Cinna le poète! tant mieux, à mort Cinna le poète ! *tuons-le pour ses mauvais vers !*' (Shakespeare).[94]

Berlioz does not give us all of Shakespeare's repetitive word play, but the last line surely made him howl. His own reaction to *mauvaise musique* was no less violent.

On 10 January 1859, Berlioz told his sister Adèle: 'Recently I was rereading Shakespeare's *Julius Caesar;* I became literally furious with admiration, I pounded my head, I pulled my hair … I am passionate about passion.'[95] Some four months later, on 23 May 1859, to a critic who had written a positive review, Berlioz wrote, in English: 'Most noble brother, give me your hand.'[96] As he does elsewhere, here, too, in a 'quotation' that makes perfectly good sense, Berlioz conflates two passages: Cassius to Brutus, 'Most noble brother, you have done me wrong' (4.2.37); and again, Cassius to Brutus, 'Do you confess so much? Give me your hand' (4.3.117). When in the 1850s his friend Liszt pledged allegiance to Wagner, Berlioz might have said it, but in his writings 'Et tu Brute' (3.1.77) seems nowhere to be found.

Troilus and Cressida

On 3 September 1856, in preparation for work on *Les Troyens*, Berlioz told a friend that he had just re-read *Troilus and Cressida:*

> that incredible retelling of the *Iliad* in which Shakespeare renders Hector even more grandiose than Homer. Nestor, rendering homage to the sublime generosity of the defender of Troy, says that in the midst of battle he had often seen him charging mightily on his chariot, then raising his sword in the air in order to spare the masses of poor Greek soldiers who, petrified by his approach, were simply incapable of defending themselves. *It was,* says old Nestor, *Jupiter dealing life.*[97]

It is in the final scene of Act 4 that the Greek commander Nestor says of Hector, 'Lo Jupiter is yonder, dealing life!' (4.5.191). If the *Aeneid* is the overmastering source of *Les Troyens, Troilus and Cressida,* too, may have played a role in its genesis. No one 'deals life' in the opera, but perhaps that notion played a role in Berlioz's conception of an utterly beneficent and welcoming Didon, with none of the ambiguities of Virgil's creation. Also, in order to assuage Didon's remorse at betraying the memory of her husband, Berlioz has Aeneas assert, in Act 4 of the opera, that Andromache now loves the very man who is the son of her husband's murderer. This detail, not in Virgil, could be an indirect reflection of his reading of Shakespeare's Cressida, who appears not to take long to find love amongst the Greeks.

Antony and Cleopatra

When, on 19 February 1859, Berlioz joked about his health with the German critic Richard Pohl, he said that he was no longer preoccupied with learning 'how best to kill himself'.[98] If he were thinking of Octavius Caesar, in *Antony and Cleopatra,* who says of the deceased queen that 'her physician tells me / She hath pursued conclusions infinite / Of easy ways to die' (5.2.354–6), then this would be a first, indirect reference to his project, concretized but never realized, of composing an opera on the play. Eight months later, he wrote to the Princess Wittgenstein about such a work:

> You wish to convince me to pursue Cleopatra! I do indeed believe that one could make of this subject something very grandiose, but also very bitter. I can think of nothing more poisonous than Antony's love for the Queen of Egypt. I can think of no man more miserable than this wretched fellow after the loss of the Battle of Actium and the cowardly flight of his infernal mistress, that *snake of the Nile*. I can only imagine with horror such an ocean of despair.[99]

On 7 November 1859, he continued the discussion:

> Of all the subjects that could inspire me, this is the one that is least accessible to French sensibilities and thus the one that is most dangerous. Do you really believe that I could be so insolent as to deform Shakespeare's inspiration to the point of turning Cleopatra into an academic, Spanish queen speaking in rhymed and measured verses and following the conventions of her court? … Not at all. It is precisely because the sizzling and capricious Egyptian is the opposite of such a ridiculous creature that I find her so enthralling. I simply adore this wild animal who wants Julius Caesar to sleep with her with his sword at his side, who assassinates poor Antony twenty times over, in ways most horrible, but who wishes not to outlive him and who in fact does not do so for long; this working girl with a crown who goes hopping in the streets of Alexandria, who has a 'salt fish' attached to Antony's line when he is fishing in the Nile, who in one hour changes her mind some twenty times; this daredevil who asks Mardian the eunuch about his amorous desires; this woman in the end at once ridiculous and cowardly who flees the field of the Battle of Actium without knowing why. What a character for a *fantaisie musicale!*[100]

And on 13 December 1859 he enlarged his vision:

> Oh, yes, it seems to me that I could make a very seductive creature out of this torpedo; she would be very different from everything else I have done. There would be room, here, for the unexpected, the strange, the outlandish! I can sense that I would limit myself to taking only certain details from Shakespeare and that I would otherwise be well advised

to allow my imagination free rein. First I would need the interior of a pyramid and the priests of Isis with their juggling and mysterious rituals. For Cleopatra I would need even greater audacity: I would need a scene in the river at Cydnus; I would need a secret orgy of women with the eunuch Mardian to create a pendant for the triumvirs' public orgy on the youthful Pompey's royal gallery. And perhaps there would be a way of having both the cold and wise Octavia and the wild Egyptian on stage at the same time. What a contrast! [101]

Berlioz's mention of a 'musical fantasy' is ironic: should his enthusiasm have led to composition, we would rather have had a five act grand opera called *Cléopâtre*, a dramatic mezzo-soprano in the title role, a mise en scène more elaborate than that of *Les Troyens*, and an orchestration as fiery and impetuous as the Egyptian queen herself.

The Comedies

The Tempest

In 1830, when Berlioz fell in love with the pianist Camille Moke, he had lately been reading *The Tempest*, and took to referring to the brilliant young artist as 'Ariel'. In a letter to his sister of 23 August 1830 he explained the appellation: 'Let me tell you, Nanci, that Ariel is the name of the airy spirit at the beck and call of Prospero in Shakespeare's *The Tempest*. I gave it to Camille because of her brilliant eyes, her sylphlike waist, and her temperament, which is sometimes joyful and sometimes forlorn.' [102] Shakespeare's Ariel is of ambiguous gender, but Berlioz's was female – and hot, as he tells us in no uncertain terms. It would not be long before Camille would jilt the Prix de Rome, after his departure for Italy, and marry the prosperous piano maker with the same forename, Camille Pleyel. In Berlioz's later 'novel of the future', *Euphonia, ou la ville musicale*, we hear the narrator say of his beloved, 'j'entends sa voix d'Ariel, agile, argentine, pénétrante … ' [103]; but the tale itself is one of revenge for this never-forgiven act of deceit. In 1830, however, while still under her spell, Berlioz composed an *Ouverture de la Tempête* that has a part for piano – the first time the instrument figures in the basically orchestral repertory – which was surely conceived for the argentine fingers of Mlle Moke. This overture will figure prominently in Berlioz's most Shakespearean work, *Lélio ou Le Retour à la vie*.

The Tempest was on his mind when, on 24 September 1857, in his regular column for the *Débats*, Berlioz expressed admiration for the director of

the casino in Baden-Baden, Édouard Bénazet, who had given him carte
blanche to conduct concerts there, saying that only with absolute power
can one produce in music something beautiful and grand. Berlioz then
quotes 20 lines (in French) from the opening scene of *The Tempest*, where
in the thick of the storm, Alonso, King of Naples, is told by the Boatswain to
keep out of the way.[104] The passage speaks immediately to Berlioz's notion
of authority. It is similar to the tale of the famous marine commander, Jean
Bart, to whom Louis XIV had given a much deserved promotion: 'Sire',
said the sailor, 'vous avez bien fait.' Berlioz, who also knew his own worth
(and who loved this anecdote), always wanted to say to a sovereign who
would have rewarded his merit, 'Sire, you have done well.'

Twelfth Night

We discover one of Berlioz's favourite quotations, from *Twelfth Night*, in
reviews of one of his favourite pieces, Beethoven's Seventh Symphony. On
one occasion, in 1834, he says, of the A-major interlude in the A-minor
slow movement, that the composer, casting aside the sombre veil of his
imagination, 'nous apparaît jetant sur le passé un regard doux et triste
de la *patience souriant à la douleur*' – the composer, that is, seems to have
'cast upon the past that gentle and heartrending gaze of *patience smiling at
grief*'.[105] One year later he applied the same words to the same passage –
'comme la patience souriant à la douleur' – thus again modifying Viola's
lines from Act 2, 'She sate like Patience on a monument, / Smiling at
grief' (2.4.114–15).[106] He repeats them yet again in 1838: the 'trio' of the
slow movement is 'a glimmer of hope'; after the frightful opening section,
it offers a vaporous melody, pure, simple, sweet, melancholy and resigned,
'comme la patience souriant à la douceur'.[107] Years later, speaking of the
recently deceased wife of his friend Armand Bertin, he said that she was
the personification of the Shakespearean ideal: 'La patience souriant à la
douleur'.[108] Of these several lines, Haydn, in 1795, had made a sensitive
setting for voice and piano.[109] Berlioz is unlikely to have known it – he
mentions much of Haydn but never the songs – and he, like the earlier
Austrian master, seems to have understood them as the embodiment of a
woman's noble abnegation.

Much Ado About Nothing

In an article published on 8 April 1834, Berlioz mocks an overture by the
German composer Ferdinand Ries by saying the orchestra 'a fait beaucoup

de bruit pour rien'[110] – his first mention in print of *Much Ado About Nothing*. But he was already familiar with the play, having announced his intention, on 19 January 1833, to take it over for 'un opéra italien fort gai'.[111] He did indeed submit an outline of such an opera to the management of the Théâtre-Italien, in January 1833, but nothing came of the effort. *Much Ado* remained in his thoughts for the rest of his career, finally becoming the source of his last opera, *Béatrice et Bénédict*, which we shall study in section III.

Five further comedies

The Merchant of Venice will figure as a lynchpin in Berlioz's grand Virgilian opera of the mid–1850s, but in his writings citations from the play are rare. Of the great German soprano Henriette Sontag, he once wrote:

> She would have been worthy of singing the incomparable love duet from the last act of *The Merchant of Venice:* "Ce fut par une nuit semblable que la jeune Cressida, quittant les tentes des Grecs, alla rejoindre au pied des murs de Troie Troilus son amant." However unlikely this may seem, Mme Sontag, I do believe, could have sung Shakespeare. I can think of no higher praise than that. [112]

Berlioz's version of Lorenzo's first words is an imprecise condensation of 'in such a night / Troilus methinks mounted the Trojan walls, / And sigh'd his soul toward the Grecian tents / Where Cressid lay that night' (5.1.1–6). He will aim higher, as we shall see, in the love scene of *Les Troyens*.

On 15 October 1854, Berlioz replied with scepticism to his Belgian friend Adolphe Samuel's hope of broadening the larger public's understanding of music: 'I'm afraid that I am obliged to repeat what one of Shakespeare's characters says of the world: "Le monde est une huître et je l'ouvre avec mon épée!" '[113] The words are Pistol's, to Falstaff, in the *Merry Wives of Windsor:* 'Why, then the world's mine oyster, / Which I with sword will open' (2.2.3–4). Once again Berlioz has lodged his scepticism of the crowd in a line from the Bard.

In a letter of 30 December 1859, Berlioz likens *himself* to a character in *Measure for Measure* – Barnardine, the stubborn and comically straight-speaking prisoner who, by dint of another hapless prisoner's natural death, is spared a treacherous beheading. Aware that Barnardine has been imprisoned for nine years, Berlioz writes to Pauline Viardot: 'so much the better if death has forgotten me for nine years ....'[114] It is fair to assume that, in Berlioz's reference to his physical suffering (from what we now believe was Crohn's disease), Viardot, one of whose intimates was the Shakespeare-admiring Russian writer Ivan Turgenev, heard the Shakespearean resonance of Berlioz's doleful remark.

In the summer of 1862, Berlioz prepared a new collection of articles that would appear in September under the title of *À travers chants* (a play on the common French expression 'à travers champs') that may be rendered in English as 'through fields of song'. Along with that terrifying line from Virgil, 'Hostis habet muros' ('The enemy holds the walls'), *À travers chants* carries as an epigraph the impenetrable Shakespearean title of *Love's Labour's Lost*. Does this mean that 'love's labour' is lost? Does it refer to the lost labours of love? Shakespeareans continue to debate the question, but Berlioz, here, seems to suggest that *his* labour of love – in defence of music – has been lost, and thus that the enemy – the philistine horde, or perhaps Wagner and the Wagnerians[115] – has indeed taken the walls. Something otherwise playful may also be at work here: the conjoining of his own imaginative title, which sounds like something else because of the homonymic 'chants' and 'champs', and Shakespeare's ambiguous and alliterative allusion to the dénouement of his comedy.

Berlioz's only regular citation from *A Midsummer Night's Dream* is 'bien rugi, lion' – Demetrius's words to Snug: 'Well roared, lion' (5.1.265). We find this, appropriately enough, in Berlioz's congratulatory letter of 26 January 1866 to the actor Jean-Baptiste Bressant, for his performance in François Ponsard's new five-act comedy, *Le Lion amoureux*.[116]

The Histories

Only one of the history plays, *Richard III*, was given by Harriet Smithson's English company in their Parisian salad days, but Berlioz surely read them all. In a story he published on 3 August 1834 entitled 'Le Suicide par enthousiasme', Berlioz borrows the celebrated quotation from *Richard III* – 'Un cheval! un cheval! mon royaume pour un cheval!' – to describe the urgency felt by the hero of his own tale (an idealist who commits suicide in the face of artistic disappointment) to get out of town.[117] But he knew the play in its entirety. On 15 August 1846 he notes that child prodigies 'live little' or become stupid in old age. Berlioz's 'ils vivent peu' is his version of Richard's cruel aside, 'So wise so young, they say, do never live long' (3.1.79).[118] And on 21 September 1862, speaking to the Princess Wittgenstein of his dislike of philosophical contemplation, *Richard III* again comes to his mind: 'If such reflections could make me weep, there would fall from my eyes (as Shakespeare puts it) only millstones.'[119] In the play, Gloucester says to the First Murderer: 'Your eyes drop millstones, when fools' eyes fall tears' (1.3.352). If Berlioz's was fond of Gloucester's outspoken malice, he was also fond of the ghosts' repeated denunciation of him in Act 5, scene 3: 'Despair and die!'

On 9 June 1834, writing of the pitifully small number of Frenchmen who glorified Beethoven, Berlioz lingers upon the word 'gloire' and thinks of Falstaff, in *1 Henry IV*, who asks: 'What is honor? A word. What is in that word honor? What is that honor? Air' (5.1.133–5). Berlioz writes, 'Falstaff is absolutely right: What is glory? Let us briefly examine the meaning of this word.'[120] In fact Falstaff – found in the *Henry* plays and in *The Merry Wives of Windsor* – much delighted Berlioz. Writing to his friend Ferdinand Hiller on 1 January 1832, Berlioz refers to the pernickety critic François-Joseph Fétis as 'ce Falstaff', seeing him at that point as rather more wicked than Shakespeare's usually comical 'round man' (2.4.140). In the last part of *Les Soirées de l'orchestre*, however, Berlioz's narrator explains the presence of Falstaff in these plays as 'the archetype of the English buffoon, the English Gascon, the English blow-hard'. In him we should see

the true English Punchinello, and the embodiment of five or six cardinal sins; that gluttony, wenching, and cowardice are his outstanding qualities; that despite his obesity, his rotundity, his avarice, and his spinelessness, he captivates women and makes them pawn their silver to satisfy his greedy appetite; that Shakespeare made him Prince Hal's companion in his wantonness and nocturnal escapades in the streets of London; and that the Prince allows Falstaff to treat His Highness with the most unbelievable familiarity, until the time when, having become King under the name of Henry V and eager to have his youthful indiscretions forgotten, 'royal Hal', as Falstaff has the insolence to nickname him, banishes from the court his fat companion in debauchery and sends him into exile.[121]

Berlioz would have known of various operas on *Falstaff*, including Michael William Balfe's 1838 setting, for Berlioz and Balfe became friends in London in the 1840s and in their later years enjoyed smoking cigars and talking about Shakespeare.[122] Berlioz did see the Falstaff who appears in Ambroise Thomas' opera *Songe d'une nuit d'été*, premiered at the Opéra-Comique on 20 April 1850 and reviewed by Berlioz five days later. The libretto, by Joseph Rosier and Adolph de Leuven, is partly based on *1 Henry IV*, but is otherwise a comical invention that has Queen Elisabeth I take shelter from a thunderstorm in a tavern and there find herself the object of Sir John Falstaff's flirtations until the arrival of … William Shakespeare himself. Berlioz, normally horrified by such licentiousness, was this time rather amused.[123]

On 5 December 1849, in a sombre letter to his sister Nanci, Berlioz writes: 'O Seigneur Diew! méchante fortune! Pour parler comme d'Orléans dans Shakespeare.'[124] Here, in another conflation, Berlioz is thinking of both the moment in *Henry V* when the French Dauphin, in the face of defeat, cries 'O méchante fortune!' (4.5.5), and the earlier moment when Katherine, daughter of King Charles VI, attempting to learn English, exclaims: 'O Seigneur Dieu, je m'en oublie d'elbow' (3.4.31). Berlioz's spelling of 'Diew,' illustrative of Anglophones' diphthongal pronunciation of the word, is probably not original.

In an article of 3 July 1857, Berlioz quotes *1 Henry VI*: 'Hélas! hélas! Shakespeare a raison: *La gloire est comme un cercle dans l'onde, qui va toujours s'élargissant, jusqu'à ce qu'à force de s'étendre il disparaisse tout à fait.*'[125] He quotes precisely the same passage in a letter to his uncle Félix Marmion of 31 July 1866, in which he laments that the violence of his love of Shakespeare is little felt elsewhere: 'La gloire est comme un cercle dans l'onde, qui va toujours s'élargissant, jusqu'à ce qu'il disparaisse tout à fait.'[126] This is his rendering of 'Glory is like a circle in the water, / Which never ceaseth to enlarge itself / Till by broad spreading it disperse to nought' (1.2.133–5). The slight difference between Berlioz's French renderings shows again that he is quoting from memory.

The meaning of Berlioz's quotations

I have registered Berlioz's interaction with nine of the 12 tragedies; he also knew *Cymbeline*, which he suggests is a source for the libretto of Weber's *Euryanthe*.[127] I have mentioned seven of the 16 comedies; he also knew *Two Gentlemen of Verona*, which he notes is *not* the source of an opéra comique by Justin Cadaux entitled *Deux Gentilshommes de Vérone*,[128] and *As You Like It*, whose celebrated line 'All the world's a stage' (2.7.139) he rendered as 'le monde est un théâtre'. And I have touched upon four of the ten histories (we are entitled to assume that he was also familiar with *2 Henry IV*). Twenty-three of 38 plays and, again, ten of the 12 tragedies, with only *Titus Andronicus* and *Timon of Athens* unmentioned. Would a professor of English literature be ashamed of this score?

In private communication Berlioz employs Shakespeare to transmit the wisdom of the ages, to intensify daily life and to establish common ground. For his friend Léon Kreutzer, Shakespeare was the 'trait d'union' or hyphen between their two minds.[129] In public writing he exploits Shakespeare to deepen insights, to fortify arguments, to further critical and aesthetic ends and 'to grant himself the permission to release the full powers of his own fantasy'.[130] Brief quotation is easily mocked – 'Just declaim a few lines from Othella, And they'll think you're a hell of a fella'[131] – but when it is true to the occasion it is peculiarly satisfying.

Berlioz clearly reads the plays with their musical potential in mind. Little given to theorizing, Berlioz does offer, in an article of 10 September 1837, a tiny treatise on what dramatic characters are most fitted to musical setting:

> Love, enthusiasm, melancholy, joy, terror, jealousy, and serenity are sentiments and passions entirely appropriate to musical development, while ambition and political intrigue, on the contrary, do not at all lend themselves to music. This is why Romeo, Juliet, Tybalt, Friar Lawrence, Othello, Desdemona, Ariel, and Caliban himself may be perfectly admirable as sung characters, while Richard III and Macbeth could never figure in an opera without giving up the principal traits of the personalities that Shakespeare gave them, or without vainly torturing the art of music by asking it to express what it is unable to say. Far more than the Earl of Gloucester and Macbeth analysing the reasons for their ambition, for example, Romeo's old monk – who casts both a philosophical and religious eye upon the physical world, on the hidden forces of nature, on fish and flowers, on life and death – can furnish the composer with material for sublime pages of music, because the melancholy gravity of the latter is readily adaptable to hymnlike or elegiac forms, that is to say to the most elegant forms that melody, harmony, and rhythm can adorn, while, applied to the cold and bitter emotions of the former, music will always seem like a robe of gold and silk draped over a cold marble statue.[132]

Here, in a nutshell, is why we have from Berlioz a *Tempest* and a *Romeo and Juliet*, and why we might have had from him an *Othello* or a *Falstaff*, to mention works carried out by a certain Italian composer ten years his junior. Verdi did discover the musical potential of *Macbeth*, but when the revised version of that opera was performed in Paris, at the Théâtre-Lyrique, in April 1865, Berlioz, in retirement, appears to have stayed at home.

Berlioz the actor

That the experience of acting the plays marked Shakespeare's writing is certain, even if how they did so will forever remain fare for conjecture.

'Shakespeare the director' is the title of a real book but is otherwise a set of unconfirmable inferences drawn from the theatrical texts.[133] Conducting as an element of Berlioz's method of composition – the musical equivalent of acting and directing the plays – is more readily analysed. Scholars have noted how performers have welcomed Berlioz's sensitivity to the 'practical issues of live-music-making'; about how Berlioz went about producing his own concerts, we know a great deal.[134]

The lesson Berlioz learned at the first rehearsal of his first large-scale work – when, in December 1824, the ill-copied parts of the *Messe solennelle* led to chaos and cacophony – is centrally responsible, I think, for the astonishing clarity of his own autograph manuscripts. Embarrassed on that day in the presence of the then well-known conductor Henri Valentino, Berlioz never again suffered disaster due to messy materials. He did suffer from others' mishandling of his music, and thus determined in 1835 to conduct his concerts himself.[135] His later handbook, 'Le Chef d'orchestre', treats both the technical aspects of the art of the orchestral and choral conductor – how to arrange the players, how to beat time, how to rehearse – and the psychological dimensions of the profession. The conductor, the captain of the ship, the commander of the army, must possess 'gifts, impossible to define, without which he will be unable to establish an invisible bond between himself and those whom he would lead, unable to transmit to them his feelings, unable accurately and powerfully to lead'. [136]

In her monograph on *Shakespeare the Actor*, Meredith Skura speaks of the nervousness, the need for equanimity, the fear of failure, the narcissism coupled with insecurity, and the necessity of pleasing an audience not always worthy of one's efforts that must have affected Shakespeare as he set down the parts of his plays.[137] One could surely say the same of Berlioz as he set down the parts of his scores. Indeed, in Chapter XLVIII of the *Mémoires*, Berlioz writes: 'Poor composers! Learn how to conduct yourselves, and to conduct yourselves well (literally and figuratively)! Because of all your interpreters, the most dangerous – never forget it – is the conductor!' 'Poor composers' has a Shakespearean ring. Did Shakespeare in a supervisory mode ever say anything of this sort? Was he frustrated by unfeeling actors? We will never really know. In *Lélio*, Berlioz has his alter-ego explicitly articulate the directorial paradox: 'As to your understanding of melodic and expressive nuance, I have nothing to say: my advice would be perfectly useless to those who have it, and even more so to those who do not.' This sounds like Coleridge, who, speaking not too many years before Berlioz, said of the opening of *Hamlet:* 'O heaven! words are wasted on those who feel, and to those who do not feel the exquisite judgement of Shakespeare in this scene, what can be said?'[138]

Berlioz the advocate

If one of the earliest biographies is to be believed, Berlioz began to read Shakespeare aloud as early as the 1830s.[139] But it was in his later years, when the rat race of writing, roaming and reviewing had wound down, that he became a regular public reader of the plays. The literal evidence only hints at the reality. On 20 December 1862, for example, he invited Mme Comettant, a singer and the wife of the influential critic and musicographer Oscar Comettant, to a reading of *Othello* that he would give at his apartment on the following day, Sunday, 21 December.[140] On 25 October 1864, he read *Othello* (in the French translation by Benjamin Laroche) to six friends, among them Mme Érard, Mme Spontini, Mme Ary Scheffer and her daughter and sister, at the Érard mansion, the Château de la Muette. Some months later, writing to his niece Nanci Suat on 3 February 1865, he mentions that Louise-Aglaé Massart, one of the close friends of his old age and she to whom he would bequeath his one-volume English Shakespeare, had asked him to read *Hamlet* aloud: 'There will be only *five* of us; we will dine at 6 o'clock, I will begin at 7, and, God willing, I will finish at *midnight*. It takes five hours. My reading of *Othello* at Mme Érard's has made the rounds; I'm gaining a reputation as an actor.'[141] Again, six days later, on 8 February, he reflected on the five persons who would hear him reading *Hamlet*: 'I am a little fearful of seeing these artistic souls suddenly confronted by this phenomenal work of genius. The circumstance makes me think of children born blind who would suddenly become sighted. I think they will understand; I know them. But to arrive at forty-five or fifty without knowing *Hamlet!!* To have lived that long in the dark!!' Berlioz then once again quotes *1 Henry VI*: 'Shakespeare said it himself: "Glory is like a circle in the water which never ceaseth to enlarge itself till by broad spreading it disperse to nought." '[142]

On 15 September 1865, he told Mme Massart that when she returned to Paris, 'we will have to recompose our little audience of men, and we will read *Coriolanus*. Nothing pleases me more than to witness the enthusiasm of people who are understanding and not blasé, and who are blessed with imagination and sensitivity'.[143] In October, he arranged a reading of the play at his apartment, inviting the painter Paul Chenavard to come along 'next Sunday at eight o'clock sharp'.[144]

Berlioz's reputation as an 'actor' apparently reached Russia. Writing from St. Petersburg on 9 December 1867, he told Berthold Damcke that the Grand Duchess Elena Pavlovna, patroness of the Russian Musical Society, had asked him to read *Hamlet*[145] – and he mentioned the reading to at least four other friends. But it seems never to have taken place. Would the Grand Duchess have been shocked by Berlioz's exuberance? Stephen Heller, the composer's close friend in the final three decades of his life, remembered that Berlioz 'read very well, but too often let his emotions get the best of him. The beautiful passages always drew forth his tears. He nonetheless continued to read while quickly wiping them away'.[146] A similar anecdote is recounted by August Barbier, who attended with Berlioz the funeral of a mutual friend. 'As we left the cemetery [Berlioz] said to me, "I'm going home; come along, we'll read some Shakespeare." We went up to his flat and, once seated, he read the scene in *Hamlet* at Ophelia's grave. His emotions were overwhelming and rivers of tears flowed from his eyes. The aesthetic emotion had accomplished what the real loss had not.'[147]

In fact and in fiction Berlioz excoriated those who reacted tepidly to Shakespeare. In the tale of *Euphonia* later incorporated into the Vingt-Cinquième Soirée of *Les Soirées de l'orchestre*, Berlioz's mock heroine is condemned by the narrator for calmly pronouncing the name of Shakespeare without turning pale or crimson: Shakespeare, for her, 'was just one more poet, like so many others .... '[148]

Berlioz's advocacy of Shakespeare was not only as a reader. In 1864, as the three-hundredth anniversary of Shakespeare's birth approached, he associated himself with those wishing to celebrate the tercentenary. On the appointed day, Saturday, 23 April 1864, *Hamlet, A Midsummer Night's Dream* and *'Falstaff'* (arranged by the writer Paul Meurice, the instigator of the event, and Auguste Vacquerie) were to be performed at the Théâtre de la Porte-Saint-Martin after the grand banquet that was to take place during the afternoon in the elegant dining room of the newly refurbished Grand Hôtel. On 11 April, the members made public the letter they were sending to Victor Hugo, in exile, whose book *William Shakespeare* was published in that very month:

Cher et illustre maître,

A meeting of writers, authors and dramatic artists, and representatives of all the liberal professions, has taken place in the effort to organize in Paris, on 23 April, a celebration on the occasion of the three-hundredth anniversary of the birth of Shakespeare.

Named to the board of the French Shakespeare Committee are: MM. August Barbier, [Antoine-Louis] Barye, Charles Bataille (du

Conservatoire), Hector Berlioz, Alexandre Dumas, Jules Favre, George Sand, Jules Janin, Théophile Gautier, François-Victor Hugo, [Ernest] Legouvé, [Émile] Littré, Paul Meurice, [Jules] Michelet, Eugène Pelletan, and [François-Joseph] Régnier (de la Comédie française). The secretaries are: MM. Laurent Pichat, [Charles-Marie-René] Leconte de Lisle, Félicien Mallefille, Paul de Saint-Victor, and [Théophile] Thoré.

The presidency of the committee, by unanimous acclamation, has been accorded to you, as is only fitting for the great poet and great citizen you are. We confidently await your acceptance, which will lend to this celebration all appropriate gravity.[149]

Of those listed here, only one, beyond Berlioz, was from the world of music: Charles-Amable Bataille, the bass singer who created and often sang the Père de famille in *L'Enfance du Christ.* Bataille – a surprising choice, considering the celebrity of the others – was a member of what in 1864 Berlioz called his regular Monday night 'Club des Insensés', or 'club of madmen'.[150] Hugo himself was pleased to think that as president he would sit in an 'empty chair' and thus be remarked upon as 'absent and present at the same time'.[151] At the meeting of the Conseil des ministres on 16 April 1864, fearing precisely this sort of recognition, Napoléon III gave the order to halt the performances and the banquet. Six hundred men had been expected to attend the events (women were excluded). Hugo took the cancellation as a victory for the anti-imperialists.[152]

Berlioz took it less seriously. During the third week of April, he wrote to his son: 'You know that the Emperor has banned the Shakespeare Jubilee … It's perhaps just as well; we would probably have done and said only a lot of silly things.'[153] The matter is more complicated than Berlioz's casual letter would suggest, however, because the anniversary was associated not only with the publication of Hugo's *William Shakespeare* but especially with the translation of the complete works (appearing serially since 1857) by his son François-Victor. We learn more from the extensive article published by Benoît Jouvin, director of *Le Figaro,* in the issue of 21 April 1864:

Among the names [of the anniversary committee members], all highly honorable, I count only two who are capable of reading Shakespeare in his own language: M. François-Victor Hugo and M. Berlioz – and even these two, were they to debate one of the great poet's problematical texts, might well quietly suggest that the other was badly informed.

Two years ago, M. Hector Berlioz, Paul de Saint-Victor, and I found ourselves dining at the same table. In the mind of the author of *Les*

Troyens, neither Beethoven nor Gluck occupies a greater place than Shakespeare. As the conversation gently drifted from music to poetry, we came to speak of the translation by François-Victor Hugo, and I asked Berlioz his opinion of it, since he knows the great English poet by heart. He gave it to us, directly and decisively, despite Paul de Saint-Victor's mild objections. If Hector Berlioz is thinking of expressing this opinion as a part of the toast he is preparing to offer to Shakespeare, the banquet on 23 April may well end as did the banquet of the marriage of Pirithous: in inevitable lapithating.[154]

This proves, first, that Berlioz was considered an expert on Shakespeare. (A few years later, another prominent journalist wrote that he had even seen Englishmen consult Berlioz 'about their poet'.)[155] It proves that as late as 20 April the Emperor's decision to cancel the banquet was unknown to the director of one of the capital's leading newspapers. And it proves that Berlioz, presumably for artistic reasons, was unimpressed by the translation of François-Victor Hugo. Politics, too, may have played a role. Berlioz, always an admirer of Napoléon Iᵉʳ, was antagonistic to Victor Hugo's republican aspirations and, despite what he called the later emperor's 'harmonophobia', was devoted as well to Napoléon III.

He did of course see the links between artistic freedom and adminis-trative policy. In June 1863, speaking of Franco–German friendship at a music festival organized by the cities of Strasbourg and Kehl, on the new bridge linking the two, he proclaimed that 'under the influence of music, the soul is uplifted, the intellect broadened; civilization progresses, and national enmities disappear'. He went on to quote *The Merchant of Venice*:

A great poet has said: "The man that hath no music in himself, Nor is not moved with concord of sweet sounds, Is fit for treasons, stratagems and spoils [...] Let no such man be trusted." Clearly Shakespeare was here availing himself of poetic licence. But the observation nonetheless demonstrates that, if his proposition is beyond the bounds of what is considered proper for particular individuals, it is far less so for individual nations, and today we must recognize that where music ends, barbarism begins.[156]

Berlioz's *géopolitique* was musical; his *géopoétique* was Shakespearean.

Shakespeare in Translation

As a boy, in his father's library, Berlioz traveled vicariously from Troy to Latium, with Aeneas, in Virgil's original Latin. He entered Babylon, with Alexander the Great, in what we presume was Jacques Amyot's French translation of Plutarch's original Greek. He later made the rounds with Goethe's Faust in the distant language of Gérard de Nerval. Berlioz knew the pleasures of reading *dans le texte* and the pitfalls of reading *en version française*. Of Shakespeare, he explicitly regrets (in Chapter XVIII of the *Mémoires*) 'les brouillards de la traduction de Le Tourneur', which he finds 'pâle et infidèle'. When his own *Roméo et Juliette* was about to be performed in Vienna, he wrote: 'Ils n'ont encore là qu'une affreuse traduction allemande.'[157] And yet he never hesitated to have his works translated as the need arose. This renders more surprising the audacity of those who came to Paris in the 1820s with Shakespeare in English. How much of the language did Berlioz possess?

From a letter he sent to his sister on 1 November 1828, we know that in the year after the shock of Shakespeare, Berlioz was studying English. 'Nothing exasperates me more', he wrote, after meeting a German visitor to Paris, 'than seeing foreigners speaking well in our language, while we cannot say a single word in theirs. I bitterly regret not being able to learn English more rapidly. It is frustrating to take a public course three times per week where one learns in an hour what in a private lesson one could learn in fifteen minutes. But I cannot afford to hire a private teacher.'[158] By January 1829, he had had to give up even the public course.[159]

At the time of his engagement to Harriet Smithson, in January 1833, Berlioz told his sister: 'I can't speak English and her French is very poor; she cannot articulate half her thoughts, and she often doesn't understand me at all. I will soon know English.'[160] They exchanged up to three letters a day, '*she in English, I in French*'.[161] Years later, and three days after arriving for the first time in England, on 7 November 1847, Berlioz reported to his father: 'I am very surprised by my knowledge of English. I can say almost everything I need to say, without too strong an accent, but I do not understand much more than half of what is said to me. I have some serious studying to do.'[162] By then married for 14 years, Berlioz must have spoken to his wife in an English that was not Shakespearean and she to him in a French that was not sure.

Here is the passage in Chapter XVIII of the *Mémoires* where Berlioz (writing in 1848) explains his first encounter with Shakespeare.

I must add that at the time I knew not a word of English, that I saw Shakespeare only through the fog of the translation by Le Tourneur, and thus that I perceived none of the poetic threads that surround his miraculous designs like a golden lattice. Unfortunately, I continue today to suffer from the same disadvantage. It is far more difficult for a Frenchman to sound the depths of Shakespeare's style than it is for an Englishman to sense the originality and finesse of La Fontaine or Molière. Our two poets are rich continents; Shakespeare is a world. But the flair of the actors, and especially of the actress, the succession of the scenes, the pantomime, and the sounds of the voices meant more to me, and filled me with thousands more Shakespearean notions and passions, than did the text of my pale and imprecise translation.

Today we enjoy asking if Shakespeare is better read or seen on the stage, but for the young Berlioz the question was not moot. The Conservatoire of which he was a graduate was *de musique et de déclamation*, the latter word implying instruction, above and beyond musical technique, in the art of interpretation. When he first encountered the English company, Berlioz was no expert on acting, but as a journalist he would spend years in the theatre of music and say much about action on the stage. It is not far-fetched to believe that the leading actress's real tears in Ophelia's mad scene would, as Hugh Macdonald has written, 'have crossed any language barrier'.[163] Speaking of the same encounter, Jacques Barzun notes that 'for life's predicaments and the feelings they arouse, Shakespeare coins definitive phrasings by the hundred; this in addition to stretches of poetry verbally and emotionally miraculous'.[164]

Could Berlioz taste those 'definitive phrasings'? As he moved into middle and old age, his knowledge and comprehension deepened – of Shakespeare, and of English. In a letter of 3 July 1855, he accomplishes some bilingual word-play of triple complexity that suggests genuine under-standing of his wife's native tongue. Mentioning to a friend that in London he found no pineapples (which Berlioz adored), he notes that strawberries were in great supply – 'Pas d'ananas! Nous sommes volés; mais force fraises; nous avons jusqu'à des fraises de veau' – and adds: '*Vile phrase!* calembourg anglais'. The sentence is untranslatable, and the joke is silly. It turns on Polonius's remarks to Gertrude that ' "beautified" is a vile phrase' (2.2.111); it turns on knowing that Shakespeare's 'vile', pronounced with a French accent, becomes the English word 'veal' (the French 'veau'), and on knowing that Shakespeare's 'phrase', pronounced with a French accent, becomes the French word 'fraises' ('strawberries'); it turns, finally, on the recurrence of 'fraises' in 'fraises de veau', which is the connecting membrane of veal intestines and a culinary delicacy for those in the know.

Still, if they demonstrate Berlioz's Shakespearean love of words, such adroit manœuvres – of which the composer would have said 'je ne trouve pas ceux de Chaix pires' (Chaixspire's are no worse than mine) [165] – prove neither that Berlioz had mastered Shakespearean English nor that he understood the potential ambiguities of Polonius's line. To probe its depths, indeed its surface, he was surely in need of occasional translation. On the other hand, even while steeped in the music of the rhymed and strictly duodecasyllabic French alexandrine, he could surely feel the formal freedom of Shakespeare's iambic pentameters and alternations of prose and verse. I would say, if pressed, that Berlioz's reading of Shakespeare, uncommonly wide, was unpredictably deep.

The translations Berlioz knew

In Chapter XVIII of the *Mémoires* Berlioz specifically mentions the translations of Pierre-Félicien Le Tourneur (1736–88), whose 20-volume *Shakespeare traduit de l'Anglois* appeared from 1776–83. Berlioz knew Le Tourneur's work but did not own those volumes, nor were they to be found in his widely educated father's library. [166] His father did subscribe to Louis-Gabriel Michaud's famous *Biographie universelle*, which appeared in 52 volumes between 1811 and 1828, and it is here that the teenager first encountered Gluck (in volume 17, of 1816), and Haydn (in volume 19, of 1817), in articles – not music – that inspired him to become a musician. Berlioz had been away at school for four years by the time of the appearance of the article on Shakespeare, by Abel-François Villemain, in Michaud's volume 42. Had Berlioz met Shakespeare there he would have told us. Villemain's admiration of the oppositions in Shakespeare that others found barbarous is suggestive of his liberal politics: at the time of Charles X's promulgation of new laws regarding censorship, in 1827, which among other things conspicuously exposed Shakespeare's embodiment of formal liberty, Villemain was the only member of the Conseil d'État to raise his voice in favour of freedom of the press. [167]

Jean-François Ducis (1733–1816) made verse 'translations' of six of the plays, solely on the basis of the prose translations of La Place and Le Tourneur. Berlioz suggests amusingly, in Chapter XXXVI of the *Mémoires*, that Ducis was to Shakespeare what Vaccai was to Beethoven. [168] Observing the fifteen reprintings of Ducis' *Hamlet* between 1769–1880, however, we see that Berlioz's jaundiced view was not that of his century.

We may assume that, when he attended the performances of *Hamlet* and *Romeo and Juliet* in 1827, Berlioz purchased the texts of the plays as printed in Paris by Mme Vergne, whose shop was in the Place de l'Odéon, at the price of 1 franc 50 centimes. These miniature brochures, whose texts were 'conformes à la représéntation' because they were intended to be read during the performance, were printed on the day of the première of each play: one in English, one in French. Between September 1827 and February 1828 Mme Vergne brought out, in order, *Hamlet, Romeo and Juliet, Othello, King Lear, Macbeth* and *Richard III*. On the front cover of the first play to be published, we read *Théâtre Anglais, Collection des pièces anglaises jouées à Paris* [...] *HAMLET*; and on the back cover (in French): 'In the press: *Roméo et Juliette, tragédie, Otello, tragédie, Macbeth, tragédie, Venise Sauvée, tragédie*. Each of the plays that will comprise this Collection will appear, if possible, on the day of the first performance. They will be published in English and in French, separately, *and in English and French within the same volume* [my emphasis].' I have looked long and hard, and have found only *two* of the promised bilingual editions, which I therefore assume were the only ones published. Their cost, double that of the single-language publications (with the same texts), was three francs.[169]

In 1828, Truchy, a publisher in the Boulevard des Italiens, also brought out English editions of the plays, some with explanatory notes in French. Theses allow us to see the words an English-speaking Frenchman would have stumbled over when reading the text.

From later correspondence we know that Berlioz came into possession of the *Œuvres dramatiques de Shakspeare* [*sic*], *traduction nouvelle par Benjamin Laroche, précédée d'une introduction sur le génie de Shakspeare, par Alexandre Dumas*, first published in Paris by Marchant in 1839 (volume 1) and 1840 (volume 2). The Laroche translation, a commercial success, was issued in seven smaller volumes in 1841–3; it was reissued in two volumes in 1844 and 1847, and in six volumes in 1859. This is the translation with which Berlioz became most familiar.

In a letter to his sister Adèle of 26 October 1856, Berlioz writes: 'J'ai trois éditions de Shakespeare, deux en anglais, une en français, une TRADUCTION! [*sic*].'[170] That first English edition is mentioned in a letter to his father of 6 May 1835: 'The day before yesterday, an amateur, returning from my concert, made me a gift of the complete works of Shakespeare in one volume, in English. This book is worth at least a hundred francs.'[171] I assume that the 'amateur' – inspired by Berlioz's concert at the Conservatoire on 3 May, which featured the *Fantastique* followed by its Shakespearean sequel, *Le Retour à la vie* – offered Berlioz a copy of *The Dramatic works of W. Shakspeare* [*sic*], *from the text of Johnson, Stevens and Reed, with a biographical memoir and summary remarks on each play, embellished with a portrait of Shakspeare*, because this 800-page tome (the first Johnson edition appeared in 1765) was published in Paris, by Baudry, in 1829, in 1830 and again in 1835.

The second English edition is presumably the one he mentions in his letter from London to his friend Théodore Ritter, dated 3 July 1855, where he notes that John Ella has just given him a complete, one-volume Shakespeare.[172] There were at the time many such one-volume editions, but if this one were recent, it would in all likelihood be *The Works of William Shakspere, containing his plays and poems*, edited by Charles Knight and published lately in London by George Cox, in 1849, in 1852 and again in 1854.

Despite the spiteful capital letters of his reference to the TRADUCTION, Berlioz did use the Laroche text in, among other places, a letter of 10 March 1859, where he cites a long passage from *Coriolanus*, Act 3, scene 3. But in a letter of 28 October 1864, this time speaking of *Othello*, he again disparages Laroche: 'And the translators are such asses. I have corrected in my edition I don't know how many absurdities by M. Benjamin Laroche, and yet he is the most faithful and least ignorant of the lot.'[173] Sixty years later an American who closely examined the text remarked that 'Laroche's mistakes are remarkably few'.[174]

Guizot's translation was issued as an eight-volume *nouvelle édition entièrement revue* in 1862–4, in time to mark the tercentenary, and to compete with François-Victor Hugo's.[175] We have no evidence that Berlioz purchased the Guizot, but on 11 December 1862 (Berlioz's birthday) his son Louis wrote to him: 'As soon as I have paid off some debts in Paris, I intend to offer myself the new Guizot edition, which I think is the best.' Three years later, when he received from the bindery several of those volumes, he wrote to his father: 'mes amis sont arrivés'.[176]

In addition to such complete editions, there were literally hundreds of translations of the individual plays, of which many were 'imités de Shakespeare' – a formula that is by no means derisive. One may find early comment on the most important of these in the encyclopedic study by Albert Lacroix.[177] Of *Othello* there were at least 20 translations published in France by the time of Berlioz's death; of *Hamlet*, at least a dozen.[178] For all of these, it is difficult if not impossible to know from which *English* edition the translators worked.

Traduttore, traditore

During Berlioz's lifetime and beyond, on the French stage and in the French operatic theatre, the use of euphemism was common, the use of common words rare. Alfred de Vigny, whose *Othello* at the Comédie-Française was a *bataille d'Hernani* avant la lettre, was ridiculed for calling Desdemona's all-important handkerchief a mere 'mouchoir'.[179] Berlioz, too, suffered the brutality of the language police for using, in the libretto of *Benvenuto Cellini*, such vulgarities as 'gueux' (beggar), 'vipère' (betrayer), 'maraud' (rascal) and 'canaille' (scoundrel).[180] While Shakespeare's eighteenth- and early nineteenth-century translators did not seek to deliver his Elizabethan English in 'period French', they did attempt to exclude lowness and lewdness and to mind the propriety that was traditional in the French theatrical arena, where the lexicon was clear about which words were sanctioned on the stage, and where *verse* was all but a sine qua non.[181] This led François-Victor Hugo, in 1865, to preface his own translation with a revealing comment:

> before one could produce a literal translation of Shakespeare, the literary movement of 1830 had to be victorious, the liberty that had been won in politics had to be won in literature, the new language, the revolutionary language, the language of the right word and the right image had to become definitively established. Because this is now the case, we have tried our hand at literal translation of Shakespeare. Have we succeeded? The reader will be the judge.[182]

The translations by François-Victor Hugo – if the classical volumes published by Garnier-Flammarion may stand as evidence – remain most common in France.

Berlioz's longest disquisition on the question of fidelity in translation comes in an article that begins as a review of a performance of Monsigny's *Le Déserteur* (1769), given at the Opéra-Comique on 30 October 1843. Adolphe Adam had made a piano transcription and arrangement of the work, whose many modifications Berlioz found deeply troubling. In the tirade that follows (it was much revised and shortened when incorporated into the *Mémoires*) he gets carried away:

> The consequences of this principle [of arrangement] are too grave and too obvious to miss, and I have no fear at all of contradicting myself in rejecting them out of hand. True, I have in fact orchestrated a work for

piano by Weber, but it happens that I merely translated the piano into the orchestra, quite the opposite of what one usually does these days in translating operas and symphonies into the piano, just as one translates plays and poems from one language into another. But translation, *when it is faithful*, permits no additions and no subtractions and no alterations whatsoever to the thinking of the author. Unfortunately what I assert here is not about translation but about *correction*, and, accordingly, about a doctrine whose deplorable consequences we see to this day in English literature – where they have tailored and corrected *Shakespeare!* But common sense tell us straight away that if such liberties are to be taken in the case of great artists (if indeed such liberties are to be taken at all), then they must be taken by artists who are themselves even greater and more immense! And who was greater, who is greater, who will *ever* be greater than Shakespeare? ...

One might wish to say, in answer to my question, that it is not necessary to be superior to Shakespeare in order to have a good idea. There is no doubt that Garrick conceived a dénouement for *Romeo and Juliet* that is an incomparably brilliant theatrical inspiration, and he substituted it for Shakespeare's, the effect of which is less striking ... But by contrast, who is the scoundrel, who is the cretin, who is the insolent fool who came up with the dénouement for *King Lear* that is sometimes and even often substituted for the final, heartbreaking scene that Shakespeare set down in his masterpiece? Who is the crude and brainless rhymester who put into the mouth of Cordelia, the sweet and honest Cordelia, that celestial creation of a superhuman genius, those coarse tirades full of vulgar passions so foreign to her chaste and noble heart? Where is he? Would that every poet and artist and father and lover on earth could come to give him a beating, and, exposing him to the pillory of public indignation, could say to him: Wretched fool, you have committed a loathsome crime, the greatest, most odious, most contemptible of crimes, because it puts to death that highest of man's faculties that we call genius. Be you scorned, be you shamed, be you cursed! Despair and die![183]

The person whom Berlioz excoriates is of course Nahum Tate, whose adaptations were long performed in England. Adaptations and arrangements, like translations, keep works alive. Berlioz knew this and made some. But other than in exceptional circumstances, his public stance was that the *arrangement*, literary or musical, was a *derangement* that ought to be punishable by death. 'Despair and die!'

Shakespeare in Berlioz's Works

In September 1827, when Berlioz discovered Shakespeare and Harriet Smithson, he was three months shy of his twenty-fourth birthday. Oddly enough, considering his later behaviour, no *music* by Berlioz – then in the second of the four years he would spend at the Paris Conservatoire – shows any obvious trace of the *coup de foudre*. In 1828, however, when similarly shattered on first looking into Goethe's *Faust*, Berlioz was immediately inspired to compose eight 'scenes' on the poetic texts of Gérard de Nerval's otherwise prose translation of Goethe's great drama.[184] To the published score of *Huit Scènes de Faust* (later revised and incorporated into *La Damnation*), Berlioz added Shakespearean epigraphs to the quotations from Goethe that frame the individual numbers of this curious miscellany. Here we see the titles of the *Scènes* with their attendant citations (from Mme Vergne's 1827 edition):

No. 1, *Chant de la fête de Pâques*
Ophelia: 'Heavenly powers, restore him' (*Hamlet*, 3.1.141).

No. 2, *Paysans sous les tilleuls, Danse et chant*
Capulet: 'Who'll now deny to dance? She that makes dainty, I'll swear hath corns' (*Romeo and Juliet*, 1.5.18–20).

No. 3, *Concert de sylphes, Sextuor*
Mercutio: 'I talk of dreams, which are the children of an airy brain, begot of nothing but vain fantasy; which is as thin of substance as the air, and more inconstant than the wind' (*Romeo and Juliet*, 1.4.96–100).

No. 4, *Écot de joyeux compagnons, Histoire d'un rat*
Hamlet: 'How now? a rat? Dead, for a ducat, dead' (*Hamlet*, 3.4.245).

No. 5, *Chanson de Méphistophélès, Histoire d'une puce*
Hamlet: 'Miching mallecho: it means mischief' (*Hamlet*, 3.2.137–8).[185]

No. 6, *Le Roi de Thulé, Chanson Gothique*
Ophelia: 'He is dead and gone; at his head a grass green turf; at his heels a stone' (*Hamlet*, 4.5.30–2).

No. 7, *Romance de Marguerite*
Romeo: 'Ah me! Sad hours seem long' (*Romeo and Juliet*, 1.1.162).

[No. 7b], *Chœur de soldats passant sous les fenêtres de la maison de Marguerite Mercutio:* 'Come, let's be gone, the sport is over' (*Romeo and Juliet*, 1.5.119: *Benvolio:* 'Away, be gone, the sport is at the best').

No. 8, *Sérénade de Méphistophélès*
Hamlet: 'It is a damned ghost' (*Hamlet*, 3.2.82).

What is the function of these epigraphs in the printed score? To whom are they addressed? At the head of the *Chants de la fête de Pâques*, we read Ophelia's plea that Hamlet to come to his senses ('Heavenly powers, restore him'), then Faust's preparations for suicide: 'Voici une liqueur que je dois boire pieusement ....' With Mephistopheles' mischievous *Histoire d'une puce* Berlioz associates 'miching mellecho'. Could he have heard Hamlet's words as nonsense syllables of the sort he soon set down in the *Chœur d'ombres* of *Le Retour à la vie* and later in *Pandæmonium* of *La Damnation de Faust*? For Marguérite's *Roi de Thulé* he cites Ophelia, who openly preceded her Goethean counterpart as a figure aroused and abandoned. The quotations may be read as illuminating the abstraction that links them – the desire for worldly release – or even, Rainer Schmusch has argued, as a dream-like psychodrama that anticipates the archetypical programme (1830) of the *Symphonie fantastique*.[186] This may be more fantastical than what Berlioz had in mind: a gathering of scenes from *Faust* not necessarily intended for complete performance and never heard by the composer in its entirety.

 Huit Scènes de Faust, seemingly Berlioz's first effort to attach Shakespeare to music, was published in April 1829 as *Œuvre 1*. *Œuvre 2*, a *Ballet des ombres* that appeared later in 1829, is a setting by Berlioz's friend Albert Du Boys of a text based on 'Der Schattentanz' from Herder's *Terpsichore* of 1795. It, too, carries an epigraph from Shakespeare: "Tis now the very witching time of night, / When churchyards yawn, and hell itself breathes out / Contagion to this world' (*Hamlet*, 3.2.388–90). Ten years later, some of this spooky music made its way into the *Queen Mab Scherzo* of *Roméo et Juliette* – a fact that has led Hugh Macdonald to suggest that the origins of the *Ballet des ombres* may lie in music for *Romeo and Juliet* that Berlioz conceived in the aftermath of seeing the play in September 1827. Macdonald's theory – based on Berlioz's documented propensity for immediate musical response – is that the composer *did* have an instantaneous musical reaction to Shakespeare, in 1827, in the form of four 'scenes' from *Romeo and Juliet* sketched and drafted in the period between the autumn of 1827 and the summer of 1828, of which this *Ballet des ombres*, its Herderian roots notwithstanding, was perhaps the first: a music initially inspired, that is, by Mercutio's Queen Mab speech in Act 1, scene 4 of the play.[187] Further *Romeo and Juliet* music may be inferred from works composed over the next several years.

Every summer from 1827–30 Berlioz entered the *concours du Prix de Rome*, the competition sponsored by the Institut de France for a five-year fellowship that would allow composers to construct, at home and abroad, their newly sanctioned professional careers. In 1828 the subject of the prescribed exercise – a short cantata on a given text – was an episode from Tasso that shows Queen Erminia torn by her conflicted love for the Christian crusader Tancred. First-time listeners to Berlioz's *Herminie* are always surprised by the main theme of the cantata's *Introduction* – which is nothing other than the so-called *idée fixe* of the *Symphonie fantastique*. Berlioz would soon describe this 'pensée musicale' as having a 'caractère de grâce et de noblesse'[188] – precisely the character of the beloved woman with whom it is associated. That woman is quite obviously Harriet Smithson – which allows us to suppose that in the aftermath of seeing *Romeo and Juliet*, Berlioz also conceived this academic 'scene', modelled on Romeo's initial passion for Juliet, and later transmogrified into the first movement of the *Symphonie fantastique*.

In 1829 the cantata text concerned the death of Cleopatra, a Shakespearean subject that Berlioz thought, as we have seen, that he might adopt as the basis of an opera. The centrepiece of Berlioz's *Cléopâtre* is a 'Méditation' in which the heroine, contemplating suicide, wonders if the Egyptian pharos or the Ptolemaic kings will allow her to sleep for all eternity in the ancient pyramids. 'Grands Pharaons, nobles Lagides', with a startling eleven-bar harmonic sequence that descends chromatically from C-sharp minor to F minor and thusly into the sepulchral darkness, is headed with an epigraph from *Romeo and Juliet* (4.3.30): 'What if when I am laid into the tomb ....'[189] Berlioz explained to his friend Humbert Ferrand the source of his inspiration: 'C'est la scène où Juliette médite sur son ensevelissement dans les caveaux des Capulets [...].'[190] Here, explicitly, is the third of Macdonald's four 'scenes' from the play. The composer Adrien Boieldieu reprimanded Berlioz for his experimental writing: 'I'll bet you're an admirer of Goethe, of Shakespeare', he apparently moaned.[191]

In 1830 the cantata text described *La Mort de Sardanapale*, the subject magnificently portrayed three years earlier in one of Delacroix's greatest masterpieces but set by Berlioz in a conventional style that led the judges to grant him the Prix de Rome. No Shakespearean epigraphs ornament this manuscript, which Berlioz completed just as the July Revolution reached its climactic last day. But one of *Sardanapale*'s principal melodies was reused nine years later in the *Scène d'amour* of *Roméo et Juliette*, suggesting that that tune, too, was conceived, in the aftermath of the revelation of 1827, as the kernel of a scene of first love.

Two further works mark the composer's official entry into the professional musical world: an *Ouverture de la Tempête*, composed between August and October of 1830 and premiered at the Opéra on 7 November (more about this work below), and the *Symphonie fantastique* itself, drafted during the first four months of 1830, rehearsed in May, and first performed on 5 December at a concert for the benefit of those wounded in July. The *Fantastique* was revised over the years, but it nonetheless remains a leading contender for the most astonishing first symphony in the history of western music. The second movement, *Un bal*, with its central recollection of the *idée fixe*, would constitute the last of Macdonald's 'lost' scenes from *Roméo et Juliette*, this one inspired (in 1827–8) by the Capulet ball in Act 1, scene 5: 'Music plays, and they dance.'

One may be sceptical of Macdonald's hypothesis and still perceive the Shakespearean influence on the cantatas and other works that punctuate Berlioz's career at the Conservatoire. But there is something more Shakespearean in the *Symphonie fantastique* than the mere reuse of materials conceived on Shakespearean themes. What has kept the work in the musical headlines, to the chagrin of those who believe its claim to fame should rest solely on its intrinsic musical architecture, is its literary programme. Fourteen different versions of this document testify to the importance Berlioz attributed to it, though most of these differ only in detail. Reduced to its essentials, the story remains the same: unrequited love, rage and jealousy; passion and betrayal; real and imagined revenge. That *la femme aimée* of the symphony is murdered by the artist-hero in nightmarish fury has led Katherine Kolb to see the work as founded on an '*Othello* paradigm'. Indeed, Kolb observes that revenge in the face of infidelity, amorous or artistic, becomes a key element of Berlioz's larger criticism and fiction, most notably in the story *Le Premier Opéra* of 1837, where an unreliable patron is left in the lurch, and in *Euphonia* of 1844, where an unfaithful lover is put to death.[192]

The unfaithful woman of the *Fantastique* would of course be Harriet Smithson – though when he sketched the programme, Berlioz had yet to make her acquaintance in person. By a twist of fate, on the day of symphony's première at the Conservatoire, 5 December 1830, a benefit at the Opéra was held for Miss Smithson herself, who had returned to Paris in March and had since that time been trying to establish a new company for the performance of English drama. Her efforts were in vain: even though

King Louis-Philippe offered Harriet an honorarium of 1,000 francs for her performance (Berlioz received an honorarium of only 300 francs for his), it was clear that her future husband's star was rising, while hers was about to fall.

The Prix de Rome, awarded in the autumn of 1830, was Berlioz's union card and ticket to an Italian expedition that would provide immediate adventure and lasting musical enrichment. The 'Voyage en Italie' became the stuff of Berlioz's books and articles, and the eventual source of at least five Italy-inspired works: the symphonies *Harold en Italie* and *Roméo et Juliette* ('Two households … in fair Verona') and the operas based on Benvenuto Cellini's *Vita*, on Virgil's *Aeneid*, and on Shakespeare's *Much Ado*. During the 15 months he actually spent on the Italian peninsula, from March 1831 to June 1832, Berlioz composed two unambiguously Shakespearean works, the *Grande Ouverture du Roi Lear*, set down in April and May 1831 and explicitly inspired by his first reading of *King Lear*, and *Le Retour à la vie*, constructed in the summer of 1831 as a Shakespeare-saturated sequel to the *Symphonie fantastique* and thus the second part of what he called *Épisode de la vie d'un artiste*.[193]

After conducting the *Lear* overture many years later, Berlioz wrote to his friend Mme Massart: 'Perhaps *father* Shakespeare would not denounce me for having dared in this way to make his old Breton king and his sweet Cordelia speak.'[194] He wrote the same thing to his niece, Joséphine Suat: 'I think that *father* Shakespeare would perhaps smile on hearing the speech I gave to his old king and his sweet Cordelia.'[195] Now, scholars and critics have spilled more than a little ink over the aesthetic question of 'programme music', and I am not innocent of spattering some of my own. But from these quotations we see with no theorizing precisely how Berlioz articulated his intention – that the voices of the king and his daughter be heard. In Chapter LIX of the *Mémoires*, Berlioz recites what King George V of Hanover heard after the overture's performance there on 1 April 1854: 'It's magnificent, M. Berlioz, simply magnificent! Your orchestra speaks, you have no need of words. I followed all the scenes: the entrance of the king into his council chamber, the storm on the heath, the terrible prison scene, and the grief of Cordelia. Oh, this Cordelia, how well have you painted her! How tender and timid she is! It is heartbreaking, and so very beautiful.'

If George V, who had a rich musical imagination, heard more than meets the eye (the king was blind), Berlioz did not contradict him. The first of two themes in the opening Andante, in the lower strings, can indeed be likened to Shakespeare's stubborn old king, and the second, in the solo oboe, to the soft and gentle Cordelia. But to suggest that the work literally follows the narrative of the play is to ignore its musical architecture – that of a modified sonata Allegro (exposition-development-recapitulation-coda) preceded by a slow introduction.

Berlioz does explain one explicitly programmatic moment: the curious drumrolls in measures 66–85 that are superimposed upon the cantankerous theme associated with Lear:

> It was customary, at the French Court, up to the time of Charles X, in 1830, to announce the king's arrival at the residence (after Sunday Mass) with the sounding of an enormous bass drum, which hammered out the strange five-beat rhythm that had been traditional since ancient times. This gave me the idea of accompanying with such a drumroll Lear's entrance into the council chamber for the scene of the division of his kingdom.[196]

But in Chapter VI of the *Mémoires* (drafted ten years before the letter we have quoted), Berlioz described the scene with a different twist, noting that Charles X withdrew 'to the grotesque noise of a fife and an enormous bass drum sounding the traditional fanfare in a quintuple metre worthy of the musical barbarianism of the very Middle Ages that begot it'. Here we find derisiveness, a fife, and no reference to *Lear* – which suggests that, in the composer's creative imagination, the thunderous *musical* gesture preceded the programmatic description, and thus that the description may be taken *cum grano salis*.

Le Retour à la vie, completed in 1831–2 as the sequel to the *Fantastique* and revised in 1855–7 as *Lélio ou Le Retour à la vie*, is Berlioz's least understood and most Shakespearean work. Here, in what he first called *mélologue* (the term borrowed from Thomas Moore) and later *monodrame lyrique*, the composer-librettist arranged six musical numbers preceded by six monologues into a series that carries forward the psychological progression of the life of the artist-hero of the symphony by transforming his nightmarish despair into a rational expression of faith in the power of music.[197] The central musical ingredient of this six-part 'Return to Life' is a *Chœur d'ombres irritées*, which is nothing other than the 'Méditation' (transplanted from the 1829 prize cantata, *Cléopâtre*) that Berlioz explicitly labelled, as we have seen, 'the scene in which Juliet meditates her entombment in the Capulets' vault'. In *Le Retour à la vie*, before this ominous chorus – now labelled as a music for the ghost scene in *Hamlet* – we hear the meditation of the artist-hero as he attempts to urge upon himself the will to live:

To live! ... but to live, for me, is to suffer! While death ... is relief. I am not overly troubled by Hamlet's doubts; I seek neither to explore *what torturous dreams may come when we have shuffled off this mortal coil* nor to know the map of *the undiscovered country from whose bourn no traveler returns* ... Hamlet! Profound and depressing conception, how much torment you have caused me! Oh, it is only too true, Shakespeare sparked in me a revolution that has afflicted my entire being [...]. And yet, I constantly return to him; I allow myself to be entranced by his terrifying genius ... How beautiful, truthful, and penetrating is that speech of the royal ghost, revealing to young Hamlet the crime that deprived him of his father! It has always seemed to me that this passage could be the subject of a grand and dark musical composition. I feel right now only too prepared to draft such a work ... Already, despite myself, I sense that the singular capacity of which I am possessed to 'think music' has been so powerfully engaged that I have at my command, so to speak, imaginary performers who move me as though I were actually hearing them. Often this is the result of reflection; sometimes, it is the result of my inflamed imagination. The ideal orchestra then takes off like lightning, without my being able to control its movements. Here ... yes ... I need a hushed instrumentation, broad and sinister harmonies, a lugubrious melody, a chorus in unison and in octaves singing in a strange language as though it were a single, powerful voice emanating from a world unknown and to us incomprehensible.[198]

The speaker is an actor who recites his lines before a curtain that conceals both the orchestra and the chorus. Like Hamlet, he holds a book in his hands, and, as in the play, we never learn what book it is, though it should obviously be *Hamlet*, since, as the words in italics demonstrate, he is quoting the 'to be or not to be' soliloquy.[199] In the 'Chorus of Shades' that follows, we hear not the text from *Cléopâtre* but the words of some unintelligible 'ancien dialecte du Nord', a language inspired perhaps by the 'squeak and gibber' that Horatio attributes to the 'sheeted dead' at the opening of the play (1.1.115–16).

After the *Chœur d'ombres irritées*, the narrator continues:

Oh, Shakespeare! Shakespeare! You, whose early years went by unnoticed, whose story is almost as uncertain as that of Ossian, or of Homer – oh, what a blinding legacy your genius has left us! Colossus fallen upon a world of dwarves, how little are you understood! A great people adore you, it is true. But by so many others are you cursed! Without knowing you, and putting their faith in brainless writers who, while denigrating you, pilfer your treasures, they accuse you of barbarism ... The author of *Romeo* and of *Coriolanus*, the creator of such characters as Desdemona, Ophelia, Juliet, and Cordelia, the father of the delicious Ariel ... a barbarian![200]

There ensues a furious tirade against so many 'profanateurs' who dare to alter works of genius and arrange them to fit current styles and tastes. 'I would rather be an outlaw', the narrator exclaims, as he pays musical tribute to the life of the desperado in a boisterous *Scène de la vie de brigand*. Then, after a touching and melancholy reminiscence of love, the narrator determines to renounce despair and to live on for the sake of his art. As composer-conductor, he assembles his forces – in the fiction they are his 'students' – and prepares to rehearse a work of his own devising. This is nothing other than the *Ouverture de la Tempête* composed in the summer of 1830 with Camille Moke in mind:

> Yes, a magician who at will stirs and soothes the elements, graceful spirits who obey him, a sweet and timid virgin, a passionate young man, a savage beast, so many varied scenes terminating in a most brilliant dénouement – I shall seize upon these many vivid contrasts! Choruses of airy spirits, cast intermittently upon the orchestra, will here speak sweetly to the lovely Miranda in a sonorous and harmonious language, and there speak to the beastly Caliban in dark and menacing tones. And I shall have the voices of the sylphs enshrouded in a feathery haze of harmony that will burnish the fluttering of their wings.[201]

In the revised *Lélio ou Le Retour à la vie* Berlioz took this opportunity – before the students' performance of what is now called a *Fantaisie dramatique sur La Tempête* – to evoke *Hamlet*'s play-within-a play: 'The curtain rises, one sees all the performers on the risers, the Artist begins to rehearse what is "real" music, giving critical advice to his interpreters just as Hamlet does in the scene with the players.'[202] 'Leave room for the piano! [...] The singers must not hold their music in front of their faces [...] Do not exaggerate the dynamics, do not confuse *mezzo-forte* with *fortissimo*!'[203] Through the lines of Berlioz's fictional composer-conductor we read his sympathy for the performing artist, which he carried, 'as Hamlet put it', he says, in his 'heart of hearts'.[204] The performance itself is preceded by the artist's private prayer: not 'May God protect me', but rather 'Que *Shakespeare* me protège!'

Le Retour à la vie, first performed in Paris on 9 December 1832, marked Berlioz's return to the worldly stage upon which he hoped to build his career. Success in France meant performance at the opera house, and that became Berlioz's immediate goal. As a winner of the Prix de Rome, and as an acquaintance of the powerful family of Louis-François Bertin (the director of the *Journal des débats* and the 'Monsieur Bertin' of Ingres' famous portrait), Berlioz had good reason to believe that he would indeed obtain a commission from the Académie royale de musique. In May 1834, Berlioz told his friend Ferrand that his affairs at the Opéra were in the hands of the Bertins. The proposed subject was no surprise: 'Il s'agit de me donner l'*Hamlet* de Shakespeare supérieurement arrangé en opéra.'[205] The librettist was to be Léon de Wailly, a man of letters from a family of government officials who had grown up with Louis Bertin's sons Armand and Édouard and who had embarked upon a translation of *Hamlet* as early as 1829. Berlioz himself, we learn from a later reminiscence, had 'written out long passages [of *Hamlet*] in translation and dreamed of translating it all'. The man reminiscing – Louis Bourgault-Ducoudray, who won the Prix de Rome in 1862, and who had a long conversation with Berlioz at that time – also remembered Berlioz saying that he 'would never dare' to write an opera on *Hamlet*.[206] I rather believe that young Berlioz would have jumped at the chance, even had he found Hamlet's broodings – like Romeo and Juliet's declarations of love – too disturbing for conventional operatic setting.

The biographers have made little of this might-have-been. But if anyone were prepared to cast in music this great play of revenge, it was Berlioz. In the 1840s Verdi cast it off as too difficult – and wrote *Stiffelio*. In 1868, Ambroise Thomas produced his version – with a happy ending. We do have *Hamlet* music by Berlioz (to be considered below), but the opera he would have written in his most youthfully imaginative period – the period, it turned out, of *Benvenuto Cellini* – might well have equalled the grandeur of the play that had long been his intellectual obsession. In December 1834, a journalist spoke of Berlioz's 'glorieuse mission': 'to bring to the art of music the genius and power of Shakespeare'.[207] Surely he had *Hamlet* in mind.

'A Shakespearean musical drama' is what Jacques Barzun calls the opera that Berlioz did write, *Benvenuto Cellini*, on the basis of its mixture of comedy and seriousness and its complex title character.[208] Conceived in the early 1830s and produced at the Opéra in the autumn of 1838, *Cellini* is also Shakespearean in its conspicuous progression to a dramatic climax – the casting in the final tableau of Perseus holding the head of the medusa.

For Berlioz, Shakespeare was the veritable 'inventor of the crescendo' in precisely this sense.[209] Be this as it may, his opera failed to secure a place in the rotation at the Académie royale de musique, less because of its unrelenting score than because of its undistinguished libretto, whose language, fashioned by Léon de Wailly and Auguste Barbier, with help from Alfred de Vigny, was deemed commonplace and inappropriate to the nation's most exalted musical theatre.

Viewed from afar, the fall of *Benvenuto Cellini* seems to portend the rise of the 'dramatic symphony' – to provoke the composer, when Nicolò Paganini bestowed upon him a generous gift, to return to *Romeo and Juliet* and to put it forth in an entirely new manner. He had seen Bellini's *I Capuleti ed i Montecchi* in Florence, in March 1831, and, under the mistaken impression that it was based on Shakespeare, found it 'ignoble, ridicule, impuissant, nul'.[210] Now, in 1839, he would cast his own setting as an instrumental composition but include sung words in order that the untexted portions of the work be properly understood. In the *Avant-propos de l'auteur*, printed with the libretto of *Roméo et Juliette* at the time of the initial performances, we find a platform – a 400-word aesthetic manifesto, the most important such document Berlioz ever produced – whose opening words, 'One will *surely* not misconstrue the genre of this work', are ironic. One will *certainly* misconstrue the genre of this work, he intends to say, because that genre is by no means self-evident. 'Although voices are often employed in it, it is neither a concert nor a cantata but rather a choral symphony.' If you associate 'choral symphony' with Beethoven's Ninth – always 'la symphonie avec chœurs' in French – then you react precisely as Berlioz intended.

The links between Beethoven's Ninth and Berlioz's Third (after the *Fantastique* and *Harold en Italie*) are significant. For the Ninth, Berlioz said, listeners must have a literal translation of the German words. Without one, 'How do you expect the public to understand the composer's full intentions, to recognize the reasons for the plan he established, or to appreciate the expressive value of his melodies?'[211] 'This symphony', he earlier remarked, 'has the misfortune of beginning with a movement of such enormous expression and form that the rest of the work suffers by comparison, and yet the rest is nonetheless colossal.'[212] Such comments may explain the plan of his own 'symphonie avec chœurs'. The first of its seven movements is in four parts (*Introduction, Prologue, Strophes, Scherzetto*) that outline via words and musical foreshadowings the essential steps of the tragedy. There follow five central movements that relate by title and purely musical content the stillness of Romeo's gloom, the brilliance of the Capulets' ball, the deserted gardens of the Capulets' estate, the wit of

Mercutio's invocation of Queen Mab and the tragedy of Juliet's death. In the production of the play Berlioz saw in 1827, Juliet's last wish, 'let me die', closed the curtain. In his symphony of 1839, a concluding movement, cast in operatic terms, tells of the reconciliation of the families.

For the love scene, Berlioz's opening manifesto offers us the last word:

> If, in the celebrated scenes in the garden and in the cemetery, the dialogue of the two lovers, the asides of Juliet and the passionate outbursts of Romeo are not sung, if in the end the duets of love and despair are confided to the orchestra, the reasons for this are numerous and readily grasped. First of all – and this reason alone suffices to justify the author's approach – what we have here is a symphony and not an opera. Secondly, vocal duets of this sort having been composed thousands of times and by the greatest of masters, it seemed wise as well as unusual to attempt a different mode of expression. Finally, the very sublimity of this love rendered its depiction so dangerous for the composer that he had to give to his imagination a latitude that the positive sense of sung words would not have allowed him, and to resort to the language of instruments, a language at once richer, more varied, less restrained, and by its very indefiniteness incomparably more powerful in such a situation.[213]

Only pure instrumental music can capture the rapture of immeasurable love. *Lélio*, its soliloquies declaimed by the Hamlet-like narrator, is his ingenious theatrical tribute to the Bard. The *Scène d'amour* is his greatest musical tribute to Shakespeare – because it is his greatest transformation of Shakespeare, and operates on a plane wholly distinct from that of the play. Years later, when Émile Deschamps, the author of the libretto, proposed that a performance of the play be interspersed with music from the symphony, Berlioz told him that the symphony was composed for an entirely different purpose: 'Music', he said, 'has no place in Shakespeare's drama.'[214]

Berlioz's words have not discouraged analysts from finding direct reflections of the text of the play in the texture of the music. Ian Kemp's impressive study of *Roméo et Juliette* argues for section-by-section and line-by-line correspondences between words and notes.[215] 'O speak again bright angel' (2.2.26) would sound, in the *Scène d'amour*, at the arrival of a 'first subject' (bar 125), which begins in C-sharp minor and moves to A major. 'What man art thou' (2.2.52) would mark a transition section (bar 181). 'Thou knowest the mask of night' (2.2.84) would sound at the arrival of a 'second subject' (bar 250), which begins in F-sharp minor and moves to A major. A final section, still in A major, would open (bar 274) at 'In truth, fair Montague, I am too fond' (2.2.98). But are the musical divisions strictly motivated by the text? That remains the question. Berlioz answered it with a crucial (and ambiguous) word: 'This is a musical *paraphrase* of the most sublime scene that poetry has ever produced.' He refers to the scene that begins, 'But, soft! what light through yonder window breaks?' (2.2.3–4) – 'Silence ! Quelle clarté resplendit à cette fenêtre!'[216]

Another model for the form of the love scene, it has been argued, is to be found in the Ninth Symphony, whose combination of vocal and instrumental forces and whose foreshadowings and reminiscences so obviously provoked Berlioz's initial conception of the whole. Like the Adagio of the Beethoven, which may be seen as composed of two main thematic elements of which one disappears (after a transition section) in the second half of the movement, while the other, remaining in the tonic key, is subject to variation, so too, Jean-Pierre Bartoli claims, may the Adagio of the Berlioz be seen as designed in two parts, with one principal theme disappearing (after a transition section) in part two, while the other, remaining in the tonic, is extensively developed.[217]

The claims of Kemp and Bartoli are subtle; they suffer from abridgement. If I prefer analysis that turns on abstract musical architecture, it is because I cannot forget the nefarious tradition, which arose in the immediate wake of the *Fantastique*, that sees *all* of Berlioz's structures collapsing without the support of words. This is simply not true – not even for the moment in *Roméo et Juliette* that is more curious than all the rest, *Roméo au tombeau des Capulets*, to which Berlioz affixed the following note at the head of the score:

> The public has no imagination. Works addressed solely to the imagination, therefore, have no public. The following instrumental scene is such a work, and I think that it ought to be omitted every time that this symphony is not performed before elite listeners who possess highly developed poetic sensibilities and who are very familiar with Garrick's dénouement for the fifth act of Shakespeare's tragedy. That is to say that this scene ought to be omitted ninety-nine times out of a hundred.[218]

In 'Romeo at the Capulets' tomb' Ian Kemp hears Romeo wrenching open the tomb, killing Paris, discovering and addressing Juliet's apparently lifeless body, and more. (The Garrick dénouement, which Berlioz prized, has Juliet awaken before Romeo dies.) But the subtitles in the score – 'Invocation, Réveil de Juliette, Joie délirante, désespoir, dernières angoisses et mort des deux amants' – tell us even more than we need to know, because the movement is clearly evocative of discovery, deliriousness and despair *in themselves*. In fact, the 'deliriousness' is self-explanatory: Berlioz conveys it by a new transformation of the main theme of the *Scène d'amour* in 60-some bars of the most ecstatic music he ever composed – an independent architectural pillar, in other words, that causes the larger musical edifice to cohere.

In his ingenious analysis of this scene, Daniel Albright finds musical expression that is 'antithetical' to musical form, as 'the orchestra becomes a sort of recording device for spastic contractions' and 'for paroxysms of the brain' in what is termed 'somatic opera' – opera, that is, of almost pure corporeal gesture.[219] Albright's account has the advantage of focusing not upon Shakespeare's words but upon Berlioz's notes. In fact, Berlioz was deeply ambivalent about an opera on *Romeo and Juliet*: 'Yes, of course, I could still write a marvellous opera, in addition to the symphony. But for whom? Who would sing it? Who would produce it? Who would appreciate it? Let us no more speak of that!'[220] Earlier he was more precise about the difficulty of finding a Romeo, 'a young man simultaneously wistful and ebullient', a 'fierce and handsome Montague who knows how to kill and to die, and whose love is *as vast and profound as the sea*'.[221]

We do have an account from Berlioz of *Roméo au tombeau*, which is found in his review of Bellini's *Roméo et Juliette* as performed at the Opéra in 1859.[222] In order to minimize Bellini's version of the tomb scene, he gives his own description – which I believe we are entitled to take as the unarticulated programme of that scene in the *symphonie dramatique*:

The tomb scene as performed by the great English artists will always remain the most sublime miracle of dramatic art. On hearing the name Romeo feebly escaping from the lips of Juliet, coming back to life, the young Montague, stupefied, remains momentarily transfixed. A second even more tender call draws his eyes towards the bier, and Juliet's stirring dissipates his doubts. She lives! He rushes to the funereal couch, wrenches from it the beloved body, tearing away the veils and the shroud, and he carries it to the front of the stage, holding it up upright in his arms. Juliet looks about languidly, her eyes pale. Romeo calls her by name, presses her to him in a desperate embrace, parts the hair that hides her wan forehead, covers her face with furious kisses, and bursts out in convulsive laughter. In his heartrending happiness he has forgotten that he is about to die. Juliet breathes! Juliet! Juliet! ... But a terrible pain reminds him: the poison is at work, it devours his entrails! … *O potent poison!*[223]

In Berlioz's score we hear the ecstasy of discovery (bars 90–147) and the agony of death (bars 148–227): we know the protagonists because the melody that is emblazoned, then torn to shreds, is *texted* in the Prologue: 'Roméo, palpitant d'une joie inquiète, se découvre à Juliette, et de son cœur les feux éclatent à leur tour' – 'Romeo, throbbing with nervous excitement, reveals himself to Juliet, and from her heart in turn her ardor explodes.'

Shortly after the completion of *Roméo et Juliette*, Berlioz and his wife, she burdened by his recurrent absence and he by her recurrent jealousy, began irretrievably to fall apart. The composer took up with a little-known mezzo soprano, Marie Récio, whom he may have met as early as 1837, and who seems to have become his mistress in 1840 or 1841, at which time, perhaps inspired by her, he completed the song cycle *Les Nuits d'été* on poems by Théophile Gautier. In 1842 he returned to *Hamlet* and made a setting for voice and piano of *La Mort d'Ophélie*, a 'ballade imitée de Shakespeare' by his friend the playwright Ernest Legouvé. The text is an elegant paraphrase of Gertrude's poetic account of Ophelia's death: 'There is a willow grows askaunt the brook, / That shows his hoary leaves in the glassy stream' (4.7.166–7). If we see the dramatic symphony as a monument to Harriet Smithson, so too may we see this melancholy song, punctuated by the expressive use of the interjection 'Ah', as a poignant memento of the demise of the composer's star-crossed love. Those *vocalises* on 'Ah', as Heather Hadlock has called them, render Ophelia 'present' in what is otherwise a recitation not by the Queen but by an anonymous narrator. It is as though Ophelia, like Romeo and Juliet in the *symphonie dramatique*, were beyond verbal representation.[224]

La Mort d'Ophélie has a complicated publication history, appearing as a solo song in 1848, reappearing in 1849 as a part of a collection entitled *Tristia*, and appearing yet again – as revised in 1848 for women's chorus and orchestra – in a second version of *Tristia* published in 1852. We find in that second version another Shakespearean composition, a *Marche funèbre pour la dernière scène d'Hamlet*, which Berlioz completed in 1844 for projected performance during a production of the play in the now completed translation by his old friend Léon de Wailly. That performance never took place. Nor did a Shakespeare concert take place at Covent Garden, in February 1848, when Berlioz was in London and again hoping to hear both *La Mort d'Ophélie* and the *Marche funèbre*, which he revised for the occasion.

At the head of the score of the March, which calls for a wordless chorus of men and women who sing (as in the song) the single vocable 'Ah', Berlioz sets down the speech of Fortinbras that closes the play: 'Let four captains / Bear Hamlet like a soldier to the stage,' etc. (5.2.395–403) – to the left, in English, to the right, in French. The final stage direction – 'Exeunt marching, bearing off the bodies, after the which a peal of ordinance are shot off' – is omitted. But at the climax of the score, at bar 85, we *hear* a peal of ordinance: the score indicates 'feu de peloton derrière le théâtre'.

The death of a hero has always inspired music. After the *Marcia funebre* of the *Eroica* Symphony and before the *Trauermusik* for Siegfried in *Götterdämmerung*, the greatest music in the funereal genre is, I daresay, this *Marche funèbre sur la mort d'Hamlet*. Berlioz's own 'symphonic life ends here', Julian Rushton has rightly observed, because, after the 1840s, he will produce no further extended, independent instrumental composition.[225] This one, rich with affecting dissonance and ferocious dynamic surprise, is impractical to perform not because of the need for gunfire, which can be simulated, but because of the need for a chorus – which has very little to do. It is based loosely on the sonata principle and anchored firmly on the obsessive rhythm of the Allegretto of Beethoven's Seventh Symphony, where the closing inconclusive harmony (on a six-four chord) caused Berlioz, as we have seen, to write, to cite, 'the rest is silence'. The *Marche* likewise concludes on an inconclusive harmony: a nod to the Beethoven, but also to Horatio, whose heartbreaking call for music – 'And flights of angels sing thee to thy rest!' – ironically contradicts Hamlet's last words.

In 1845 Berlioz drafted in a notebook a list of his works that includes *three* 'Morceaux d'Hamlet'. I have mentioned two, *La Mort d'Ophélie*, and the *March funèbre*, which he here calls *Coronach*, an Irish word for 'dirge' that he may have heard from Harriet Smithson or found in Sir Walter Scott. The third is a now lost or hidden *Scène de la comédie*, which suggests the *Hamlet*-inspired scene in *Lélio* prior to the playing of the *Fantaisie sur La Tempête*, even if it is difficult to imagine a musicking of Shakespeare's play-within-a-play.

Although we may find Shakespearean elements in them, the major musical works of the late 1840s and early 1950s, *La Damnation de Faust*, the *Te Deum*, and *L'Enfance du Christ*, do not overtly project Berlioz's fascination with Shakespeare. (This is the period of the drafting of most of the *Mémoires*). Of the *Te Deum* Berlioz did say, to Liszt, that 'yes, the *Requiem* now has a brother, a brother come into the world with teeth in its head, like Richard III (only without the hump)'.[226] During the long genesis of

Les Troyens, in Berlioz's imagination and workshop, the Bard was of course never far away.

Berlioz's great five-act French grand opera represents the culmination of the passion for Virgil he developed as a child. It is a work rich in the *contrastes et oppositions* that characterize much of his music and that have been associated, perhaps too facilely, with Shakespeare's famous indifference to generic purity. In fact there is but a single bead of comedy in *Les Troyens*, which is essentially faithful to its Virgilian source and almost unremittingly tragic – despite the presence of dance, pantomime and procession – in recounting the inescapable demise of Cassandre, the Trojan princess, and the inevitable death of Didon, the Carthaginian Queen. That bead occurs in Act 5, before Énée, having consummated his love for Didon in the previous act and been reminded *post-amorem* that his sacred foundational mission lies elsewhere, gives in to the ghosts of the gods (ghosts are *ipso facto* Shakespearean) and sets sail for Italy.

At the opening of this final act, Berlioz gives us a gentle aria in which a Trojan sailor longs for the homeland he will never see again, and a violent chorus in which the Trojan soldiers urge immediate departure, for they, too, have heard the voices of the gods. Immediately thereafter we find a delightful little march rendered jocular by pairs of clarinets and bassoons in counterpoint over a walking bass, in which two sentinels express cynicism about the mission to Italy: 'Par Bacchus! Il sont fous avec leur Italie! ...' – 'They've gone bonkers with their "Italy"'; 'We lead a fine life right where we are' (I paraphrase); 'We have found good wine, good food, and accommodating women. Why leave now?' Even as a part of a strict alexandrine verse, 'ils sont fous' is hardly elevated poetry. But in the theatre, the contrast between the 'heroic aspirations of the royal personages', as Berlioz put it, and these 'low soldierly instincts', is hilarious.[227]

The sentinels' scene is readily associated with such comedic moments in Shakespearean tragedy as the cobbler's scene at the opening of Act 1 of *Julius Caesar*, and the gravediggers' scene at the opening of Act 5 of *Hamlet* – both of which (as Berlioz knew) Voltaire found lacking in good taste.[228] Had Berlioz's watchmen engaged with Énée, as the gravediggers do with Hamlet (and as the cobbler does with the tribunes), the musical moment would more obviously recall the theatrical event. Still, like Shakespeare, Berlioz here reduces the larger-than-life world inhabited by the principals to the level of ordinary humanity, and to an experience we can imagine undergoing ourselves: the sentinels' message – the 'folly' of exchanging Carthaginian caresses for the violence of the sea – is hardly difficult to grasp. The score, however, which the composer called 'a musical proposition to be resolved', is not without sophistication.[229] Adding to the levity of the wind instruments and walking bass is the phrase structure: the first twelve bars, for instance, fall into units of 2 [introduction] + 2 [antecedent] + 2 [consequent] + 6 [= 2 + 4] – which provides a simulacrum of regularity that in the end reflects Berlioz's lifelong allergy to everything in music that is 'expected'. Furthermore, the stage action is designed for special mirth, as the soldiers are instructed to take precisely two steps per measure, the one marching from right to left, the other from left to right, in a not quite regular 'march of complaint'.

The supreme Shakespearean moment in *Les Troyens* is the supreme moment of passion, in the Act 4 love duet, 'Nuit d'ivresse et d'extase infinie'. On 10 June 1856, Berlioz wrote of the borrowing to his friend Legouvé: 'I have just finished the fourth act duet. I have appropriated the scene from Shakespeare's *Merchant of Venice*, and I have "Virgilized" it' – 'je l'ai virgilianisée.'[230] He tells Legouvé, and others, because he was proud of his *trouvaille*, that for Dido and Aeneas Virgil provided no 'radotages' or 'ramblings of love' such as those Shakespeare composed for Jessica and Lorenzo. So he pilfered the Shakespeare (5.1.1–25) and poured it into the Virgil. Shakespeare's conceit – the repeated invocation of 'in such a night' to evoke the lines between such lovers as Troilus and Cressida, Dido and Aeneas, and Jessica and Lorenzo themselves – becomes in Berlioz the repeated invocation of 'par une telle nuit' to evoke the links between lovers such as Troilus and Cressida, Venus and Anchises, Diana and Endymion, and Dido and Aeneas themselves. The eight-fold reiteration in Shakespeare is playful, as Jessica – 'I would out-night you' – makes plain. The repetition in Berlioz is less insistent and also less free: the three-line stanzas with 'par une telle nuit' – a rhymed couplet of alexandrines followed by a six-syllable line – constitute a perfectly regular form and rhyme-scheme. These are surrounded and separated by an equally regular, thrice heard refrain, although the exquisite opening image, 'nuit d'ivresse et d'extase infinie' (an improvement over the initially sketched 'nuit d'amour, nuit d'angoisse parfumée') is by its sound anything but ordinary.[231]

Along with the form, Berlioz borrows the reference to Troilus and Cressida, and as we noted earlier, while working on *Les Troyens* Berlioz did reread Shakespeare's play. The mention of Dido and Aeneas in Shakespeare is, of course, a mere mythological allusion. In Berlioz, the 'real' Didon and Énée refer to themselves in the third person, thus 'translating their love into the realms of story'.[232] For those aware of the original Shakespearean reference, the irony is doubled.

A final borrowing from *The Merchant of Venice* is similarly literal: just as Lorenzo forgives Jessica for 'slandering' his love, so, too, does Énée forgive Didon for coldly greeting his affection. Indeed, as this nocturne runs its course, we are led to believe that love will vanquish duty and destiny, as Didon, neglecting her queenly responsibilities, and Énée, disregarding his predestined mission, live out their passion. In Shakespeare, Jessica, too, rejects Shylock's patriarchal authority, she 'deceives, disobeys, robs, and abandons her father', and exclaims to Lorenzo: 'If thou keep promise, I shall end this strife / Become a Christian and thy loving wife' (2.3.20–1).[233] In Berlioz, however, Énée disobeys nothing as he sails off à la recherché d'Italie. This leads to a poignant reference to *Othello*, at the end of the sublime aria in A-flat major near the close of Act 5, when Didon intones her farewell, 'Ma carrière est finie' – than which there is no finer rendering in French of '[Othello's] occupation gone'.

With the appropriation from *The Merchant of Venice*, Berlioz nearly completes his musical incarnation of some of Shakespeare's greatest female characters: Miranda, Desdemona, Juliette, Ophelia and Jessica – the very characters whom Alexandre Dumas singles out in his imaginative introduction to the first volume of the Shakespeare translation by Benjamin Laroche.[234] But surely the character of Beatrice also belongs on this list. It is she, and her equally mordant opposite, Benedict, who inspired Berlioz to prepare what turned out to be his final work for the theatre. Indeed, his original title (it was Shakespeare's, too) of *Bénédict et Béatrice*, set down in a letter of 10 November 1860, was soon reversed as he condensed Shakespeare's *Much Ado About Nothing* to the story of these two characters alone. 'You ask me how I could reduce Shakespeare's five acts to a single-act *opéra comique*', he wrote to his son on 21 November 1860. 'I took up only one aspect of the play; all the rest is of my own invention. It consists quite simply of convincing Beatrice and Benedict (who despise each other) that each is in love with the other, and thus to inspire in both of them what is truly love.'[235]   On 22 July 1862, he expanded his description: 'To Shakespeare's scenario I added a musical caricature, a grotesque Kapellmeister named Somarone (a big fat ass), whose asinine behavior provokes laughter.'[236]

The plot of Berlioz's comic opera – a pendant to *Les Troyens*, one might say, as is Beethoven's classically-proportioned Eighth Symphony to his mighty Seventh, or as is the Académie imperial de musique (for which theatre *Les Troyens* was designed) to the intimate rooms in Baden-Baden (for which Berlioz's take on *Much Ado* was prepared) – does indeed develop only the tale of Beatrice and Benedict tricked into matrimony, while entirely ignoring the story of Don John and his attempt to foil the love of Hero and Claudio. We need to ask why. A lady falsely accused of infidelity – Desdemona, or in this case Hero – would surely have aroused his sympathy. But as we have seen, he was disinclined to create characters of 'cold and bitter emotions' (Richard III, or in this case Don John, and even a Beatrice capable of saying, or singing, 'Kill Claudio'), and in the slender circumstances of this commission was surely averse to pursuing not an underplot, for that is what he composed, but a second plot. Somarone, the added character of whom Berlioz was so proud, is based on Shakespeare's self-important constable, Dogberry, who opens Act 4, scene 2 with the incongruous vocabulary that is his charm: 'Is our whole dissembly appear'd?' 'Which be the malefactors?' asks the town clerk, to which Dogberry, misinterpreting the word, replies: 'Marry, that am I …'

Berlioz transforms such misunderstanding into a complex musical situation: Somarone, not constable but chorus master, has composed a celebratory ode for the forthcoming wedding, an 'Épithalame grotesque', with a Dogberrian text: 'Mourez, tenders époux / Que le Bonheur enivre ! / Mourez, mourez! / Pourquoi survivre / À des instants si doux ? / Qu'une mort bienheureuse / Descende paisible sur vous / Comme la nuit calmes et rêveuse!' ('Die, tender spouses, May happiness intoxicate you! Die, die! Why outlive such delightful moments? May a blissful death come down peacefully upon you, like a calm and dreamy night.') For Somarone, flattening the union of orgasm and death, this is 'un chant de bonheur', a 'chant d'amour'. In fact it is a fugue, first played in an intentionally flat-footed way, then played expressively, with an oboe obbligato of genuine charm. Invoking his Shakespearean model by inventing a malapropitious linkage of lowly dance and High Communion, Berlioz has Somarone tells the oboist: 'You're a fine fellow. I will write a lovely saltarello for you … in my new *Mass*.'

For his libretto, Berlioz used the translation of Benjamin Laroche.[237] When a critic found that the spoken dialogue lacked imagination, Berlioz retorted: 'The dialogue is almost entirely copied from Shakespeare … ' – which it is.[238] Unlike opera, which links musical numbers via sung recitative, opéra comique links them via spoken dialogue. The quantity of lines necessary for such linkage is surely what discouraged Berlioz from making his own translation. That quantity also explains why *Béatrice et Bénédict*, which Andrew Porter called 'a play with music', is rarely performed – because if many non-native singers can *sing* French, few can *speak* it satisfactorily on the stage.[239]

Purist though he often claimed to be, Berlioz was not averse to rearranging Shakespeare's original text. 'They say the lady is fair' (2.3.230), observes Bénédict in the opera, but *after* and not before noting that 'the world must be peopled' (2.3.242). In the play, Beatrice now invites Benedict to dinner; in the opera, Berlioz gives us a *Rondo*, 'Ah! Je vais l'aimer', with a verbal crescendo worthy of his source – 'je vais l'admirer, je vais l'adorer, l'aimer, l'adorer, l'idolâtrer' – with a musical climax on that final, superlative word.

Like Shakespeare, Berlioz concludes the action with the newfound lovers' cautious jousting: 'Do you not love me?' – 'Why no, no more than reason'; 'M'aimez-vous?' – 'Non, pas plus que de raison.' The play closes on Benedict's last line, 'Strike up, pipers.' In the opera, 'pipers' strike twice. First, with a mocking dirge on 'Ici l'on voit Bénédict l'homme marié' that derives from Benedict's pledge to Claudio that if ever he married, 'let them signify under my sign, "Here you may see Benedick the married man"' (1.1.266–8). Berlioz's messengers parading large signs – 'Ici'; 'l'on voit'; 'l'homme marié' – capture Shakespeare's theatricality in a way that everyone can see.[240] Second, with a Scherzo-Duettino for the principals that epitomizes what Berlioz had in mind when setting down the description that commentators have applied to the opera in its entirety: 'a caprice that is written with the point of a needle and that requires an extraordinarily delicate execution'.[241] The main sections of the overture are derived from this final number, set in G major, Berlioz's favourite key, and lending the quality of capriciousness to the whole.

Envoy

If the close of the opera completes a rounded musical form, so too does *Béatrice and Benédict* complete a biographical circle, because setting *Much Ado About Nothing* had occurred to Berlioz early in his career, when, hopeful of a commission from the Théâtre-Italien, he wrote to Joseph d'Ortigue, as we have seen, that he intended 'to compose a charming Italian opera' on Shakespeare's witty comedy.[242] The project could never have used the French rendering of the title, *Beaucoup de bruit pour rien*, because the word 'bruit' means both 'ado' and 'noise' – of which Berlioz had already been accused of making far too much. The composer returned to the subject in 1852, when he drafted an outline of a libretto to be completed by Ernest Legouvé.[243] We hear of it again eight years later, in 1860, when he suggests that the opera commissioned by Édouard Bénazet for the new theatre in Baden-Baden be composed not on the previously agreed upon historical subject of the Thirty Years' War, but rather on the psychological war waged by Shakespeare's dissimulating duo. In August 1862, 30 years after imagining an opera on the play, Berlioz conducted the première of *Béatrice et Bénédict*.

This was not his *opus ultimum*. That honour is reserved for the arrangement of the *Marche troyenne* that Berlioz completed in January 1864, after the 21 performances of *Les Troyens à Carthage* that had taken place during the previous fall. These closed a larger creative circle more than 50 years after the young Berlioz had begun to construe Virgil, with his father, as a boy in the village of La Côte-Saint-André. Unlike his mother, who was a devout Catholic, Berlioz's father was a broad-minded thinker whose scientific research as a physician impacted his son's scepticism of religion and received ideas, and whose intellectual curiosity inculcated in the boy a love of learning and a thirst of discovery. Berlioz would eventually find acceptance abroad, in England, Russia, the various German-speaking kingdoms, and even in America, more readily than he would in France. And yet he was secure in his Frenchness and 'proud to be French'.[244] Not for a second did he fear accusation of disloyalty for citing Shakespeare, despite those who viewed the poet as the metaphorical ally of Wellington, or as 'très anglais – trop anglais'.[245]

In a recent study of Shakespeare's influence 'on the minds and works of the major English Romantic poets', Jonathan Bate finds no better way to summarize Shakespeare's inspirational power than to cite the secular 'Our Father' of the artist who has been the subject of our endeavour:

> Shakespeare! Shakespeare! Where be he? Where art thou? I feel as if he alone among all intelligent beings must have understood us both; that he alone could have pitied us, poor unhappy artists, loving yet destroying one another. Shakespeare! Shakespeare! You were a man. If you yet exist, you must be a refuge for the wretched! It is thou who art our father, it is thou who art in heaven (if there is a heaven). God standing aloof in his infinite indifference is revolting and absurd. Thou alone for the souls of artists art the living and loving God. Receive us, father, unto thy bosom, deliver us! *De profundis ad te clamo.* What are death and nothingness? Genius is immortal![246]

Berlioz loved Shakespeare and imagined that Shakespeare loved him. He encouraged us to see him now as a dolorous Hamlet, now as a Benedict with tongue in cheek. He knew his Shakespeare and became known as an expert. Others' bardology declined – 'We have renounced Shakespeare and his pomps and vanities', wrote Philarète Chasles in 1855[247] – while his endured. He became a writer out of financial necessity, necessity became the mother of invention, and he became a man of letters – but only incidentally of a Shakespearean sort. For Berlioz's writings are mosaicist documents – admiring essays, fantastical tales, humorous dialogues, intimate portraits, improbable encounters, dispatches from abroad – that privilege the wise aperçu, the ironic anecdote, the *bon mot*, the awareness of the moral ambiguity of life.

Berlioz turned to Shakespeare to examine existence, to explain thinking, to energize imagination, to encapsulate truth. 'Shakespearean', for Berlioz, was the apical adjectival accolade; quotation from Shakespeare was grist to the quill. A biographer might wish to suggest that the composer, like Hamlet, was haunted by the ghost of his father, but what is ultimately 'Shakespearean' about Berlioz is his love of *contrastes et oppositions*, if I may use the phrase yet again, and of what he identified as the preeminent quality of his *music*: 'l'imprévu' – 'the unexpected'. The poet 'wrought havoc' in the young composer, as we have seen; the 'profanateurs' – the cleavers, the clots, the clowns with no imagination – wrought his rage. But for Berlioz, music remained supreme: 'Because only music speaks at once to the imagination, to the intellect, to the heart, and to *the senses*: the action of the senses upon the intellect and the heart, and the reciprocal action of the intellect and the heart upon the senses, give birth in those gifted with exceptional discernment to extraordinary sensations that others (the barbarians) will simply never ever know.'[248]

Appendix I

Berlioz's 1861 'paraphrase' of 'To be or not to be'

Berlioz found the words in [my] italics in the *Œuvres dramatiques de Shakspeare* [*sic*], traduction nouvelle par Benjamin Laroche, vol. 2 (Paris: Marchant, 1840). To allow for comparison, I have much modified the spacing of the paragraphs.

Berlioz (translation by Peter Bloom)	Berlioz (original text)
To be, or not to be, that is the question. Whether 'tis nobler in the mind to suffer the slings and arrows of outrageous operas, ridiculous concerts, mediocre virtuosos, mad composers, or to take arms against this sea of troubles and by opposing end them?	*Être ou ne pas être, voilà la question. Une âme courageuse doit-elle supporter les* méchants opéras, les concerts ridicules, les virtuoses médiocres, les compositeurs enragés, *ou s'armer contre* ce torrent de maux, et, en le combattant, *y mettre un terme ?*
To die, to sleep, no more. And by a sleep to say we end the ear-ache, heart-ache, head-ache, and the thousand natural shocks to our senses and intelligence that the métier of the critic is heir to. Tis a consummation devoutly to be wished. To die, to sleep, to sleep, perchance to hallucinate. Ay, there's the rub.	*Mourir, — dormir, — rien de plus. Et dire que par ce sommeil nous mettons fin aux* déchirements de l'oreille, *aux souffrances du cœur et* de la raison, *aux mille douleurs* imposées par l'exercice de la critique à notre intelligence et à nos sens! — *C'est là un résultat qu'on doit appeler de tous ses vœux. — Mourir, — dormir, — dormir, —* avoir le cauchemar peut-être. — *Oui, voilà* le point embarrassant.
For in that sleep of death, what torturous dreams may come when we have shuffled off this mortal coil, what absurd theories we may come to judge, what discordant scores to hear, what morons to praise, what indignities upon masterpieces to witness, what inanities to sermonize, what pigmies to take as giants?	*Savons-nous quelles* tortures nous éprouverons en songe, *dans ce sommeil de la mort, après que nous aurons* déposé le lourd fardeau de l'existence, quelles folles théories nous aurons à examiner, quelles partitions discordantes à entendre, quels imbéciles à louer, quels outrages nous verrons infliger aux chefs-d'œuvre, quelles extravagances seront prônées, quels moulins à vent pris pour des colosses ?

This must give us pause; there's the notion that renders feuilletons so numerous and the lives of the wretches who write them so long.

For who would bear the whips and scorns of a senseless world, the sight of its delirium, the disdain and illusion of its ignorance, the injustice of its laws, the glacial indifference of its heads of state? Who would bear the cyclone of the most ignoble passions and the most petty interests hiding behind the name of love of art? Who would stoop to discuss what is absurd, to be a soldier and to teach his general to command the maneuver, to travel and to guide his guide (who will nonetheless get lost)—when he himself might his quietus make, to put an end to such humiliating tasks, with a bare flask of chloroform or a steel-tipped bullet?

Who would fardels bear to see in this base world despair borne of hope, weariness of inaction, anger of patience, but for the dread of something worse after death, the undiscover'd country from whose bourn no critic returns?...

Il y a là de quoi faire réfléchir ; c'est cette pensée qui rend les feuilletons si nombreux et prolonge *la vie des malheureux* qui les écrivent.

Qui, en effet, voudrait supporter la fréquentation d'un monde insensé, le spectacle de sa démence, les mépris et les méprises de son ignorance, l'injustice de sa justice, la glaciale indifférence des gouvernants ? Qui voudrait tourbillonner au souffle du vent des passions les moins nobles, des intérêts les plus mesquins prenant le nom d'amour de l'art, s'abaisser jusqu'à la discussion de l'absurde, être soldat et apprendre à son général à commander l'exercice, voyager et guider son guide qui s'égare néanmoins, *lorsqu'il suffirait* pour se délivrer de cette tâche humiliante d'un flacon de chloroforme ou d'une balle à pointe d'acier ?

Qui voudrait se résigner à voir dans ce bas monde le désespoir naître de l'espoir, la lassitude de l'inaction, la colère de la patience, *n'était la crainte de quelque chose de pire par delà le trépas, ce pays ignoré d'où nul* critique *n'est encore revenu ?...*

Thus conscience does make
cowards of us all…

— Soft you now! We may not
meditate for even a few moments,
for here's the fair singer Ophelia,
armed with a score and wearing a
forced smile.

[Hamlet]
—What do you wish of me?
Flattery, is it not? Well, well, well.

[Ophelia]
—No, my lord, I have a score of
yours that I have longed long to
re-deliver. I pray you, now receive
it.

[Hamlet]
—No, not I; I never gave you
aught.

[Ophelia]
—My honour'd lord, you know
right well you did, and with it
words of so sweet breath compos'd
as made the thing more rich. Take
it again; for to the noble mind rich
gifts wax poor when givers prove
unkind. There, my lord.

---

*Voilà ce qui ébranle et trouble la
volonté…*

— Allons, il n'est pas même
permis de méditer pendant
quelques instants ; voici la jeune
cantatrice Ophélie, armée d'une
partition et grimaçant un sourire.

[Hamlet]
— Que voulez-vous de moi ? des
flatteries, n'est-ce pas ? toujours,
toujours.

[Ophélie]
— Non, *monseigneur ; j'ai de vous
une partition que depuis longtemps
je désirais vous rendre. Veuillez la
recevoir, je vous prie.*

[Hamlet]
— *Moi! non certes, je ne vous ai
jamais rien donné.*

[Ophélie]
—*Monseigneur, vous savez très-bien
que c'est vous qui m'avez fait ce don,
et les paroles gracieuses dont vous
l'avez accompagné en ont encore relevé
le prix. Reprenez-le, car, pour un
noble cœur, les dons les plus précieux
deviennent sans valeur du moment
où celui qui les a faits n'a plus pour
nous que de l'indifférence. Tenez,
monseigneur.*

[Hamlet]	[Hamlet]
—Ha, ha! Are you honest?	— Ah ! vous avez du cœur ?
[Ophelia]	[Ophélie]
—My lord?	— *Monseigneur ?*
[Hamlet]	[Hamlet]
—And are you a singer?	— Et vous êtes cantatrice ?
[Ophelia]	[Ophélie]
—What means your lordship?	— *Que veut dire Votre Altesse ?*
[Hamlet]	[Hamlet]
—That if you be honest and a singer, your honesty should admit no discourse to your voice.	— *Que si vous* avez du cœur et si vous êtes cantatrice, *vous devez interdire toute communication entre* la cantatrice et la femme de cœur.
[Ophelia]	[Ophélie]
—Could voice have better commerce than with honesty?	— *Quel commerce sied mieux* pourtant à l'une que celui de l'autre ?
[Hamlet]	[Hamlet]
—Ay, truly; for the power of voice such as thine will sooner transform honesty from what it is to a bawd than the force of honesty can translate voice into his likeness. This was sometime a paradox, but now the time gives it proof. I did admire you once.	— *Tant s'en faut ; car l'influence* d'un talent comme le vôtre aura plutôt perverti les plus nobles élans du cœur, que le cœur n'aura donné de la noblesse aux aspirations du talent. *Ceci passait autrefois pour un paradoxe ; mais c'est aujourd'hui un fait dont la preuve est acquise. Il fut un temps où je vous admirais.*

[Ophelia]	[Ophélie]
—Indeed, my lord, you made me believe so.	— *En effet, monseigneur, vous me l'avez fait croire.*
[Hamlet]	[Hamlet]
—You should not have believ'd me. I admired you not.	— *Vous avez eu tort de me croire.* Mon admiration n'avait rien de réel.
[Ophelia]	[Ophélie]
—I was the more deceived.	— *Je n'en ai été que plus trompée.*
[Hamlet]	[Hamlet]
—Get thee to a nunn'ry. What wouldst thou want? A celebrated name, a great deal of money, the applause of fools, a titled spouse, the rank of duchess? Yes, yes, they all dream of marrying a prince. —Why wouldst thou be a breeder of idiots?	— *Allez-vous enfermer dans un cloître.* Quelle est votre ambition ? Un nom célèbre, beaucoup d'argent, les applaudissements des sots, un époux titré, le nom de duchesse. Oui, oui, elles rêvent toutes d'épouser un prince. —*Pourquoi vouloir donner le jour à une race* d'idiots ?
[Ophelia]	[Ophélie]
—O, help him, you sweet heavens!	— *Ayez pitié de lui, ciel miséricordieux!*
[Hamlet]	[Hamlet]
—If thou dost marry, I'll give thee this plague for thy dowry: be thou an artist as chaste as ice, as pure as snow, thou shalt not escape calumny. Get thee to a nunn'ry, go; farewell. Or, if thou wilt needs marry, marry a fool, this would be most wise, for wise men know well enough the suffering you reserve for them. To a nunn'ry, go, and quickly too. Farewell.	— *Si vous vous mariez, je vous donnerai pour dot cette vérité désolante :* qu'une femme artiste soit *froide comme la glace, pure comme la neige,* elle n'échappera point *à la calomnie. Allez au couvent. Adieu; ou s'il vous faut absolument un mari, épousez un* crétin, c'est ce que vous avez de mieux à faire ; car les hommes d'esprit savent trop bien les tourments que vous leur réservez. Allez au couvent, sans tarder. *Adieu.*

[Ophelia]	[Ophélie]
—O heavenly powers, restore him!	— *Puissances célestes, rendez-lui la raison !*
[Hamlet]	[Hamlet]
—I have heard of your vocal adventures, your amusing pretentions, your ridiculous vanity. God hath given you one voice, and you make yourself another. He hath entrusted you with a masterpiece, you defile it, you mutilate it, you alter its character, you adorn it with shoddy ornaments, you cut it insolently, you add horrible roulades, preposterous arpeggios, and ludicrous trills; you insult the composer, persons of taste, art, and common sense. Go to, I'll no moe on't. To a nunn'ry, go.	— *J'ai aussi entendu parler de* toutes vos coquetteries vocales, de vos plaisantes prétentions, de votre sotte vanité. *Dieu vous a donné une* voix, vous vous en faites une autre. On vous confie un chef-d'œuvre, vous le dénaturez, vous le mutilez, vous en changez le caractère, vous l'affublez de misérables ornements, vous y faites d'insolentes coupures, vous y introduisez des traits grotesques, des arpèges risibles, des trilles facétieux ; vous insultez le maître, les gens de goût, et l'art, et le bon sens. *Allez, qu'on ne m'en parle plus.* Au couvent! au couvent! (Il sort).
Young Ophelia is not entirely wrong, Hamlet has indeed gone a little crazy. But this will not be observed in our musical world, where everyone these days is totally mad. Besides, this poor prince of Denmark does have moments of lucidity. He is but mad north-north-west. When the wind is southerly he knows a hawk from a hand-saw.	La jeune Ophélie n'a pas tout à fait tort, Hamlet a bien un peu perdu la tête. Mais on ne s'en apercevra pas dans notre monde musical, où tout le monde à cette heure est complètement fou. D'ailleurs, il a des instants lucides, ce pauvre prince de Danemark; il n'est fou que lorsque le vent souffle du nord-nord-ouest; quand le vent est au sud, il sait très-bien distinguer un aigle d'une buse.

Chapter 2

Verdi

Daniel Albright

The composer Giuseppe Verdi (1813–1901) claimed that he had an
especially intimate relation to Shakespeare. On 28 April 1865, after the
première of the revised version of *Macbeth*, Verdi wrote a letter complaining
that a newspaper critic

> states that I didn't know Shakespeare when I wrote *Macbeth*. Oh, in this
> they are very wrong. It may be that I have not rendered *Macbeth* well, but
> that I don't know, don't understand, and don't feel Shakespeare — no,
> by God, no. He is a favorite poet of mine, whom I have had in my hands
> from earliest youth, and whom I read and reread constantly.[1]

But it took Verdi some time to become a Shakespearean in the fullest sense
of the word.

Verdi wrote three operas to Shakespearean texts, one fairly early in his
career, and the others his last two operas: *Macbeth* (1847, revised 1865),
Otello (1887), and *Falstaff* (1894). Of the three, the first is by far the closest
to its Shakespearean original, partly because the mild-mannered librettist,
Francesco Piave, was too tame to challenge either Verdi's or Shakespeare's
authority –whereas the librettist of the two late operas, Arrigo Boito, was
an extraordinarily self-assertive character, as we shall see. On the other
hand, *Macbeth* is one of Shakespeare's most atypical tragedies: short, swift,
severe, a single action with few of those swervings toward subplots and
subject-rhymes, extraneities, that mark most of Shakespeare's best work. In
his youth, Verdi was an instinctive Aristotelean, determined to pare down
his libretti to some terse contagion of pity and terror; his most common
instruction to his librettists was, Make it shorter. In some ways the young
Verdi resembled his American contemporary Edgar Allan Poe, striving for
unity and simplicity of affect; and in other ways he resembled his German
contemporary Richard Wagner, trying to fuse artistic media to achieve

maximum emotive force – in fact, Verdi remarked in 1875, when asked about Wagner, 'I too have attempted the fusion of music and drama, and that in *Macbeth.*'[2]

But no Shakespeare play, not even *Macbeth*, has the punishing linearity of, say, Sophocles' *Oedipus Rex*, and Verdi had no use for many of Shakespeare's striking scenes: there is nothing in the opera of the Porter's little game, in which he pretends to be in charge of the gates of hell; or of Malcolm's pretense of wickedness in order to test Macduff. Shakespeare's soliloquies often look like arias, but Verdi had little interest in poetry detached from dramatic action, and so 'Tomorrow and tomorrow and tomorrow' is reduced to a single casual line of recitative, stating that life is a poor idiot's tale. (Since Verdi read Shakespeare in a prose translation, this is perhaps unstartling.)

Macbeth is an opera saturated in black blood: Verdi tries to make every scene cooperant to the single tragic effect. The usual method of Italian opera is to maximize contrast: for example, in Gaetano Donizetti's *Lucia di Lammermoor* (1835), music for the wedding festivities is hearty and warm, so that when the bride appears, holding a knife, her dress stained with blood, the shock value will be high. But in *Macbeth*, the music for Lady Macbeth's toast at the banquet – a merry moment as far as most of the participants are concerned – is thick, glaring, heavy-lidded: the evil of the Macbeths infects everything. All the music is stained with tragedy: this is one of the ways in which Verdi attempted to fuse, and infuse, music with drama.

According to Verdi's intellectual world, however, such procedures were profoundly un-Shakespearean, since Shakespeare was considered less a master of tragedy than a master of mixed, impure dramatic forms. Indeed for the most influential Continental critic of the eighteenth century, Voltaire, Shakespeare was the enemy of dramatic art. Voltaire lived for a time in England, and had far more experience with Shakespeare than most of his European contemporaries; and what he found in Shakespeare was simply chaos – a barbarous disregard for the unities of time and place, and a vulgar love for mixing the noble and the ignoble. Voltaire cringed to hear the jokes of Roman cobblers in a scene from *Julius Caesar* where Brutus and Cassius discoursed; and he was sickened by the gravediggers in *Hamlet*, singing ballads as they dug up old skulls. According to Voltaire's *Letters Concerning the English Nation* (1734), Shakespeare was a genius of disgust:

> *Shakespear* boasted a strong, fruitful Genius: He was natural and sublime, but had not so much as a single Spark of good Taste, or knew one Rule of the Drama.... the great Merit of this Dramatic Poet has been the Ruin

of the English Stage. There are such beautiful, such noble, such dreadful Scenes in this Writer's monstrous Farces, to which the Name of Tragedy is given, that they have always been exhibited with great Success. Time, which only gives Reputation to Writers, at last makes their very Faults venerable. Most of the whimsical, gigantic Images of this Poet, have, thro' Length of Time ... acquir'd a Right of passing for sublime.[3]

But in a century's time, these censures would start to sound like praise. When the Romantic movement began, Shakespeare's neglect of the classical unities, his taste for the whimsical and monstrous, would seem like a heroic repudiation of stale Art in favour of abundant Nature.

The key year for the French Romantic revaluation of Shakespeare is 1827. In October of that year, Victor Hugo published his play *Cromwell* together with its famous preface: a paean to Shakespeare and a manifesto of Romantic drama. The main thesis of the preface concerned the virtue of the mixed. Hugo recommended a mixture of verse and prose, the tragic and the comic, the sublime and the grotesque – since, according to the Christian religion, man is intrinsically a mixture of pure soul and transitory flesh. This leads Hugo to a ringing defence of the ugly as a necessary aspect of art – a defence that will be taken up again and again through the nineteenth century, by Flaubert, Chekhov, and many others, and will become a prime tenet of Expressionism in the twentieth century. And the locus classicus of the ugly is the canon of Shakespeare:

> ... as a point of view with respect to the sublime, as a means of contrast, the grotesque is (according to us) the richest source that nature can open to art. Rubens doubtless understood this, when he was pleased to mix with his unfoldings of royal pomp, coronations, splendid ceremonies, some hideous figure of a court dwarf. This sort of universal beauty which antiquity solemnly spread out over everything wasn't without monotony; the same impression, always repeated, can at length be fatiguing. The sublime on top of the sublime produces a poor contrast, and one needs to rest from everything, even from the beautiful. It seems, on the contrary, that the grotesque is a stopping-place, a term of comparison, a point of departure from which one is lifted toward the beautiful with a fresher and more excited perception. The salamander throws the undine into relief; the gnome makes the sylph beautiful....
>
> ... in [Christian] poetry, while the sublime will represent the soul just as it is, [the grotesque] will play the role of the human beast. The first type, disengaged from every impure bond, will carry with it every

charm, every grace, every beauty: it must create Juliet, Desdemona, Ophelia. The second will take every ridiculous thing, every infirmity, every ugliness. To this division of humanity and creation will come passions, vices, crimes; there will be the lecher, the groveler, the glutton, the miser, the traitor, the bungler, the hypocrite; there will be by turns Iago, Tartufe, Basile; Polonius, Harpagon, Bartholo; Falstaff, Scapin, Figaro. There is only one type of the beautiful, but the ugly has a thousand types. The beautiful ... is merely form considered in its simplest relation, in its most absolute symmetry, in the most intimate harmony .... It offers to us a finished ensemble, but circumscribed, as we ourselves are circumscribed. What we call the ugly, on the contrary, is a detail of a great ensemble that escapes our grasp, and which harmonizes itself, not with man, but with creation in its entirety. That is why it presents us ceaselessly with new aspects, but incomplete aspects. [4]

Beauty is narrow, exclusive, thin-lipped, thin-hipped, a little tedious and faintly repellent; ugliness is rich and diversified and evil and generous, life itself. It is little wonder that Hugo would come to write a drama in which the star player would be a hunchbacked jester (Rigoletto, as Verdi renamed him); or to write a novel in which gypsies mutilate children in order to make them more compelling objects of pity when begging for alms: for beauty is locked in itself, while ugliness is connected to the whole of mankind, and the whole of the inanimate universe as well. Through pondering the ugly we know what it feels like to be a misshapen rock, or a sand dune, or a heap of logs, or the solar system. Though Hugo loosely equates the sublime with the beautiful, it is the ugly that is (as Burke or Kant would have understood the term) sublime.

In due time Verdi would become a Shakespearean in Hugo's sense: by 1862 he was adding dwarves to the corners of his canvas (so to speak), in the form of the comic Fra Melitone in *La forza del destino*, whose fussy exasperations and heavy-handed puns give the force of destiny a bit of time offstage to regather its dark energies. And in his last two operas Iago and Falstaff and other grotesques take over the stage: the beautiful characters, the ingénues, are almost squeezed offstage in a general triumph of the ugly. But for now, we study *Macbeth*, and Verdi's way of handling Shakespeare in a mode of univocal forward thrust.

Macbeth

In *La forza del destino* and elsewhere, Fate is an implicit character in the opera, with its own musical motive, irresistible, implacable, a vector aimed at the heart of all we love. But in *Macbeth*, Fate is an explicit character, or actually characters – the little band of witches. The witches, even in Shakespeare's original play, have an operatic quality to them: they giggle, they intone incantations, they look like music.

The stage history of *Macbeth* is a horror story in which the role of the witches keeps expanding, and frantic attempts are made to restrain their magic power. Even by the time of *Macbeth*'s first publication, in the First Folio of 1623 (seven years after Shakespeare's death), someone seems to have spliced into Shakespeare's text a new witch, or witchmaster, Hecate (3.5 and 4.1.39–43). In both her scenes, Hecate is associated with music: the stage directions instruct the witches to perform songs, 'Come away' at the end of 3.5, and 'Black spirits' at 4.1.43. The Folio doesn't give the text of either song, but each can be found both in Thomas Middleton's *The Witch* (c. 1609) and in the Davenant version of *Macbeth* (1663–4, publ. 1674). It is possible that the Hecate scenes and songs are the work of Middleton; in any case they greatly distend the spatial range of the witches. It seems that even in the 1610s *Macbeth* was beginning to move toward opera. The witches not only want to fly, but also want to sing; they need to push the play into the dimension of music theatre, just as they sail through the unroofed theatre building to the height of the moon. It is the witches who motivate the opera lurking near the surface of the drama.

The most vexing problem the witches presented was their destabilizing of such terms as *realistic* and *fantastic*, or *fatal* and *trivial*. They impinge on the most august realms of the moral universe, and seem intimate with Necessity itself, and yet slime clings to them. And listen to the way they speak. Coleridge writes:

> The exquisite judgment of Shakespeare is shown in nothing more than in the different language of the Witches with each other, and with those whom they address: the former displays a certain fierce familiarity, grotesqueness mingled with terror; the latter is always solemn, dark, mysterious.[5]

Though Coleridge would like to denature and metaphysicize the witches, dignify them, he is deeply conscious of their divided nature: part Gothic, part Greek-tragic; part ugly gossip, part will toward annihilation. But he refuses another possibility for understanding their twiformed character: the possibility that they might be at once both vile and silly, a clown-show in Satan's circus. Similarly, Shakespeare's German translator, August Wilhelm Schlegel, who noted in 1808:

> With one another the witches discourse like women of the very lowest class [*aus dem Pöbel*] ... when, however, they address Macbeth they assume a loftier tone: their predictions ... have all the obscure brevity, the majestic solemnity of oracles, such as have ever spread terror among mortals....[6]

Schlegel felt acutely the incommensurability of the witches' two styles of speech: that of the 'women of the very lowest class' and that of the Delphic Oracle. But precisely in that discrepancy, he thought, there lay the power of the play: Shakespeare combined the rudimentary terror of popular superstition (old women with the power of the evil eye, for example) with an intelligent, philosophical sort of terror, the 'Destiny of the ancients.'

Schlegel's criticism of *Macbeth* was to have important consequences in the history of opera, because an Italian translation was appended to Carlo Rusconi's 1838 translation of the play – Verdi's principal source. (Indeed the English translation printed above has been revised to reflect what Verdi actually saw.) Verdi peered at Shakespeare's witches through Schlegel's optic; and Schlegel is partly responsible for some of the disturbing features of Verdi's treatment.

For one thing, Verdi's witches, like Schlegel's, are compound creatures: 'women of the very lowest class' and yet solemn oracles. Their moods shift quickly, as if they dwelt in a continual mad scene, or enacted the insanity of fate itself. Near the beginning of the *Macbeth* project, Verdi sent his own draft of a libretto to the official librettist, Francesco Piave, with the instruction to 'adopt a sublime diction, except in the witches' choruses, which must be vulgar, yet bizarre and original [*triviali, ma stravaganti ed originali*].'[7] One might have thought that self-conscious triviality was a twentieth-century phenomenon (as in Poulenc's *Banalités*); but Verdi wanted his witches to sound at once fantastical and coarse – perhaps as close as the vocabulary of the age could come to the term 'camp'.

How trivial are Verdi's witches? Historically, listeners have answered, Much too trivial. By the standards of the finest *Schauerromantik* of Verdi's age, such as the Wolf's–Glen scene in Weber's *Der Freischütz* (1821) or Emmy's romance from Marschner's *Der Vampyr* (1828), Verdi's witches can seem comically underhorrified – peppy, freakishly high-spirited but harmonically tame. On the other hand, Verdi's contemporaries greatly enjoyed the witches; on the night of the première, 14 March 1847, the numbers for which the audience demanded an encore were the first-act grand duet – by common consent one of the triumphs of the whole Verdi canon – and the witches' choruses.[8] Verdi approached the problem of witch music from an angle wholly different from that of Weber or Marschner – but it is arguable that Verdi's imagination of the fantastic is equally successful. I don't mean at all to belittle the critics of previous generations: they were responding to the fact that there is something wrong, uneasy-making, about Verdi's depiction of witches – as indeed there is.

By 1847, Verdi was an experienced hand at writing fantasy-music, and at writing just about everything else relevant to opera. In Verdi's previous operas, the closest analogue to the witches of *Macbeth* is the chorus of demons in *Giovanna d'Arco* (1845). These demons, tempting Joan of Arc to open her heart to a tenor's love, instead of pursuing her high mission to save France from the troops of England, are easy to ridicule, and the older critics did ridicule them: Toye comments, 'they indulge in a 3/8 lilt, intended, as is so often the case with this rhythm, to be seductive, but actually suggesting comic-opera peasants and fishermen.'[9] Budden finds this 3/8 section 'Tu sei bella' 'bland and tuneful .... It has an innocent vulgarity which reeks of the Neapolitan café'; concerning the demons' most remarkable music – the *Vittoria* chorus at the end of the first act, a paean to their success at forcing Joan to fall in love, to compromise herself – Budden remarks, 'The entire episode is a tasteless and feeble excrescence.'[10]

But it's possible that Verdi liked an altogether different sort of demon from those that conform to old-time standards of diabolic propriety. It is the business of a tempter to tempt; a seducer who accompanies his subtle coaxings and blandishments with loud string tremoli, diminished sevenths, trombone rumblings and piccolo shrieks, is not likely to succeed. There is an operatic convention that demons should wear a musical badge proclaiming DEMON at every instant of their time on stage. But Verdi was under no obligation to follow this convention by compelling the orchestra to ironize the seduction with heavy demon tropes. Perhaps Joan of Arc, or her Italian alter ego Giovanna d'Arco, might plausibly find the *tinta* of a Neapolitan café more conducive to sexual surrender than that of the Flying Dutchman's zombie crew. When at last the demons reveal themselves as demons, they are transformed into figures of wholehearted evil: they sing a fanfare that is simply a buildup of a diminished-seventh chord. (Verdi was self-conscious about the stock effect of such chords: in 1871, he called them 'that rock and refuge of all those of us who can't compose four bars without half a dozen of those sevenths'.)[11] There is no ambiguity, no tension in the demons' ways of presenting themselves: first they were guitar-strumming café flatterers – a role they played so well that they even fooled the orchestra – and now they are obvious demons. The ambiguity and the tension belong entirely to Joan, who, during the first act finale, is audibly nervous: the music reproduces her gooseflesh, her irregular heartbeat, her panting. This is the Italian model of the supernatural: simple musical stimuli and a complex musical response – as opposed to the Franco-German model of building the listener's response (bristling hair, popping eyes, intake of breath to scream) into the stimulus itself. Berlioz's or Gounod's Méphistophélès is richer than his Faust; but Verdi's Joan is richer than his demons.

Verdi, then, is a literalist of the supernatural, in that he presents the fantastic creature to the audience in a way that simulates the creature's appearance to the other characters on stage – Verdi always understands that terror pertains not to the creature (why would it be terrified of itself?) but to those onstage who behold it. Whether the creature represents a fraud or a genuine apparition from the beyond, Verdi is sensitive to the fact that a fantastic contrivance should be simple: the contriver, like most magicians, works toward a single supreme effect (it flies; or it is enormous; or it is transparent; or it breathes fire) without adducing too many complications. For Verdi, fantasies can be powerful, even overwhelming, but they are not subtle. Five days after the première of *Macbeth*, the poet Giuseppe Giusti sent Verdi a thoughtful critique, warning him against foreign influences, and noting, 'The Fantastic is something that can challenge the intellect [*provare l'ingegno*]; truth challenges both the intellect and the soul';[12] Verdi was so impressed with this sentence that he copied it into an album. What interests Verdi is the soul that tries to cope with the fantastic, not the fantastic *per se*.

Macbeth shows two souls that are challenged with more fantasy than they can bear. Joan of Arc had to cope with one, and only one, sort of fantastic deception; but the Macbeths have to deal with Houdini's whole battery of tricks. I say tricks, but the witches are remarkable for their utter frankness about their prestidigitergiversations. In Marlowe's *Doctor Faustus*, as in many subsequent Faust-plays, Mephostophilis is imperturbably open about the worthlessness of the gifts he offers: he replies, when Faustus asks him how it is that he can leave hell, 'Why this is hell, nor am I out of it…. O Faustus, leave these frivolous demands, Which strike a terror to my fainting soul' (1.3. 76, 81–2). Verdi's witches do everything they can to expose their triviality, their sheer facetiousness of being.

The mid-twentieth-century critics are offended precisely because they don't want witches to sound trivial. Where the modern ear wants something deviant and exciting, Verdi provides disgustingly normal-sounding music. But the disgust of the ordinary was exactly the sort of disgust Verdi meant. His witches gain a certain strength from having their coarseness so blatant. Here Verdi's practice anticipates Freud on the uncanny, *das unheimliche*, a condition in which slight displacements of the familiar achieve a state of terror: the very commonplaceness of the witches makes them insidious. If Verdi's demons and witches rarely stray from the cafés of Naples, it is because the scariest things happen there. Verdi's witches seem most at home when singing nondescript music in major keys; when they sing in the minor, it is often part of a show put on in order to befool Macbeth, a piece of conscious hokiness – they veil themselves in the musical equivalent of robes painted with mysterious emblems.

One of the defining moments in Verdi's witch-music occurs early in the opera, when the witches hail Macbeth as thane of Glamis, thane of Cawdor, king of Scotland. By 1847, Verdi had developed a specific style for epigram: a way of thickening a terse melody into a sort of stage-object, something to be wielded, just as a character might wield a sword. Epigrams can be found in eighteenth-century music, such as Mozart's *Die Zauberflöte*, where the priest sings to Tamino the oracle 'Sobald dich führt' to a solemn laconic melody-unit, an expansion of a simple cadential formula; but in the nineteenth century they become a standard feature of music drama. A conspicuous example can be found in *Ernani* (1844), when Ernani makes a strange bargain with the man who is on the point of murdering him: in order to gain some temporary life, Ernani hands Silva a hunting horn, and says:

Ecco il pegno: nel momento	When the time comes – here is my pledge –
in che Ernani vorrai spento	when you want to see Ernani dead,
se uno squillo intenderà	if he hears the sound of this horn's cry,
tosto Ernani morirà.[13]	that instant will Ernani die.

This musical phrase becomes part of the furniture of the opera: the sound itself is a stab in the heart. A similar epigram can be found in *Attila* (1846), when Attila dreams of a huge old man who bars his path to Rome, saying:

Di flagellar l'incarco	You have been given the one task
contro i mortali hai sol,	to scourge the wicked race of men,
t'arretra! Or chiuso è il varco;	turn back! You now face a closed path;
questo de' numi è il suol![14]	this is the land of god alone!

Soon Pope Leo will confront the army of the Huns, and speak those very words. The music acquires a cybernetic force, and Attila, for all his barbaric might, trembles before a minor scale with an augmented fourth. During the 1840s Wagner was making similar experiments with musical epigrams, such as the Pope's curse on Tannhäuser. Neither Wagner nor Verdi used these epigrams as *leitmotif*: they are stiff, self-contained phrases, with none of the plasticity, the combinatorial ease typical of the *leitmotif*, in most cases they are expanded cadences with a sharp melodic profile, not a continuation of the previous musical discourse but an interruption of it. An epigram is not an episode in a symphonic development but a unit of music-theatre, in which music objectifies itself into something abrupt, hieroglyphic, legible. Often it follows the exact contours of words: but it is the meaning of the words, not the phonetic structure, that the epigram seeks to memorize, to freeze.

Verdi's fascination with epigram can be seen as a Shakespearean aspect of his art. The plays of Shakespeare, and of many other canonical playwrights, are full of soliloquies and formal speeches that lend themselves well to the format of nineteenth-century Italian opera; as Gary Schmidgall has pointed out, some of Shakespeare's heroic speeches seem to have *avant la lettre* the cantabile–cabaletta structure of the nineteenth-century Italian opera aria – a lyric meditative section followed by a fast exciting section.[15] But it is also true that these plays are full of single flinty lines, sudden revelations, sharp bursts of meaning, that are poorly suited to the format of nineteenth-century Italian opera. 'Absent thee from felicity awhile'; 'she looks like sleep'; 'cut him up in little stars'; 'we are such stuff as dreams are made on'; 'I could be bounded in a nutshell and count myself king of infinite space' – what can Italian opera do with such material? There was only one resource that came readily to Verdi's hand for imitating the trajectory of Shakespeare's quasi-extemporized scenes leading toward or receding from riddle, proverb, painful wisdom, poetic insight: arioso or recitativo occasionally punctuated by epigram.

The two great scenes in Verdi's *Macbeth* – the grand duet and the sleep-walking scene – have a texture quite distinct from normal Italian operatic practice: they seem assembled out of musical pebbles and rocks, with a peculiar sort of continuity that's more like the flow of gravel from a dump truck than the flow of a river.

In *Macbeth* Verdi uses epigrammatic music-speech for all sorts of oracles and sentences of terror – just as the witches' sashes are figured with runes, so their prophecies are conveyed through epigrams:

Salve, o Macbetto, di Glamis sire!	Hail, O Macbeth, thane of Glamis!
Salve, o Macbetto, di Caudor sire!	Hail, O Macbeth, thane of Cawdor!
Salve, o Macbetto, di Scozia re!	Hail, O Macbeth, king of Scotland![16]

The rudiment of this epigram is a half-cadence, with the tonic-dominant progression interrupted by a diminished chord; at each repetition it rises a third. This is a very simple thing; in the construction manual of opera, it isn't much more than a standard-issue brick; but Verdi shows great resourcefulness in promoting this little cadential chunk into the rawest element of horror, the Mark of Cain itself.

Soon the witches turn from Macbeth to Banco, and utter another epigram:

Men sarai di Macbetto e pur maggiore!	You will be less than Macbeth, yet greater!
Non quanto lui, ma più di lui felice!	Not so much as he, but happier than he!
Non re, ma di monarchi genitore!	Not king, but father of monarchs!

Here each phrase is chanted to a single note, rising a half-step on the last syllable, which become a chant-tone of the next line. This sort of upward crawl had long been a useful formula for oracular speech. But at this point comes something unexpected and characteristically Verdian: the witches instantly abandon their mood of vatic trance and break out in a frivolous jingle, 'Macbetto e Banco vivano!' ('long live Macbeth and Banco!'). It is as if the Cumean Sibyl, wreathed in incense, sitting on a throne hewn out of cave rock, muttering incomprehensible sentences with her eyes shut in ecstasy, suddenly rose, danced a little grinning jig, clicked her heels, and held out her arms to invite applause. Verdi has a similar effect in *Falstaff*, when Alice continues Quickly's creepy-crawly story of the hunter at Herne's Oak, full of strange string tremoli and brass blats, but then laughs it off as a mere fairy tale to entertain children before bedtime.

Why do the witches behave in such an undignified, even unwitchlike manner? One explanation is that they are deriding at any human attempt to solve their riddles, to evade their power. But, in the light of Verdi's comment on the mixture of the solemn and the coarse in Shakespeare's witches, another possibility presents itself: the witches are deliberately undermining themselves, exposing the fatuity at the heart of their spectacles of terror. The sash with its mystifying alphabet is fastened loosely, and tends to fall off, exposing the witches as silly raggedy old women with a gift for freak shows. They dismiss Macbeth, the human race and finally themselves. Beginning as instruments of tragedy, agents of a divinity that shapes our ends, rough-hew them how we will, the witches end as vehicles of a universal inconsequentiality. Here Verdi, and perhaps Shakespeare too, go beyond tragedy. Tragedy depends on some sense that Fate has dignity, even if human beings have none; but the witches of *Macbeth* impinge on a vision of the random. What if Fate itself is a threadbare woman putting on cheap theatrical tricks to tease us with the hope that disorder might be understood as malevolent order?

The bite of a vampire can turn the victim into another vampire; and similarly Verdi's witches exert a field of force that turns others into witches – especially (as we shall see) Lady Macbeth, who has no direct contact with them. Even the witches' oracular rhetoric is strangely contagious: the great Act I scene and duet for Macbeth and his wife occurs not long after the scene with Macbeth and the witches, and it is remarkable how much both the protagonists start to sound like witches. They start to talk to one another in epigrams.

Just as the witches could hardly keep a straight face as they delivered their prophecies, so the Macbeths' epigrams retain their serious demeanor with a certain difficulty – they tend to decay into gestures of meaningless fuss. The Macbeths tend to get stuck on a single musical phrase, unable to proceed. For a first look at the operations of a repeated epigram, let us examine the *Scena e Marcia* (1.2). Macbeth enters –Lady asks him when the king will be leaving, and he replies, 'Domani' ('tomorrow'); this news inspires her to devise a memorable omen, 'Mai non ci rechi il sole un tal domani' ('may the sun never bring us such a tomorrow'), her vocal line inching up the first fifth of the C minor scale, then falling back from G to E♭. The melody of this black prayer will often reappear, in blacker forms: later in this act, when Macbeth addresses a request to the 'immobil terra, a' passi miei sta muta!' ('unmoving earth, be mute to my footsteps!'); and at the very beginning of the second act, Macbeth and his wife (whom Verdi and Piave call simply 'Lady') mull over the consequences of the assassination in a short passage that is simply a tissue of this epigram, repeated over and over. First Lady tells Macbeth, 'Why worry? Il fatto è irreparabile!' ('The deed is irreparable!'); but Macbeth remains worried, and announces, to the same tune, 'Forza è che scorra un altro sangue, o donna!' ('It is fated that other blood [Banco's and his children's] must flow, O lady!'); Lady agrees that these secondary murders must happen quickly, and asks Macbeth, again to the same tune, 'Immoto sarai tu nel tuo disegno?' ('Will you be firm in your intention?'). The Macbeths have become stuck on this little obsessive figure, a circumflex mark that rises through a fifth or a third, and finally drops a third, over (in all its appearances except the first) a sin-coloured half-cadence from a minor chord to its dominant in the major, the insigne of terror. Immobile words such as 'immobil', 'immoto', 'irreparabile' tend to activate this figure; it is a musical exclamation point, a needle that gouges these sentences into the surface of the mind. Here we have the epigram of evil resolution, a musical image of the irreversibility, the unundoability, of acts. The music proclaims, What's done is done.

In a remarkable essay, Marjorie Garber has found many traces of the Medusa legend in *Macbeth* – a severed head, a battery of mirrors, hair standing on end.[17] I see evidence of petrification in Verdi's handling of this epigram: the music has simply stopped, and Macbeth and his wife keep repeating the same little phrase together – they're caught in a *folie à deux*, at least for a moment, prefiguring the monomania of Lady in the sleep-walking scene in the last act, when she is caged up in her handful of tiny musical phrases. Macbeth and his wife are gorgons to one another – both seem to turn to stone.

Macbeth-music tends to be too static, as in the prison-of-echoes scene, or too mobile, chaotic. In Act I, Macbeth's command to the immobile earth to be mute to his footsteps comes just after the apparition of the dagger, as if Macbeth were begging the far-too-active, disturbed, disorderly orchestra to stop making noise – for as Macbeth sees the apparition of the dagger ('Mi si affaccia un pugnal?!'), the orchestra is contributing a whole consort of aural hallucinations: ferocious but unsteady and fugitive rhythms; a chromatic cello line, insinuating, rising to light like a bad intention ('A me precorri sul confuso cammin': 'You lead me on a confused road') – at last the twisty melodies gutter out into a shadowy intricacy of diminished chords ('Sulla metà del mondo o morta è la natura': 'Over half the world nature now is dead'). This passage is near Verdi's limit of derangement in musical thought: the witches' love of random spastic phrases seems to have infiltrated all speech, leaving only a heap of stray ominousnesses. In these hectic gestures Macbeth, like a witch, reads the future: he will be king.

Macbeth leaves, intending to kill Duncan; when he reenters, 'as if choking', he announces 'Tutto è finito!' ('All done!') to a simple rising and falling minor-second figure at the threshold of recognition as an epigram. As many critics have noticed, Verdi will construct a number of important figures along identical lines: we can hear 'Tutto è finito' in Macbeth's description of the voice that says Macbeth doth murder sleep ('Allor questa voce'); in the opening of the great choral lament in the finale to the first act ('Schiudi, inferno'): and the first three bars of the prelude to the second act, obviously recalling 'Tutto è finito', note for note; and even the words 'Una macchia' ('a stain') in the sleepwalking scene, a subtle recollection. The accompaniment to the chorus of Scottish refugees, 'Patria oppressa', is full of intricate traceries of such figures. This little figure is the music-icon of the stain that can't be washed out – and since in a tragedy falling minor seconds, the basic figure of desolation in Western music, are likely to be everywhere, Verdi teaches us to read them as an omnipresence of blood. Verdi spatters his score with incriminating spots.

In some ways the 'Grand scena e Duetto' of Act I is far more of a black sabbath than anything found in the witches' own music. At the beginning, Verdi notes in the score that the singers must sing in a hushed and dark voice, unless instructed otherwise. Verdi wanted something that was, as far as I know, unprecedented in the domain of nineteenth-century Italian opera, a set-piece that was melodically intense – not recitative – and yet took place in some boundary region between speech and song. A letter of Verdi's to the baritone who created the role of Macbeth, Felice Varesi, makes this point clear: 'I'd rather you served the poet better than you serve the composer .... In the grand duet ... Note that it's night; everyone is asleep, and this whole duet will have to be sung sotto voce, but in a hollow voice such as to arouse terror.'[18] Verdi was often to repeat this advice. The word 'hollow' ('cupa') governed Verdi's whole imagination of *Macbeth*; it is a subterranean sort of opera, as if the performance were constituted within a cave, or as if the singers each sang from within a private abyss. Indeed words such as 'cupo' and 'gufo' ('owl') seem to brood over the text – perhaps the epigrams about immobility and irreparability, with their soft falls of a third, in some sense reproduce the sound-tint of these very words. In this opera, even more than *Otello* and *Falstaff*, Verdi comes closest to realizing the old dream of the inventors of opera, a tragedy in which speech rises effortlessly, imperceptibly, into song. In those late operas he approached Shakespeare through the highly wrought, semi-opaque medium of Boito's poetry and dramaturgy, whereas Piave provided a fairly clear image of the original Jacobean text.

Verdi's great achievement in this liminal area far beneath *bel canto*, where singers make whispery harsh sounds, is the grand duet 'Fatal mia donna!' – an astonishing psychological study of the tremors of spiritual remorse combined with the hilarity of gratified ambition. The orchestral accompaniment of much of the first section of the duet consists of continual arpeggiations of F minor and C major; the tonic-dominant pattern, instead of organizing the harmony into intelligible paragraphs, simply continues compulsively, obsessively, unable to terminate in any satisfying resolution. Punctuation is supplied instead by irruptions of diminished chords – 'O vista, o vista orribile' ('horrible face'). There; are;;; far t!o!o many brrks in the line, crammed in at odd moments. The grand duet is grand in its psychic trajectory, but hacked-up, choppy, in its local textures; it is a duet pasted together from epigrams, spasms of fear.

The large-scale dramatic rhythm of the duet is terror followed by mockery of terror. When Macbeth, fresh from killing Duncan, tells his wife that he felt like saying Amen as the footmen were praying 'May God help us', Lady interjects 'Follie!' ('follies!'), decorating her line with bright little grace notes, as if she were playing the role of his private Vice, an internal voice laughing at his scruples. When Macbeth tells her of the voice that accuses him of murdering sleep, 'avrai per guanciali sol vepri, o Macbetto' ('you will have only thorns for a pillow, O Macbeth'), Lady quotes the tune back to him, suggesting that the phantom voice was really saying 'Sei vano, o Macbetto, ma privo d'ardire' ('you are vain, O Macbeth, but not bold enough'); Lady recasts Macbeth's B♭ minor phrase in a garishly cheerful B♭ major – a parody that again suggests the effect of psychic intimacy that Lady is trying to achieve, as if she were a second point of view inside Macbeth's skull, offering alternative interpretations for the same event. 'Avrai per guanciali', the voice in Macbeth's head, is set as a three-part epigram, using a variant of the harmonic pattern of the witches' three-part epigram 'Salve, o Macbetto'. Both Macbeths are starting to talk witch-talk.

Lady infects Macbeth's imagination by echoing him. She attempts to regularize his musical discourse, to fetch him out of a traumatic realm of minor keys, diminished chords, black cadences, sudden silences and hesitations, fragmentary phrases, oracular ambiguities, into a straightforward, major-key domain of resolute action. But by quoting Macbeth she seems less to shake him out his madness than to join him in it – as if she were a psychiatrist beset by counter-transference, following her patient a little too far into psychosis. By encouraging Macbeth to bring the witches' prophecy to pass, she becomes in effect another witch – her very lack of a first name seems to abstract her from society, from the realm of namable deeds. Near the climax of the duet, Lady, exasperated, decides to incriminate the footmen herself; she manages to exit the stage, smear blood, and return to the stage in a space of 16 bars of quick music – she works in witch's time, foreshortened and accelerated, not human time. Time is becoming unnatural; the clock is out of whack.

Despite her recommendations of directness, forward thrust, Lady seems strangely shapeless and helpless, *informe*, as if she had no identity except what she could borrow from others. She is happiest when singing other people's music, or preexisting public display pieces such as the *brindisi*; left to her own devices she tends to adopt the musical mannerisms of the witches – she has never heard the witches, but it seems that she can hear everything Macbeth hears, even hallucinatory voices. Near the beginning of the first act, the witches utter dark spells, then laugh at themselves; near the end of the first act, Macbeth utters dark spells, then Lady laughs at him. The Macbeths effortlessly fall into a sort of actors'-class exercise in playing witches – an exercise itself devised by witches.

By the Italian standards of the 1840s, *Macbeth* is nearly an anti-opera, since no one falls in love, the lead singers were carefully chosen for their unattractive voices, and the few pieces that invite vocal display often have an undertone of something hideous or stupid, as if vocal display were forced to confess its own meretriciousness.

The centre of *Macbeth* is the *Gran scena del sonnambulismo*, a *scena* without an aria – perhaps it could be called an anti-aria, even an anti-mad-scene. As Verdi advised the first Lady, Marianna Barbieri-Nini, on 31 January 1847:

> the sleepwalking scene ... so far as the dramatic situation is concerned, is one of the most sublime [*più alte*] theatrical creations. Bear in mind that every word has a meaning, and that it is absolutely essential to express it both with the voice and with the acting. Everything is to be said sotto voce and in such a way as to arouse terror and pity. Study it well and you will see that you can make an effect with it, even if it lacks one of those flowing, conventional melodies [*canti filati, e soliti*], which can be found everywhere and which are all alike.[19]

The Aristotelean words 'terror' and 'pity' show how far Verdi had gone in trying to force an Italian opera back into some pre-operatic, archaic model of tragedy. In the first three acts, terror predominates; but in the fourth act, terror is giving way to pity. The Scottish refugees are figures deserving pity; 'pity' is the first word of Macbeth's wheedling fourth-act aria 'Pietà, rispetto, amore'; and the sleepwalking scene is a psychiatric case history of a mind so blasted by terror, so burnt out, so evacuated, that the spectator's pity must be evoked to fill the empty space. Lacking 'flowing, conventional melodies', Lady must rely for expression on prettily arpeggiated accompaniment figures, filling the empty spaces between the ghosts of tunes.

One of the main elements of the sleepwalking scene, the double-dotted, gently stumbling figure in F minor over which the Doctor says 'O, how her eyes gape wide', appeared early in the opera – in fact, it was the second theme in the prelude to the first act. The prelude's first theme was that of the witches' chorus at the beginning of the third act, 'Tre volte miagola la gatta' ('Thrice meowed the cat'). This was Verdi's way of mounting sound-placards, in the opera's first minute, announcing TERROR and PITY: the witches provoke terror, and Lady begs for pity. The rapid switch reveals the co-presence, the interdependence of terror and pity; just as there is an intimacy between the witches and Lady, there is an intimacy between mania and depression, the brutal and the abject, *concitato* and *molle*. The opera investigates their peculiar simultaneity of operation of terror and pity, and describes the rhythms by which terror grows larger and more hollow until it collapses into pity.

Verdi spent a great deal of time coaching Barbieri-Nini, the first Lady, in operatic somnambulism. She claimed that she worked steadily for three months on the part – this was an exaggeration, and may have been misreported, but time distortions and sleep deficits figure everywhere in the role of Lady, even in the life of the singer who enacted it: 'for three months, morning and evening, I tried to imitate those who talk in their sleep, uttering words (as Verdi would say to me) while hardly moving their lips, leaving the rest of the face immobile, including the eyes. It was enough to drive one crazy'.[20] On 11 March 1865, Verdi provided a similar recipe for the revised version, partly informed by his experience of watching the Italian actress Adelaide Ristori in Shakespeare's play:

> we reach the sleepwalking scene, which is always the high point of the opera. Anyone who has seen Ristori knows that it should be done with only the most sparing gestures, even being limited to just about a single gesture, that of wiping out a bloodstain that she thinks she has on her hand. The movements should be slow, and one should not see her taking steps; her feet should drag over the ground as if she were a statue, or ghost, walking. The eyes fixed, the appearance corpse-like; she is in agony, and dies soon after. Ristori employed a rattle in her throat – the death-rattle. In music, that must not and cannot be done; just as one shouldn't cough in the last act of *La traviata* .... Here there is an English-horn lament that takes the place of the death-rattle perfectly well, and more poetically. The piece should be sung with the utmost simplicity and in *voce cupa* [a hollow voice] (she is a dying woman) but without ever letting

the voice become ventriloquial. There are some moments in which the voice can open up, but they must be brief flashes ...[21]

To Verdi, 'Ventriloquial' seems to mean 'toneless' (elsewhere he speaks of a voice 'with tone in it, not "ventriloqu[i]al" '[22]); the Garzanti Italian dictionary defines 'ventriloquo' as a manner of speaking *a labbra semichuise* ('with lips half-closed'). But according to another definition, in which ventriloquism refers to throwing one's voice on to an inanimate object, Lady is quite ventriloquial: much of the burden of expression has been reassigned to the orchestra – the English horn performs a surrogate death-rattle. Parts of her voice have been thrown into the distance: indeed Lady has attained a state of far removal from herself, a sort of ecstasy of despair. She has contracted. Her single gesture, her brief flares of passion, are inter-missions in a state of gesturelessness, paralysis, aphasia. If a corpse could sing, it would sound like this.

Jonas Barish has argued that Verdi's sleepwalking scene is not a mad scene: it is an organized, coherent piece, without the discontinuities that usually represent madness, and without the musical reminiscences to be found, for example, in the famous mad scene in Donizetti's *Lucia di Lammermoor* – 'here the music does not remember very much'.[23] Barish has noticed a crucial feature of the scene: it turns the normal conventions for raving sopranos upside-down, as if Verdi had set out to write the exact opposite of a mad scene. But perhaps Verdi did this, not to stress Lady's sanity, but to portray a different species of madness. The extroverted Lucia became a better singer as she went mad, more urgently expressive, more dizzyingly melodic. The introverted Lady, on the other hand, is moving not toward a fantastic rapture but toward catatonia: fining herself down to an almost musicless state, she is losing expressivity, losing any power to sing. Donizetti's mad scene was full of pretty quotations from early scenes, as Lucia remembers how she and her lover met at the fountain in happier days; Lucia, so to speak, embraced her opera. But Lady relinquishes her opera, loses any connectedness to her own previous actions. With her words she helplessly returns to the past, but she can't recall the right tunes any more. Verdi's sleepwalking scene is a study in amnesia: the music illustrates the erasing of Lady's mind, its blanching into a state of silent candor. The text shows that great gaps are opening in Lady's intelligence; the music anticipates the final condition, pure extinction of faculty – 'Out, out, brief candle!' says Macbeth (5.5.23), but his wife is the one holding the taper.

Catatonia is a disease in which a general paralysis occurs because nerve signals are firing too rapidly to transmit feasible commands to muscles: and

Verdi's sleepwalking scene is an astonishing exercise in the kinesthetics of catatonia. The tempo is *largo*, slow: the dynamics hover around *ppp*, but we hear continual allusions to fast tremblings, thready pulses, aborted nerve-spasms, unscreamed screams. The scene begins in the fatal F minor of the grand duet 'Fatal mia donna' and so much else in the opera. The important musical elements in this opening section, a nearly athematic delirium, are these: (1) a staccato tracery of a slightly altered F minor scale, anticipated in the first-act prelude – a bit of musical gooseflesh, a sort of *petit pas* for mice on tiptoe; (2) a double-dotted sway, an important theme in the first-act prelude, accompanied by arpeggios of an F minor triad and a C dominant chord, a slow-motion replay of the opera's i-V motto-progression – here Lady seems to be falling into her private rhythm, a humming self-hypnosis, a state of acedia; (3) a reedy chromatic descent, recurring when the doctor notes that she keeps rubbing her hands – this may be one of Verdi's musical equivalents to Lady's ceaseless hand-wringing, her vain attempt to wash away the blood; or an anticipation of the death-rattle, for Lady is steeped in death, in the midst of death, throughout this scene. Hand, voice, faculty of sight, seem to be growing displaced into orchestral gestures. Jane Bernstein, who has closely studied descriptions of the hand movements of actresses playing Shakespeare's Lady Macbeth from Sarah Siddons to Adelaide Ristori, notes that in Verdi's sleepwalking scene 'her hands take on a preternatural life of their own ... [the opera] is centred not on the voice but on the body of the prima donna'[24] – a description that beautifully captures the way in which the disintegration of customary melody reflects the disintegration of the body.

Barish is right to say that there are no direct quotations, here or elsewhere in the sleepwalking scene, from earlier melodies; but Lady's opening phrase is full of the ghosts of quotations, quotations in the process of effacing themselves, losing salience. In the first two bars of the Db major section, the orchestra plays, in combination, the falling semitone of the epigram 'Tutto è finito', and the scalar rise and octave drop-off that marks Lady's ambition in several places in the opera, notably (in the 1865 version) Lady's cry of 'È necessario' (from La luce langue). Verdi places great emphasis on the falling semitone by putting the first note in a position where it desperately needs to fall. In some sense, the whole scene is simply stating 'tutto è finito', 'IT'S ALL OVER', in huge letters. When Lady starts to sing, her vocal line doesn't dissonate with the slow paroxym s in the orchestra, but it doesn't pay much attention to the orchestra, either – the heavily emphatic voice, singing the spluttery vagrant line 'Chi poteva in quel vegliardo tanto sangue immaginar?' ('Who could have imagined so much blood in that old man?'), seems disconnected from the accompaniment, disconnected from normal patterns of melodic development, disconnected from itself – a musical equivalent to the involution of Lady's mind, its self-immural in foot-thick walls. She's snatching at a tune that she can't quite find; the witch is self-bewitched, lost in her own labyrinth. Sometimes it feels as if Lady is an extraneous figure in her own *scena*: the orchestral music provides a stunned accompaniment for a zombie ballet, which Lady helplessly figures with vocal graffiti. The sleepwalking scene offers no abrupt changes in mood – indeed Lady seems to have fallen into some state almost beneath mood, a dead calm; but Verdi has managed to transfer the notion of mad discontinuity to other aspects of his musical discourse, while retaining the sense of a single vast arc of drama. Verdi was a composer who noted that madness is not pretty.

When the doctor, perceiving something like a confession of murder, interrupts ('Che parlò?'), the key shifts to D♭ minor, a turn to the tonic minor that seems to indicate how appalling her speech sounds to a public ear; the whole harmonic structure starts to get dangerously unstable, and by the time Lady is noticing 'Di sangue umano sa qui sempre' ('Here's the smell of blood still'), the broken and syncopated accompaniment is in F♭, an unusual key generated as the relative major of D♭ minor. As Lady's whole perceptual world is fracturing into spasms of hallucinations, the music follows her by a series of disturbing musical gestures, patterns of harmonic progression that seem to be the musical equivalent of magical thinking. The schizoid detachment of the music from the text is demonstrated in a particularly harrowing fashion when Lady sings 'Batte alcuno!' ('Someone is knocking!'), while the orchestra utterly refuses to knock. In the grand duet from Act 1, the knocking – the knocking at Hell Gate, according to Shakespeare's Porter – was clearly, obsessively imaged in the orchestra. In the sleepwalking scene, the unknocked knocking is as striking as the loud knocking in the duet.

The harmony does start to stabilize toward the end: Lady exclaims 'A letto' ('To bed') over chords in A♭ and D♭ major, as if her bed were the dominant of her emotional life, the only hope for relief and release. Lady's voice fades out on a cadenza, 'Andiam, Macbetto', as if she were sinking into complete rhythmlessness, her private time outside all clock-time. And the sleepwalking scene ends with the tiptoeing-mouse theme from the beginning, now in D♭ major, not F minor, as if Verdi were imagining Lady stepping into Lethe, entering the tranquility of oblivion. If this theme were in F minor, the sleepwalking scene would be a segment of an endless purgatorial loop; but in D♭ we feel that Lady has reached The End.

After the sleepwalking scene, we return to Macbeth, who sings a self-pitying aria, 'Pietà, rispetto, amore', in which he acknowledges that he will die, and fears that curses and not mourning will sound at his burial. This is in the same key, D♭, as Lady's sleepwalking scene, and Verdi may have intended the arias to be complementary: the hypnotized Lady and the blustery Macbeth, one thinning into reverie, the other exclaiming against fate. The recitativo before the aria even begins with the same sort of double-dotted figure that we hear in the sleepwalking scene, but faster and more excited. Again we note, in this recitativo, how little Macbeth's voice is his own voice, how much of what he sings is borrowed – as if he were a sort of amplification-device for prompters inside his head: he quotes the apparition's prophecy that no man born of woman can hurt him, in a vain attempt to shore up his failing self-confidence. The sinking of his courage, the faltering of his energy, can be heard through the aria: one might expect a certain vehemence as he anticipates the curses that will fall on him, but instead Macbeth seems droopy, listless ('ahi lasso!') – and his aria, like the sleepwalking scene, dribbles out into a cadenza. Here he seems like Shakespeare's dwarf, trying out a text a few sizes too big for his musical resources. Verdi found a good musical correlative to the way in which Shakespeare shows Macbeth, like Antony, dislimning, as water is in water.

In the 1847 version, the drama remains focused on Macbeth until the end; but in 1865 Verdi rewrote the whole conclusion of the act, cutting Macbeth's death solo, and providing a new orchestral piece to represent the battle, as well as a new final chorus. In neither version does the great Shakespeare speech 'Tomorrow, and tomorrow, and tomorrow' count for more than a few lines of perfunctory recitativo; but by finding effective forms of deletion for both Lady and Macbeth, Verdi illustrates the speech's themes: Verdi crushes, undoes his protagonists, reduces them to psychotics or to tales told by an idiot. Lady retained a certain dignity in her inanition, but Macbeth becomes first a hateful fool, and then a vacuum, as Macduff and other nobles rush in to reassert credible forms of moral action, a new wide-awake sort of reality.

The opera ends, in 1865, with dazzling feats of compositional craft. The battle interlude is a fugue, and Verdi delighted in its audacity:

You will laugh when you hear that I wrote a *Fugue* for the battle!!!! A *Fugue?* ... I, who detest everything that smells of school, and it has been nearly thirty years since I wrote one!!!! But I can tell you that in this case that musical form fits quite well. The subjects and countersubjects that follow each other, the dissonant clashes, the uproar, etc., etc., can express a battle quite well.[25]

What is the alternative to nightmare, to the hectic jerky music-speech of the witches and the Macbeths – fragmentary epigrams, stuck cadences, tempos too fast or too slow? A fugue – something at once rousing and erudite, a composition in which all elements may seem to fly apart in frenzy, but in fact fit together in an ostentatious state of control. (It is noteworthy that Berlioz's *Roméo et Juliette* begins with a battle-fugue, and Verdi's *Macbeth* ends with one: to the nineteenth-century musical imagination, the battle-fugue was a near-ideal trope for Shakespeare's peculiar ability to coordinate, to organize, the most vast and varied, conflictual, aspects of human life.) The fugue announces a victory of intelligence over desperate fantasy. Terror is dependent on tacky special effects; the antidote to terror is a display of verifiable and authoritative voice-leading. Music finally asserts itself as a medium at once absolute and humanly expressive, solid, reliable, having little to do with the tenuities and hollownesses of the Macbeths. The fugue is Verdi's metaphor for catharsis itself.

The new (in 1865) final chorus, 'Macbeth, Macbeth ov' è?' ('Macbeth, where is Macbeth?') is the headiest, most exultant chorus Verdi was ever to write; rapid, double-dotted, springy, it has it something of the built-in political activism of Hanns Eisler's marches from the 1930s. The people of Scotland delight that a thunderbolt from the God of victory has destroyed the usurper; then they honour their new king. The soldiers, the women, all eventually join in, but the hymn is first sung by a chorus of *bardi* – and bards seem appropriate, with the suggestions of inspiration, ecstasy, prophecy, that the name implies. The bards are the sequel to the witches, possessing an access to the transcendental but without any implication of malice; the witches have no further role to play in a post-Macbeth Scotland, so they transform themselves (so to speak) into an innocuous and public-spirited band of poets. The bards play the role of Eumenides to the witches' Erinyes: furies tamed into spirits of justice. The key structure of the final chorus is of interest: it begins in C major, as if to confirm that the entire opera is a huge expansion of a cadence from F minor to C major. But the second half of the chorus is in A major, a key not often heard previously. It forms a satisfying span to an act that began with the 'Patria oppressa' chorus in A minor. But it is also a key closely related (the subdominant) to the witches' key of E. The witches' eyes perhaps glimmer faintly from the joyous last bars of the opera, an ongoing force of destiny.

If the witches were demons, the play would end with their slinking back, defeated, into hell. But the witches of *Macbeth* nowhere gnash their teeth or rage at the triumph of justice; in fact their plan succeeds in every last detail, and the army of Macduff and Malcolm is as much an instrument for expediting their wishes as the magic cauldron is. This can be understood, in the orthodox Christian fashion, as the subsumption of partial evils into the universal good; but it can be understood less effortfully as an allegation of something distasteful – petty and deformed – in the action of Providence itself. Teleology colludes with the willful; the abyss is full of maggots.

Otello

After overseeing the Italian première of *Aida* in 1872, Verdi was not sure that he wanted to continue to write operas. He was 59 years old; he had written some two dozen operas, often at the rate of two or three a year; he was tired, tired of dealing with the philistine, shady, ignorant, meretricious or barbaric behaviour of impresarios, critics and tenors. And he felt that the whole genre of Italian opera was changing in ways uncongenial to him: especially since a certain vogue for Wagner and Wagnerism had begun with the first Italian performance of a Wagner opera (*Lohengrin*) in 1871. But Verdi may have felt that he had some unfinished business with Shakespeare, the dramatist he esteemed above all others – his cherished project of writing an opera on *King Lear* had, to his regret, come to nothing. And it was through his fascination with Shakespeare that he was ultimately led back to composing opera. The man most responsible was a glitteringly gifted writer and composer, Arrigo Boito.

The librettists with whom Verdi had worked over the 40-year-span from *Oberto* to *Aida* were, for the most part, experienced craftsmen, with a canny knowledge of the European theatre. At least one of them, Salvatore Cammarano, the librettist of *Il trovatore*, *Luisa Miller* and a few lesser operas, had even earned a bit of respect from Verdi. For the most part, however, Verdi had a low opinion of their talents – the two traits he valued most were terseness of expression, and compliance to his will. He expected his librettists to jump when he barked – and it is possible that his hard insistence on passivity was not the ideal recipe for bringing great operas into being, though it is hard to quarrel with a method that gave the world *Macbeth*, *Rigoletto*, *La traviata*, *Il trovatore*, *Un ballo in maschera*, *La forza del destino* and *Don Carlos*. With Boito, however, things would be different; now, at last, Verdi had a collaborator with a first-rate dramatic intellect.

Not far from Venice, in Padua, there is a fragment of a building called the Cappella degli Scrovegni. When you enter this dismantled thing you find yourself under a vault painted overhead with eight-pointed stars on a dark blue background; portholes in the sky show haloed figures that seem to dangle scrolls down at you. On the walls you see one of the chief monuments of Renaissance art, the 36 frescoes of Giotto illuminating scenes from the life of Mary and Jesus; at the east end there is an Annunciation, at the west end a Last Judgment – it is as you have stepped into the New Testament itself.

When I visited Padua, long ago, I spent some time wondering at Giotto's hard precision, tense restraint, lavish apprehension of things unseen; then I stepped out into the sunshine and wandered into a nearby park. There I saw, on a pedestal, a bust of Boito, born in Padua in 1842; and just behind the bust a gardener had laid out a large floral arrangement in the shape of the smiling head of Mickey Mouse. The ensemble seemed an elegant summary of Boito's creative character: on one side the classicist Boito, whose prodigious mind was illustrated with panels encompassing much of European culture; on the other side, the Boito of the Silly Symphony, relishing the grotesque, the vulgar, the *niais*. Of course, the same tension can be found in the creative personality of many others, not least William Shakespeare.

Boito's career began with fireworks, and slowly tapered off into the respectable. At first, he was part of an Italian artistic movement eventually known as the *Scapigliatura*, the band of the disheveled: its *chic* included bohemianism in behaviour, anarchism or socialism in politics, verism or symbolism in art, and teutonicism in music – Wagner was one of its heroes. (In some ways, it was a first run for the Futurist movement for which Marinetti struck up the band in 1909.) By his early twenties, Boito already was conspicuous for offending the bourgeoisie, as a poet and newspaper editor. And he always already deeply involved in the world of Italian music: he wrote the libretto for Franco Faccio's opera *Amleto* (1865), and the libretto *and* the music for *Mefistofele* (1868) – there were no significant precedents in Italian opera for a composer acting as his own librettist. The premiere of *Mefistofele* began well – the Prologue was received with some enthusiasm – but it turned out to be a very long opera, and as the hour approached midnight, and passed midnight, the audience grew restive and unhappy. (It was not until an 1875 revision that *Mefistofele* found a stageworthy form, and it has remained in the international repertoire ever since.) In any case, by 1868, Boito was feeling the romance of decadence less keenly, and he started to turn conservative – by 1914, he was so presentable to the public that he was made a senator of the Kingdom of Italy. He never lost his taste for music, and he found the great work of his middle age in writing distinguished libretti of a peculiar character, at once swift in action and baroque in language – in 1876 for Amilcar Ponchielli's *La gioconda*, and then for the two last Verdi operas *Otello* and *Falstaff*. He also wrote a libretto first intended for Verdi, then for himself, *Nerone*; and though he laboured on the music for decades, the opera remained unfinished at his death in 1918.

The first Verdi–Boito collaboration was a patriotic hymn, the *Inno delle nazioni* of 1862 – Boito was 20 years old, Verdi almost 50. They might have continued a productive working relationship, but for an unfortunate event in 1863: as a toast in honour of his friend Franco Faccio, Boito read an ode in which he hoped that there was already born a man who would restore the pure art of Italian music, 'Su quell'altar bruttato come un muro / Di lupanare' ('On this altar made ugly as a wall / Of a brothel'). This poem was published in a newspaper shortly afterward, and Verdi took it as a personal insult – and Verdi was a man who could hold a grudge.

It was not until 1879 that Verdi's publisher, Giulio Ricordi, hatched the idea of tempting Verdi to write an Othello opera in collaboration with Boito. Boito and Verdi began to trade ideas about adapting Shakespeare's play, in a somewhat noncommittal manner. Meanwhile, Boito wrote a Council Room scene for the revised version of Verdi's *Simon Boccanegra* (1881) – this preliminary operatic collaboration turned out extremely well, and, as Ricordi and Boito, with infinite steadfastness, removed every obstacle toward *Otello* that Verdi saw in his path, including imaginary ones, Verdi gave his heart to the project. Verdi insisted that the stale features of Italian opera should be discarded; he was particularly emphatic that the libretto should contain no choruses, though, in the end, Verdi's choral writing turned out to be one of the particular brilliancies of the score. Boito had been long urging operatic reform: as early as 1863 he had written that the old formulae – aria, rondo, cabaletta, stretto, ritornello, and so forth – had to be obliterated, and opera writers ought to devise their tragedies straight, without dilution or conventional articulation. Verdi and Boito, then, could agree on the principle of overhaul: opera should be written, not for the convenience of singers or for the sake of gratifying the expectations of a complacent audience, but for the intensification of drama.

But the drama that *Otello* intensifies turned out not to be quite Shakespeare's.

To gain some insight into the ways that Boito read Shakespeare, it's helpful to look at the motor rhythms of his plots. Like most playwrights,

Boito tended to return, again and again, to certain perplexities he found particularly thrilling. I'm tempted to think that the purest expression of the Boito Situation occurs in the first scene of *Nerone*. Simon Magus and Nero are walking at night in a field by the Appian Way; Nero, neurasthenic, spooked, is carrying the ashes of the mother he murdered, and trembling at the Furies that he feels around him. Simon Magus instructs him to pour a libation of blood over the grave; but as he pours, a spectral figure rises out of the ground, holding a torch, her face wreathed with snakes – Nero screams, and runs. The spectral figure tries to chase him, but Simon Magus blocks her way:

> Simon Magus.   I've caught you.
> Asteria.   Who loves death may touch me.
> Simon Magus.   Don't hope to make me afraid. The snakes twisted
>   around your neck are dead or dying. [26]

Don't try to con a con man. The apparition of the Erinyes is a hoax, but hoax created as a genuine expression of madness – for Asteria is a sort of goth groupie of Nero's, sick with love for the sick emperor; eventually she will proclaim, at the Wildean climax of this scene, 'Love that does not kill is not Love!' Even Simon Magus wonders at her eerie look: 'In this torchlight you could be Medusa, Hecate, Sphinx' (*Nerone*, p. 17)

I once saw a magician who rolled up his sleeve, pulled out a knife, and announced to the audience, 'It's going to look as if I'm cutting open my arm, but it's just a trick.' He then put the knife to his wrist and slowly slashed his arm all the way to the elbow – as a bloody gash seemed to appear along the track of the blade, he said, 'Don't worry, folks, it's just fake blood … You don't think I'd really hurt myself, do you?' The cheerful patter had the odd effect of intensifying my anxiety – it was such a violation of the protocols of stage magic that it made me wonder if he might actually be cutting himself in some act of ghastly performance art. Boito's dramas tend to be like that: he erects elaborate theatrical hoaxes that confess their hoaxing nature, but make us shiver anyway. It's as if Snug the Joiner, his head peeking out from his lion costume as he begs the ladies not to be afraid, roared so brilliantly that he provoked actual terror.

The aesthetic effect of *Mefistofele* is unlike that of any other opera, because it insinuates that heaven and hell are nothing but extremely impressive *son et lumière* shows. In Gide's novel *Les caves du Vatican* (1914), a hopeless gull is led into a complicated swindle based on the premise that the real pope has been kidnapped, and a fake pope in league with the freemasons has taken his place; eventually the situation becomes so metaphysical confusing that one character remarks, 'Et qui me dira si Fleurissoire en arrivant au paradis n'y découvre pas tout de même que son bon Dieu non plus n'est pas *le vrai?*'[27] ('And who's going to tell whether [the gull], arriving in paradise, won't discover that God himself isn't the *real* one?') *Mefistofele* is written according to a similar premise.

Boito's Mefistopheles is an obvious clown, a clown of the void. In his Credo, 'Sono lo spirito che nega' ('I am the spirit that denies'), he decorates his great cry for universal annihilation with violent whistles, as if he were not only a participant in some low-brow circus, but also a critic denouncing the whole creation as wretched theatre. Later, in the Walpurgisnight scene, he hold up a glass globe and says, 'Behold the world' ('Ecco il mondo'); soon he throws it to the ground, and it shatters. Throughout the score, the Mefistopheles-music is usually skipping, hopping, pizzicato, or heavy, thick, laboured 'Su, cammina, cammina, cammina' – he's either an acrobat on a trapeze, or a Pierrot dragging something almost too heavy to move.

But we expect the devil to be full of stupid little miracles – though Boito omits the scene in Goethe's *Faust* where Mephistopheles makes wine flow from holes bored in the edge of a table. The daring part of the opera is Boito's treatment of God – represented as a *Chorus mysticus*, a plural God, like that of Schoenberg in *Moses und Aron*. Verdi put his finger on the problem, after hearing the 1875 revision of *Mefistofele*: 'I've always read, and heard people say, that the Prologue *in Heaven* was a thing of genius ... yet when I hear the piece, these harmonies supported almost always on dissonances certainly don't seem very *heavenly.*'[28] This is especially noticeable in the *Salve regina* section of the Prologue, where the Cherubim sing of the angelic spirals turning and turning and turning – Boito's music offers chromatic slithers of the sort more often associated with the devil. Heaven and hell are alike deliria, without any firm basis of support. Boito closely modelled his Prologue on the Prologue to Goethe's *Faust*, a rethinking of the Book of Job, where God and Satan wager about human salvation. Many have thought that Job's God and Job's Satan were, ethically speaking, hard to distinguish, and Boito gives us a God uncomfortably close, musically speaking, to Mephistopheles.

Boito had a strong tendency to conceive all plot lines as variants of an archetypal plot – this may account for the striking recurrence of themes throughout his dramatic work. When critics wondered, after the 1868 premiere of *Mefistofele*, why he had written an opera on such an overfamiliar theme as Faust, Boito replied that (in effect) it was the official plot line of Western literature:

My friend, even the Bible is full of my subject. If we forget Darwin's system, just for this evening, we would have to believe that Adam is indeed the first man — then, look! Adam is the first Faust, and Job is the second, and Solomon is the third. … any man burning with the thirst for knowledge and life, any man impelled by curiosity about good and evil, is Faust. … Just as Solomon is the Biblical Faust, so Prometheus is the mythological Faust. Any man panting after the Unknown, the Ideal, is Faust; you can discern a spark of his great soul under the deep-set eyes of the English Manfred, under the grotesque visor of the Spanish Don Quixote. … Mephistopheles is as old as the Bible and Aeschylus. Mephistopheles is Eden's serpent, and Prometheus' vulture. Mephistopheles is the doubt that gives birth to knowledge, and the evil that gives birth to the good. Wherever you find the spirit of negation, there is Mephistopheles. Job has a Mephistopheles called Satan, Homer has one called Thersites, Shakespeare has one called Falstaff. Mephistopheles is the incarnation of the eternal No to the True, the Beautiful, the Good.[29]

What Boito does not say here is his deepest, most occult theme: that Yes will be difficult to tell from No, and God from the Devil. The reference to Shakespeare is important, because, as we'll see, Boito likes to reconfigure Shakespeare's plots along Faustian lines.

For Boito, the boundary lines that separate one character from another, one play from another play, are vague and permeable. This habit of mind is clear even as early as his youthful libretto for Faccio's *Amleto*: when Hamlet stages *The Mousetrap*, Boito provides for Claudius and Gertrude the following dialogue:

Re.	Regina nel core – mi lacera il morso
	D'un negro pensiero – d'un bieco rimorso.
	Regina, m'aita – mi sento tremar.
	Quel vecchio che dorme – non posso guardar.
	Quel vecchio… nol'vedi? – orrenda figura!!
	È un morto che spezza – la sua sepoltura …
	Mi sento paura.
Regina.	Paura, o pusillo – di fatua fiamma
	Di vana chimera – che i sensi t'infiamma!
	Paura d'un dramma![30]
Claudius.	It tears at my breast – queen of my heart –

A grim remorse – bite of black thought –
Help me, queen – I'm starting to shake.
That sleeping old man – I can't bear to look.
That old man … do you see? – my hair stands on end!!
He's a corpse that breaks – out of his tomb…
                    I am afraid.

Gertrude.   You coward, you fear – a vain chimera.
             A will-o'-the-wisp – inflames you with horror!
                    You quake at a play!

Shakespeare's Gertrude says nothing except 'How fares my lord?' when Claudius blanches and exits; but Boito feels the scene so strongly as a recasting of the banquet scene in *Macbeth* that he supplies dialogue straight out of that play. The player king becomes Banquo's ghost; Gertrude becomes Lady Macbeth, urging her husband to be a more self-possessed criminal; and Hamlet becomes the Wayward Sisters, devising a spectacle of catastrophe out of sheer glee at the prospect of ruin. Boito sees *Hamlet* as he sees nearly every play, as a drama about the cheesy claptrap of evil.

Boito's theatre of fakes and charades, of hallucinations relished for their hallucinatory character, of thrillingly meaningless spectacles, has many precedents in Shakespeare's work. Charlatans and pranksters are everywhere. In the Induction to *The Taming of the Shrew*, a Lord dresses up a dead-drunk idler in fancy clothes, and, when he awakes, pretends to be the drunkard's servant. In *1 Henry IV*, Hotspur meets a Welsh rebel, Owen Glendower, versed in the old Celtic magic:

Glendower.   I can call spirits from the vasty deep.
Hotspur.   Why, so can I, or so can any man;
              But will they come when you do call for them?
              (*1 Henry IV* 3.1)

But the Shakespeare play that best fits Boito's special dramaturgy was *Othello*.

Othello is, of course, a play about jealousy, a most theatrical emotion: every man suffering from sexual jealousy is a kind of playwright, who stages for himself a pornographic theatre in which the beloved flesh is fondled by someone else's hand, kissed by someone else's lips. The special agony of this internal peepshow arises from doubt: since the jealous man is often unsure to what extent this manufactured drama corresponds to reality: is it pure fiction, or a glimpse of a documentary film? In this sense, jealousy is one of the most creative of emotions: it continually erects elaborate and often flimsy superstructures of anxiety, complete with scenarios involving whispered assignations, guttural words of love and tense contortions of bodies; and these disturbing fantasies are all the more obsessive in that the jealous man may find them arousing. Jealousy is an act of imagination, and may be most intense in the most imaginative.

What can provide the means for resisting jealousy? What can calm the jealous man's fears, un-imagine these painful images? Only something that can render improbable the jealous man's scenarios of betrayal, dismiss them as fictitious. One could argue that there was no opportunity for the beloved to commit adultery. But this argument cannot soothe very success-fully, for, unless the beloved is kept in chains behind a locked door, there's *always* opportunity to commit clandestine adultery – as Iago points out, correctly,

> It is impossible you should see this
> Were they as prime as goats, as hot as monkeys,
> As salt as wolves in pride, and fools as gross
> As ignorance made drunk. (3.3.463)

The only real bulwark against jealous suspicion is reputation: the jealous man's conviction of the integrity, the steadfastness, of the beloved's character; his sense that the whole law of her inner being would rebel against the idea of committing any infidelity.

But is any reputation really secure? How much can we really know about another person, and how certain are we that past good behaviour will predict a future of good behaviour? Reputation is based on observation, both the jealous man's own observation, and the sum of what other people tell him they've observed about the beloved. But not all human behaviour is observable, as Iago just said; and what other people know is, from the jealous man's point of view, only hearsay; and, furthermore, other people, who paint the beloved as an angel of probity, may not be telling the truth. Reputation is largely gossip – an artifice, a fiction, not a reliable truth that can neutralize and appease jealous suspicion. Reputation pertains to the theatrical aspect of social life – to our sense that the *dramatis personae* whom we meet on our daily business have sturdy, invariant masks, and will not depart from their assigned character – he's a slut, she's a clown, he's a nerd with a pocket protector for his pencils, she's a stuck-up priss who won't let any man unbutton her blouse. But people are not simply set masks

– there's an improvisatory quality to human life (and no one knew that better than Shakespeare). Sometimes the nursing student will inflict bodily harm; sometimes the wise and prudent person will crash his car into a tree. Reputation is fragile, and often a poor predictor of conduct. Reputation, like jealousy, is a construct of the imagination.

The conflict between reputation for virtue and jealous suspicion is, then, a conflict between two opposing models of the theatre: a semi-allegorical theatre in which people are well-defined incarnations of various traits (Honesty, Folly, Wit, Spitefulness, etc.), and a kind of actors' workshop in which all roles are provisional, easily reassigned. Reputation hopes that all social roles are fixed; jealousy fears that roles are arbitrary and exchangeable, that she who plays the madonna might just as easily play the whore. *Othello* is an experiment in the boundaries between these two theatrical modes. Into the comfortable, predictable, semi-allegorical theatre of Venetian social life, in which Desdemona is Marital Chastity, Roderigo is Infatuation, Othello is something like Reputation personified, there enters Iago, a pure actor, an actor-for-acting's-sake, who proposes to all the extremely uncomfortable thesis that everyone's an actor: and quickly the settled theatre of assigned roles fractures into an actor's workshop, in which the characters are compelled to improvise uncongenial roles. W. H. Auden thought that Iago was simply a negation, a facile actor who was nothing at all, a soulless metaphysical zero, when he wasn't playing a role; therefore Auden thought that Iago should seem a virtuoso actor when in the company of others, but should read his soliloquies in the halting, hammy fashion of a poor actor, since when alone Iago has no role to play, and therefore can only dramatize his non-entity.[31] I'm not sure we need to conceive Iago in such transcendental terms; but it's helpful to conceive his approach to life as essentially histrionic, a continual experimenting in roles. 'I am not what I am' (1.1.65) might be the motto engraved over every actor's dressing-room. It is also Satan's motto, in that 'I am that I am' is the motto of God (Exod. 3:14).

The characters differentiate themselves quite clearly on the axis of Rigid Mask vs. Histrion. At the far right of the scale lies the chameleon Iago, with his enormous negative capability. He has spent his life impersonating a honest man; he can easily impersonate voices of suspicion in Othello's mind; indeed he's such a gifted mime that even Cassio's voice, and Desdemona's body, are well within the range of his clowning:

And then, sir, would he gripe and wring my hand,
Cry, 'O sweet creature!' then kiss me hard,

As if he pluck'd up kisses by the roots
That grew upon my lips; then laid his leg
Over my thigh, and sigh'd, and kiss'd, and then
Cried, 'Cursed fate that gave thee to the Moor!' (3.3.421–6)

At the far left of the scale lies Desdemona, who is too settled in virtue for her own good. Not only does she herself possess authenticity of being, but she has the sort of eyesight that sees the essences of others – perhaps not always quite correctly; she attends, not to surface coloration, but to deep character, moral quality: 'I saw Othello's visage in his mind' (1.3.25). Desdemona's noble indifference to the superficial is one of those virtues that Iago can blacken to pitch: Iago can claim that Desdemona's attraction to Othello is not a matter of loving him in spite of his skin colour, but of loving him because of his skin colour, owing to her irregular sexual appetite:

Not to affect many proposed matches
Of her own clime, complexion, and degree,
Whereto we see in all thing nature tends –
Foh, one may smell in such, a will most rank,
Foul disproportions, thoughts unnatural. (3.3.229–33)

Like many of Shakespeare's virtuous characters, she is a somewhat untheatrical creature; Iago gives her colour and interest by ramming her into the fake theatre of jealousy. She is capable of being playful, even fun-loving, as in her wit-contest with Iago (2.1); and she can stretch her acting skills far enough to play the role of the abandoned maid Barbary, whose Willow Song she sings in the last act.

Still, she's an actress of limited talent, so caught up in her own authenticity that she's incapable of feigning anything – a dangerous state for any Shakespearean character, as Coriolanus proves. When she briefly places herself in the fantasy role of an adulteress, she finds the part wholly incomprehensible, outside her imaginative range: she 'would not do such a wrong / For the whole world' (4.3.78–9). Her central error in dealing with Othello is that she doesn't know how to play the role of a wrongly accused wife: she keeps pressing Cassio's suit, oblivious to the danger of incriminating herself further. She simply can't accept the fact that her husband could relabel her – but in the dereferentialized world inspired by Iago, labels easily drift: 'Was this fair paper, this most goodly book, / Made to write "whore" upon?' (4.2.71–2), as Othello inquires.

But if Desdemona can't feign, and can only utter her authentic being, Othello is a more gifted thespian, a superb monologuist, inventing all sorts of wonderful stories starring himself. In some sense he's a great actor, like Iago, but only in a specialized genre, the monodrama. He has to occupy the whole stage – it's as if he's simultaneously Mark Twain at the lectern, telling anecdotes about his life, and Hal Holbrook impersonating Mark Twain in a theatre. 'Othello' is a grand part that Shakespeare's Moor grandly plays. But when he's forced to depart from his rehearsed script, he can have trouble improvising – sometimes he succeeds brilliantly, but at other times he's overwhelmed, utterly at a loss for words and acts, and sinks into an infantile, chaotic state of being. When events happen that don't fit into his private mythography, Othello is reduced almost to nonentity – just as Antony, after his defeat, puddles out into a kind of human amorph: he compares himself to cloud that keeps reshaping itself as a dragon, a bear, a lion, a blue promontory – 'that which is now a horse, even with a thought / The rack dislimns, and makes it indistinct, / As water is in water' (*Antony and Cleopatra* 4.14.9–11).

From the beginning, Othello is a man looking for direction, and watching for cues: 'Were it my cue to fight, I should have known it / Without a prompter' (1.2.83–4) – he's oddly dependent on cues, and therefore manipulable, despite his valour and strength. He keeps searching not only for cues to act, but also for cues to tell stories: indeed his whole notion of courtship is to woo via narratives of hair-raising exploits; though he claims 'Rude am I in my speech' (1.3.81) – an old orator's trick – he's in fact an extremely talented fabulist:

> I spoke of most disastrous chances ...
> Of hair-breadth scapes i' th' imminent deadly breach,
> Of being taken by the insolent foe
> And sold to slave, of my redemption thence
> And portance in my travel's history;
> Wherein of antres vast and deserts idle,
> Rough quarries, rocks, and hills whose heads touch heaven ...
> And of the Cannibals that each other eat,
> The Anthropophagi, and men whose heads
> Do grow beneath their shoulders. (1.3.134, 136–41, 143–5)

Not only can he recount well-rehearsed impossible autobiography, but he can make up tales on the spot to further his schemes:

> That handkerchief
> Did an Egyptian to my mother give;
> She was a charmer, and could almost read
> The thoughts of people. She told her ... if she lost it,
> Or made a gift of it, my father's eye
> Should hold her loathed, and his spirits should hunt
> After new fancies. She, dying, gave it to me. (3.4.55–8, 60–3).

The murder itself is committed in a kind of delirium of story-telling: Othello tries hard to persuade himself that he's not an avenging husband, but a judge and jury and executioner in a legal process:

> It is the cause, it is the cause, my soul ...
> O balmy breath, that dost almost persuade
> Justice to break her sword! ...
> O perjur'd woman, thou dost stone my heart,
> And mak'st me call what I intend to do
> A murther, which I thought a sacrifice ... (5.2.1, 16–17, 63–5).

And Othello's suicide is a kind of surprise ending to heighten the effect of a narrative: first he imagines the story that people will tell about him in the future:

> Then must you speak
> Of one that lov'd not wisely but too well;
> Of one not easily jealous, but being wrought,
> Perplexed in the extreme; of one whose hand
> (Like the base Indian [so Q1 – according to F1, Iudean] threw a pearl away
> Richer than all his tribe) (5.2.54–8)

and then Othello ends in a blaze of autobiographical reminiscence of his service to Venice:

> Set you down this;
> And say besides, that in Aleppo once,
> Where a malignant and a turban'd Turk
> Beat a Venetian and traduc'd the state,
> I took by th' throat the circumcised dog,
> And smote him – thus. (5.2.351–6).

Just as Iago could occupy all roles in his drama, including Cassio and Desdemona, so Othello can occupy all roles in his monodrama: he is at last the murderer and the murdered. In a sense both Iago and Othello are like the Bottom of *A Midsummer Night's Dream,* eager to play not only Pyramus, but also Thisby and even the lion. Othello's story of the Turk is at once a diversion to keep people's attention away from the knife, and a kind of induction to suicide, as if the only logic that counted to Othello were the logic of narrative. Suicide is the only real act available to a monodramatic hero.

The psychic irony of Othello's plight is that he makes himself a monster – an uxoricide, a suicide – in order to avoid becoming a monster. He clings to a vision of himself as a heroic protagonist because he knows that there are dragons within him. Antony, at the end of his strength, nebulizes himself into a dragon before he dissolves and is lost; and Othello may like stories of cannibals, and men who are a mishmash of head and torso, because he fears that he cannot hold on to his shape, the shape of the admirable warrior Othello. He fears a monster inside Desdemona too: he thinks of her reproductive organs as 'a cestern for foul toads / To knot and gender in!' (4.2.61–2), as if she were a sort of Duessa–Charybdis, a vagina belching an endless swarm of little hideous things.

It is easy for Iago to substitute the difficult-to-fight monster of jealousy for the creatures that decorate Othello's tall tales: jealousy is a monster with green eyes and a large stomach, that 'doth mock the meat it feeds on' (3.3.166–7) – it draws its strength from the strength of the love it perverts. There's a certain cannibal-like quality to Iago's famous description, a quality also latent in Emilia's speech to Desdemona:

> Jealous souls … are not ever jealous for the cause,
> But jealous for they're jealous. It is a monster
> Begot upon itself, born on itself. (3.4.159–62)

Jealousy eats itself, has sex with itself, gives birth to itself; it erects a whole self-engorged microcosm of anxiety, self-sustaining.

Iago seems to have listened to Othello's stories about cannibals with an attention as close as Desdemona's, and with a cannier critical intelligence. Iago invites Othello to conceive his lovely new wife as just another misbegotten hideous thing much in need of slaying – Iago teases out the monster in Othello by teasing out the monster-slayer. Othello is an ideal hypnotic subject, infinitely susceptible, carried away by Iago's suggestions to the point of epileptic raving: 'Pish! Noses, ears, and lips. Is't possible? Confess?

Handkerchief? O devil!' (4.1.42–3); and when Emilia tells him the truth about the handkerchief plot, Othello exclaims 'O, O, O!' and falls on the bed (5.2.198). In this sense the story of the Turk is an attempt at self-hypnosis, as if Othello could substitute, through sheer power of invention, a glorious death in battle for the ignominy of judicial proceedings against a man who strangled his wife. There's a part of Othello that's deeply gratified by the whole unwinding of the plot: he's a man who has at last found an action worthy of his dramatic gifts – not merely an honoured warrior and a skilled diplomat, but a *tragic hero*. T. S. Eliot thought that Othello, at the end, was trying to cheer himself up; that seems almost right, but I think that Othello has been cheerful throughout the play, a maniac pleased with his own vehemence.

Othello is credulous, or half-credulous, of the phantasmagoria of narrative; Iago, of course, is acutely conscious of the fictitiousness of fiction. This is one of the features that Boito found attractive in Shakespeare's play: Iago is not only another Mephistopheles, but also another Asteria: I mean that Iago is at once evil and the master-of-ceremonies of a charade of evil, a conjuror of dead snakes. Ever since the seventeeth-century critic Thomas Rymer sneered that the moral of *Othello* was that good wives should look to their linen, spectators have wondered at the flimsiness of Iago's contrivance. But the grace of evil lies in parsimony: how can I damn my victim with the least effort? The Faust story is a maximalist tale: Mephistopheles is willing to do anything, anything, even to transport Faust to the Empyrean in a chariot of dragons, to capture Faust's soul. Iago is a far thriftier devil, able to ruin Othello with a scheme made of duct tape and chewing gum.

Students of the Elizabethan theatre have always understood that Iago descends from the Vice figure of the old morality and mystery plays – dramatizations of scenes from the Bible, or scenes of good and evil spirits at war for the human soul, a genre in decline by Shakespeare's time, though the boy Shakespeare might have seen one of the last performances of a mystery cycle performed annually in Coventry, not far from Stratford, until it was discontinued in 1579. When Boito rewrote Iago (now spelled as Jago) to accommodate the nineteenth century's notions of proper theatre, he had to stretch and cramp Jago into the shape of a devil that Shakespeare would have found partly familiar and partly unfamiliar.

Credo in un Dio crudel che m'ha creato
Simile a sé, e che nell'ira io nomo.
Dalla viltà d'un germe o d'un atòmo
Vile son nato.

Sono scellerato
Perché son uomo,
E sento il fango originario in me.
Si! questa è la mia fe'!
Credo con fermo cuor, siccome crede
La vedovella al tempio,
Che il mal ch'io penso e che da me procede,
Per il mio destino adempio.
Credo che il guisto è un istrïon beffardo,
E nel viso e nel cuor,
Che tutto è in lui bugiardo:
Lagrima, bacio, sguardo,
Sacrificio ed onor.
E credo l'uom gioco d'iniqua sorte
Dal germe della culla
Al verme dell'avel.
Vien dopo tanta irrision la Morte.
E poi? – La Morte è il Nulla.
È vecchia fola il Ciel.[32]
I believe in a cruel god, a god defiled,
Who made me just like him, a raging thing,
From an atom, from a vile seed, I spring,
I was born vile,
Full of guile,
For I'm a human being,
And the smell of original mud is strong in me.
Yes! That's what I believe!

I believe with a firm heart, as firm
As the heart of the widow kneeling to pray,
That when I think harm and when I do harm
I fulfill my destiny.
I believe that the just man is a jeering player,
And in his face and in his heart
Everything, everything is a liar:
The tear, the kiss, the gazing-higher,
Sacrifice, honour – practiced art.
And I believe man the toy of unjust fate
From the germ of the cradle
To the worm of the grave-hole.

After so much derision comes Death.
And then? Death is just nothingness.
And Heaven an old wives' tale.

This is the famous text of the aria that Boito wrote for Jago near the beginning of Act 2 of *Otello* – all of the soliloquies of Shakespeare's Iago rolled into one and outfitted with contemporary clothes. In Shakespeare's play, Iago spends most of his private time toying with jaunty explanations of his own conduct, what Coleridge called the motive-hunting of a motiveless malignity. But Boito's Jago, though fringed like Shakespeare's with a certain aura of supernatural malevolence, is a nineteenth-century atheist, who understands Heaven and Hell as symmetrical fairy tales. Shakespeare's Iago apostrophizes Hell (2.3.350); Boito's Jago dismisses it. He scarcely needs to concern himself with his motives, since he rejects the concepts of good and evil.

In the *Credo* I find Jago's expression 'fango originario' ('original ooze') of particular interest. Here Boito plays with the term 'peccato originario' ('original sin'), but displaces it in an odd direction. You may remember that Boito, in his 1868 justification of his use of the Faust legend, noted that the Bible was full of Fausts: 'If we forget Darwin's system, just for this evening, we would have to believe that Adam is indeed the first man.' But in devising the strange poem of Jago's *Credo*, Boito did not forget Darwin for a moment. Jago derives himself, and the whole human race, from a single-celled organism in archaic slime. The up-to-date devil scoffs at God, scoffs (so to speak) at himself, and wears the honest face of Charles Darwin.

Like Robert Browning's Caliban (in 'Caliban upon Setebos'), Boito's Jago reverses creation, making up a god in his own image. Jago is, in some ways, even more shapeless and casual than Browning's Caliban. Browning wrote his poem in the most flexible and neutral of English meters, blank verse, but the poem's rhythm is still fairly regular. Boito, on the other hand, incorporated the randomness of Darwinian mutagenesis into the very texture of the *Credo*'s verse: the syllable-count varies unpredictably from one line to the next, and the rhymes come in unexpected places. It is a meter of chaos – Jago is so decadent that he experiments with *vers libre*. As James Hepokoski has noted,[33] this 'metro rotto e non simetrico' ('broken asymmetrical meter', Boito's own term) had appeared in Boito's 1866 poem 'Case nuove', concerning the mishmash of ugly new buildings in Milan. The *Credo* is a poem of deliberately substandard architecture, a contraption meant to fall down.

When Verdi came to set it to music, he too sought the broken and asymmetrical.

The music begins with a mighty unison four-octave phrase in F minor – the key that Verdi long ago assigned to Macbeth's evil: it consists of the notes F–G♭–B♭–C–A♭–B♭–C–F–C, with trills on F and A♭. In this phrase the great discords of the semitone (F–G♭) and the tritone (G♭–C, the *diabolus in musica*) are prominent. Perhaps Verdi based the music of the scene on a unison phrase because Jago harmonizes with nothing – he's a solitary agent, without intimate relations. His vocal line is almost athematic, as if he were, when alone, beneath melody: he either chants on a monotone, or slightly above and below a monotone – or he makes wide angular leaps; the voice-line is clownish, gawky, unsteady, as if tunefulness were dismantling itself, returning to the aboriginal slime of sound, a tar pit with a few fossils of melody sticking out.

The orchestra is far more varied than the voice: in addition to the unison phrase, there's a phrase marked *aspramente*, sometimes decorated with military fanfares. Jago has a whole heap of razzes and Bronx cheers, bitter little chuckles that can turn quite jaunty at times, as if he were Rossini's Figaro in hell. In some sense the *Credo* is a bundle of broken proverbs, since the voice can't coordinate well with the orchestra; Jago lurches from one spasm to the next, because his religion of discontinuity, filth and extinction doesn't permit any sort of smooth discourse. The devil may quote scripture, but he deliberately makes a botch of quotation. The one moment of consonant harmony is a joke, just before *Vien dopo tanta irrision la Morte,* where the unison theme is outfitted with sombre harmonization suitable for a dignified funeral, as if Jago were imagining his soul flying up, enhaloed, to a parody heaven; but he can't long dissemble to himself his gleeful atheism: *La Morte è il Nulla.*

All of these musical gestures seem perfectly appropriate to Jago. But, oddly, they are appropriate to Othello as well. The *Credo* is full of the musical tropes of madness (discontinuity of phrase, discontinuity of implied affect), but Jago is perfectly sane; it is Othello who has epileptic fits, whose speech breaks down into gibberish. Verdi has ways of making musical differentiations between Jago and Othello: Othello is a trumpet in the shape of a tenor, occasionally mellowing into the lyrical or breaking down into empty blatting, whereas chameleon Jago feigns any music useful to his purpose, but tends to decorate his fictitious music with a recognizable vocabulary of rude noises. Verdi's systems of differentiation, however, vanish at certain key moments: Verdi seems aware that Shakespeare's characters like to switch masks at key moments, play one another's roles.

When I try to imagine the single most characteristically Shakespearean scene in all Shakespeare, I think of the scene in *1 Henry IV*, where Falstaff and Hal, lounging at the Boar's Head tavern, enact a fantasy-scene where Hal and his father, King Henry, are discussing Hal's friendship with Falstaff: first Falstaff plays the king and Hal plays himself, then they swap roles, replay the same scene with Falstaff as Hal and Hal as king. I spoke earlier of the dialectic between rigid masks and actor's workshop plasticity of role: in scenes such as this one, Shakespeare's love of acting games takes centre stage, and all identity becomes liquid. At the end of the scene, Falstaff says that to banish plump Jack is to banish the world, but Hal, speaking as his father the king, say, 'I do, I will' (*1 Henry IV* 2.4.481), anticipating Hal's real banishment of Falstaff, long afterward. For Shakespeare, all things pre-occur in the labile, shimmering world of play, and history is just a game that actually happens.

Verdi has his methods for stressing the uncanny intimacy of Jago and Otello. Particularly remarkable is the little game that Jago and Otello play in the second act, a version of the game from *Duck Soup* in which Harpo and Groucho Marx face each other in an imaginary mirror: Othello notes that Cassio conveyed presents from Desdemona, and Jago replies, 'Dassenno?' ('Indeed?') and Otello says, 'Sì, dassenno. Nel credi onesto?' ('Do you think her honest?') and Jago repeats 'Onesto?' and Otello says 'Che ascondi nel tuo core?' ('What are you hiding in your heart?') and Jago repeats, as if the sentence didn't have any meaning, 'Che ascondo in cor, signore?' ('What am I hiding in my heart, lord?') and Otello reflects the same words back at him, to the same tune, like a parrot, 'Che ascondo in cor, signore?' From 'onesto' on, these phrases all begin with the same three notes – it is not easy to tell who is the singing coach and who the slow-witted pupil, but the audience knows that Jago, usurping Otello's voice, is calling the tune. Temptation scenes play in Verdi's head as a form of echolalia.

The second act ends with an emphatic duet of male bonding ('Sì, pel ciel'), as Jago and Otello swear by marble heaven and contorted lightning and death and the dark exterminating sea that they will take vengeance on the adulterous pair. This duet can be compared to other excited all-for-one-and-one-for-all moments in Verdi's earlier works, but the tune is convulsive, clenched, and a listener attending not to the text but to the melody might imagine that the two singers were enemies preparing for mortal combat, in the manner of the Edgardo–Enrico duel–duet 'O sole più rapido a sorger t'appresta' in Donizetti's *Lucia di Lammermoor*. At this moment Otello and Jago are indistinguishable, caught up in a savage concord, an intimate discord. Earlier in Act 2 Jago referred to jealousy as 'un'idra fosca, livida, cieca' — a blind, bruise-black hydra – and just before the duet Otello announces that he feels himself in the hydra's grasp. The hydra is a beast with many heads, but during the duet we sense that Jago and Otello constitute a beast with two heads, heads at war with the world and with one another.

For some time Verdi intended to call the opera *Jago*, on the grounds that Rossini's successful opera *Otello* (1816) had given the earlier composer permanent claim to the title. If Verdi had retained his working title, the nature of his achievement might have been clearer. For one thing, by making the villain the protagonist, Verdi would have stressed the affiliation between his opera and Boito's own *Mefistofele:* and indeed there are some important connections. The chromatic slither in Verdi's setting of the green-eyed monster passage ('Temete, signor, la gelosia!') can be found in *Mefistofele,* in the orchestral prelude to the Walpurgisnight scene. Indeed the whole combination of the angular and the unctuous, the effortful and the insidious, that marks the Jago music is conspicuous in Boito's devil music.

For another thing, to name an opera after a villain is a provocation. *Mefistofele* is an uneasy-making opera for many reasons, not least because it attacks the genre of opera itself: the overwhelming irony undercuts any sense of the dignity of emotional display – tender cooing, snarls of rage, yelps of despair, heaven and hell themselves, are all theatrical claptrap. Mephistopheles is a demon, not a human being, and the opera is written from a Martian's cold perspective on mankind. *Otello* is also an attack against opera. In this Verdi is being an excellent Shakespearean, for no one felt the prejudice against theatre more keenly than Shakespeare.

Verdi first conceived *Otello* as an opera of pure drama, stripped of the devices that he considered extraneous or disreputable. In the end he included almost all the old conventional things, but in a way that makes us uncomfortable with them. You need a love duet? Well, at the end of Act 1 Verdi gives you a Love Duet, long, leisurely, beautifully spun out, maybe the most melodically intense number of his entire career. But its gorgeousness seems not an expression of ardor but a substitute for it. It's a love duet in the past tense:

Te ne rammenti!
Quando narravi l'esule tua vita
E i fieri eventi e i lunghi tuoi dolor,
Ed io t'udia coll'anima rapita
In quei spaventi e coll'estasi in cor.

You remember!
When you told me your life in exile,
And savage actions, and the long torment,
And I heard you with enraptured soul,
With what fear and ecstasy in my heart.

This duet is more appropriate for a golden wedding anniversary than for two newlyweds. There is no urgency in it; it takes place in a crystal Elysium of melody. When, near the end, Otello and Desdemona sing Amen, it seems the right culmination to this chaste celebration of erotic love. When happy, Otello seems old, exhausted; it is only the prospect of fighting monsters that kindles his zeal. By providing Otello with a hydra to confront, Jago rouses him out of lyrical sloth.

Another convention of Italian opera was the grand act-finale, the *pezzo concertato*, in which the soloists and the chorus blaze out in a triumph of despair, or rage, or joy, or any combination of such vehemences. Verdi generally enjoyed writing such scenes, and expected his librettists to provide himself with richly active material – he wanted the characters on stage to *do* something, not just to stand around and sing. Some of Verdi's earliest correspondence with Boito concerns the big finale to Act 3, where the Doge of Venice arrives in Cyprus to congratulate Otello for his victory over the Turks (and to order him back to Venice) – a scene gone horribly awry when Otello turns the ceremony into a public shaming of Desdemona. Verdi thought that Shakespeare's scene could be improved if Boito wrote some verses on the following theme:

> Suddenly in the distance are heard drums, trumpets, cannon fire, etc., etc … 'The Turks! The Turks! Populace and soldiers invade the stage. All are surprised and frightened! Otello recovers himself and stands erect like a lion; he brandishes his sword and, addressing Lodovico, says: 'Come! I will again lead you to victory. Venice will then reward me *with dismissal!…*' All abandon the stage except Desdemona. Meanwhile the women of the populace, rushing in on all sides, terrified, fling themselves down on their knees, while from off stage the shouts of the warriors are heard, cannon fire, drums, trumpets, etc., all the fury of battle. Desdemona in the centre of the stage, isolated, motionless, her eyes fixed on Heaven, prays for Otello.
>
>   The curtain falls.[34]

Verdi had qualms about his own proposal: he noted that the Turks were thought to have been convincingly defeated in Act 1, and he wasn't sure that the devastated Otello could credibly rouse himself to heroic action. But Verdi was willing to abandon many sorts of plausibility for the sake of ending the Act with an Event, instead of the loud massive musing on the situation that Boito had originally provided.

Boito's qualms went further than Verdi's, and he responded with a gently persuasive letter (the second letter he had ever sent to the composer):

> ... you ask me, or rather, you ask yourself: 'Are these scruples, or serious objections? I must say further: *They are serious objections.* You have hit the nail on the head. Otello is like a man moving in a nightmare, and under the fatal, mounting domination of this nightmare he thinks, acts, moves, suffers, and commits his dreadful crime. Now if we conceive an event that must necessarily rouse and distract Otello from such a tenacious nightmare, we thus destroy all the sinister spell Shakespeare created, and we cannot arrive logically at the denouement. That attack of the Turks seems to me like a fist breaking the window of a room where two people are about to die of asphyxiation. That private atmosphere of death so carefully created by Shakespeare suddenly vanishes. ... In other words: *We have found the end of an act, but at the expense of the effect of the final catastrophe.*[35]

Verdi accepted this line of argument, and in the end created a *pezzo concertato* that (to some degree) reverses the old purpose of choral reinforcement of affect – an opening-out, a making-public of the protagonists' knot of feelings. Instead, the chorus and the soloists become a box of living walls, inside which Otello and Desdemona choke, gasp for lack of oxygen. At the beginning, the music seems puzzled, slightly aimless, as if the music, like the spectators, doesn't know what to make of Otello's barbaric treatment of his wife. But as soon as Jago says, 'Una parola' ('A word'), a little four-note figure, falling down through narrow intervals, starts to take command of the whole immensely complicated musical texture; Desdemona and some of the other singers try to escape it by singing urgently lyrical counter-melodies, but no one can escape. Though the choral text sympathizes with Desdemona, the music constructs a sort of infernal machine in which the husband and wife are crushed.

Just before the chorus sings 'Quel viso santo' ('What a holy counte-nance'), the staccato eighth-notes in the orchestra take the shape of a melody we've heard earlier in Act 3, in the trio, when Jago teases Cassio about his sexual conquest, while waving the handkerchief at the concealed

Otello, as a matador might wave a red flag in front of a bull. The melody quoted in the finale is a bit of chromatic chatter sung to the words 'Questa è una ragna' ('This is a spider'): Jago is ostensibly complimenting Cassio for his luck with women, while gleefully spinning the plot-web that will catch Otello. Through the third act the web keeps tightening. The space in which Otello can operate is growing smaller and smaller, until finally it contracts to zero, and he faints, and Jago stands over him, sneering 'Ecco il Leone!' ('Behold the Lion!') to the now-familiar razz-trill in the vocal line. The chorus is still singing 'Long live Otello', because it has already moved on, and has witnessed nothing of the hero's final ignominy – the private and public, instead of growing interresponsive to each other in the usual *pezzo concertato* manner, have separated into two distinct zones of being, each ignorant of the other. After the great singing mass has constructed a suitable cage for Otello, it has no more use for him, until it returns to express shock after the murder of Desdemona.

Verdi's experimentation with aria-form is no less daring than his rethinking of the *pezzo concertato*. The arias have an odd way of opening large spaces around the characters, spaces in which they tend to get a bit lost. Much of Otello's solo music consists of heroic declamation that doesn't shape itself into the symmetrical phrases of a normal aria; and when he does sing something recognizable as an aria of sorts, it tends to go wrong. His very short Act 2 aria, 'Ora e per sempre addio' ('Now and forever farewell') is decorated with brass fanfares that seem to come at us from varying distances, some close by, some remote, as if Otello's military career were receding into the distance before our own ears. His longer Act 3 aria, 'Dio! mi potevi scagliar' ('Dear God! You could have flung every evil at me') is a continual permuting of a short falling figure, as if a sob were being examined from every possible angle; the middle section is written in the odd key of A♭ minor – seven flats – as if the flattenedness of Otello's being were expressed even in the key signature. A normal aria in Italian opera is divided into a slow lyrical section (sometimes called the *cavatina*) and a fast excited section (the *cabaletta*); but in this aria Verdi elides the two, makes it difficult to tell where one ends and the other begins, as Otello's dejection gradually reorganizes itself into rage. Verdi reshapes the aria-form to match more closely the psychological trajectory of the text.

In the case of Desdemona, Verdi wrote a Big Aria, corresponding to Shakespeare's willow song, but a Big Aria that degenerates into flitters as it concludes. Of course, in Shakespeare's own text, the willow song is already a sort of interpolated aria, in that the song is a revised version of a pre-existing song, presumably sung to one of two melodies familiar in

Shakespeare's day. To understand what Verdi has done, we might first take a glance at what might be called Shakespeare's own operatic practice.

The famous songs in the plays are the ones that call attention to themselves – the star turns. Sometimes Shakespeare brings a specialist on to the stage, like a contestant on *American Idol*, for the sole purpose of singing a song. In *Measure for Measure*, Mariana, seduced and abandoned, enters with a Boy, who first sings a song appropriate to her condition ('Take, O, take those lips away' – 4.1.1) and then promptly exits; in *Henry VIII*, Queen Katherine asks a stray wench to sing ('Orpheus with his lute' – 3.1.3), and then turns her attention to weightier matters. But not all of the great songs are relegated to specialists. The boy who played Desdemona must have been proficient both as singer and actor, for he was entrusted with the task of singing 'Willow, willow', perhaps the most lyrically intense moment in all Shakespeare.

Sorely grieving at her husband's accusations, Desdemona remembers a song that Barbary, her mother's maid, died while singing – 'he she lov'd, prov'd mad, / And did forsake her':

> The poor soul sat sighing [so Q2; singing F1] by a sycamore tree,
>   Sing all a green willow:
> Her hand on her bosom, her head on her knee.
>   Sing willow, willow, willow. (4.3.40–3)

Literary critics like to find intricate and dense networks of meaning, and it is not hard to discover connections between 'Willow, willow' and the rest of the play: Desdemona has always been vulnerable to the charms of romantic stories – Othello wooed her with tales of the anthropophagi and men whose heads do grow beneath their shoulders – and the story of the lover whose tears softened the stones would appeal to her taste for extravagance; and by placing her misery among the accustomed traditional miseries of ruined maids and weeping willows Desdemona may ease the sting of her pain.

On the other hand, part of the effect of 'Willow, willow' comes precisely from its *inappropriateness*. Desdemona is not a maid whose lover has proved false; she is a married woman accused of falseness by a faithful husband. It is commonly noticed that Shakespeare reversed the genders of the pronouns in the original song, which concerns a man abandoned by a false woman; 'Willow, willow' is exactly the song that Othello should be singing, as he fantasizes about his presumed sexual betrayal. In her ecstasy of sorrow, Desdemona has weirdly usurped a male song pertaining to her husband's state of mind and turned it against its singer. The strangest moment in the whole role of Desdemona comes at the end of the song:

> I call'd my love false love; but what said he then?
>   Sing willow, willow, willow;
> If I court moe women, you'll couch with moe men. (4.3.55–7)

As far as I know, Shakespeare simply made up the last line: no text of 'Willow, willow' contains it. The timbre of Iago is insinuating itself into Desdemona's voice: earlier in the play Iago told Desdemona that an ideally fair and chaste woman was, in the end, fit only to 'suckle fools and chronicle small beer' (2.1.160); and now Desdemona seems on the extreme verge of disillusionment, as she pushes 'Willow, willow' toward a prosaic cruelty not in the original. At moments of crisis, roles tend to become more fluid – the actors' workshop model grows more vivid, and finite masks start to dissolve.

Shakespeare wanted a song for Desdemona; but her revising, her misre-membering, is more important than the song itself. 'Willow, willow' was no more and no less useful for this purpose than any number of songs about abandoned lovers; if Mariana's 'boy' were to sing 'Willow, willow', and Desdemona were to sing 'Take, O take those lips away', it wouldn't make much difference. There are some songs in Shakespeare, such as 'Full fathom five', that are so specific to the dramatic situation that no one would think of altering them; but most of Shakespeare's star turns are fungible commodities, permitting easy substitutions. The significance of 'Willow, willow' has less to do with willows and soft stones than with the long chains of 'will ow will ow will ow will ow' – I mean that the cantabile, the la la la, is the chief thing, the deliquescence of grief into descant. (The power of the more famous old melody comes from the way in which the descending scales slink their way from D minor, first to D Dorian, then to D major.) Othello can find no worse term of abuse to spit on Desdemona than 'admirable musician! O, she will sing the savageness out of a bear!' (4.1.1889). Desdemona indeed turns out to be an admirable musician, and the fact that she sings means more than the content of her song.

Verdi was not the first operatic composer who noticed in singing 'Willow, willow' Desdemona seems to recede into some fiction of infinite melodic space. Rossini's finest moment as a dramatist occurs in the last act of his *Otello*, when, as Desdemona is preparing to sing the willow song, a gondolier is heard outside, singing the famous lines from Dante's *Inferno* where Paolo and Francesca lament their lost adulterous joy:

Nessun maggior dolore
Che ricordarsi del tempo felice
Nella miseria

No greater pain
Than to remember times of delight
In times of misery.

Rossini set this to a haunting little epigram of a tune – it was left to Liszt to develop its musical potential in a piano piece, 'Canzone del gondoliere nel "Otello" di Rossini', part of a supplement to his second book of *Années de Pèlerinage*. By interpolating this motto from Dante, Rossini opens up space around the willow song, as the abandoned maid and her seducer take their place at the end of an immense series of wretched lovers. Paolo and Francesca themselves were caught up in passion after reading a book together, a romance of Lancelot and Guinevere: and surely Lancelot and Guinevere imagined their tormented love as recapitulating who knows what legendary lovers' pangs?

Verdi got his spatial effect by different means. One of the most notable features of his willow song is the 'Salce' ('willow') refrain, a repeated B-minor droop, like a dove cooing on a branch; Verdi marked this *come una voce lontana* ('in a faraway voice') and a little later he marked the orchestral repeat of 'Salce' as *come un eco* ('like an echo'); but Desdemona's echoes of herself are not like the distorted echoes we've heard in the parrot-games of Jago and Otello, but limpid and exact. She constitutes a whole world of pathos herself, as she's rejected by Otello's world – she's already remote from herself, halfway to heaven, a discarnating spirit. Just as spaces of reverberation open around Otello in his arias, so spaces open around her: Boito spoke in his letter of the sense of claustrophobic enclosure, and the echoey music echoes the whole theme of being lost in a hollow space. The second verse of her song is still more ravishing, ravished, as orchestral simulations of nature-noises – brook-trickles and wind-rustles – embellish the line: a glimpse of Arcadia in the midst of hell, a region whose borders are enforced by the sheer purity of her will. But, as in Shakespeare, she keeps interrupting her song as her attention turns to the sounds, not necessarily pleasant sounds, that she hears around her – Is someone at the door? And, in due course, the tatters of her song blow away in the wind, and she sings a simple prayer, 'Ave Maria', and she goes to bed.

After Otello kills her and realizes just what he's done, he sings out an anguished finale: at the unaccompanied words 'come sei pallida! e stanca, e muta, e bella' ('how pale you are! and wan, and mute, and lovely'), Otello repeats a little figure three times, dropping a minor third from D to B. When Desdemona sang her willow song, she kept repeating her refrain-word three times, 'Salce, salce, salce', to the same notes, D and B. It's as if Otello were vanishing into Desdemona's own cave of echoes; and the opera ends with Otello's recollection of 'Un bacio' ('A kiss'), from the love duet in Act 1, as he abandons himself to one last echo, and recedes into the status of a personage in his own tragic fable. There is no greater pain than recalling times of delight in times of misery.

Falstaff

Otello was a great success at its première in 1887, some 16 years after the première of Verdi's previous opera, *Aida.* Verdi was of course pleased, though evidently a little vexed that the public seemed more drawn by the lead tenor, Francesco Tamagno, than by the opera; when anyone else sang the role, fewer people bought tickets. (Verdi considered that Tamagno, thrilling in loud sustained high notes, didn't sing the love duet with any great steadiness of voice.) Not long after the premiere, Boito started thinking about ways to extract yet another opera out of the septuagenarian composer: Boito wrote to a friend that he was 'eager to make that bronze colossus resound one more time.'[36]

Boito now played on two points where Verdi seemed manipulable: first, his continuing love of Shakespeare; and second, his irritability concerning his presumed lack of talent for comedy. Verdi's one and only comedy, his second opera *Un giorno di regno,* had been a failure; and Rossini had been one of many who said out loud that Verdi's genius was restricted to the tragic mode. There were comic scenes in some of Verdi's operas, such as *La forza del destino,* where the grumpy Fra Melitone keeps spouting laboured puns; and, from the point of view of the Duke, *Rigoletto* is a comedy, maybe all the funnier in that the hunchbacked jester winds up hiring someone to murder his own daughter. But Verdi's audiences, in 1887, might be forgiven for thinking that elegant sparkle was not his strength.

The gestation of *Falstaff* was not as slow as that of *Otello,* but Verdi took his time. On 3 December 1890, Verdi wrote to a friend,

> For forty years I've wanted to write a comic opera, and for fifty years I've known *The Merry Wives of Windsor* ... Now Boito has taken away all my *buts,* and has made for me a lyric comedy like none other ... *Falstaff* is a sad man who commits every sort of wicked deed ... but in a delightful

way [*forma divertente*]. He's a *type!* Types are so various! The opera is completely comical. *Amen.*[37]

A comedy about a sad bad man who amuses the audience, then, is what Verdi first had in mind. Phrased in this way, Verdi's letter seems to posit Falstaff as the successor to Rigoletto, a professional comedian and amateur villain, full of inner pain about his concealed daughter; and something of the glare, the artificial frenzy, the forced laughter, of the opening of *Rigoletto* will be heard in the *Falstaff* music. At the end of *Rigoletto*, the jester, about to throw into the river a sack containing a body, opens the sack and discovers his dying daughter; 40 years later, Verdi (so to speak) opens the same sack and discovers Falstaff, shivering and loudly wretched after being tossed into the Thames. Falstaff is the gaily promiscuous Duke and the deformed clown Rigoletto in one; and, as an occasional singer of falsetto ('Io son di Sir John Falstaff' – 'I am Sir John Falstaff's' – he twitters, imitating one of his imaginary conquests), he seems capable of impersonating a woman as well. Earlier Falstaff operas by Salieri and Nicolai made good use of the episode in *The Merry Wives of Windsor* where Falstaff dresses up in drag as the old witch of Brainford; Verdi and Boito omitted this episode, but the fat zany's Oliver-Hardy-like daintiness is on full display in his wooing song in Act 2, scene 2. And one of Verdi's best jokes is to assign as Falstaff's only aria his account of his life as a slender young page, 'Quand'ero paggio del Duca di Norfolk', a tripping wisp of an tune that can take less than a minute to sing.

The poet William Butler Yeats was fascinated by the mythological figure of the Hunchback, and wrote that the Hunchback, or Multiple Man, conceals in his hunch every human identity: 'A Roman Caesar is held down / Under this hump' ('The Saint and the Hunchback'). Falstaff's paunch operates in a similar manner: Falstaff is a lump of silly putty capable of taking any shape, from the slender page of the Duke of Norfolk to the King of England (whom he pretends to be in Shakespeare's *1 Henry IV*). Like Bottom and Iago, he's an actor so versatile that the whole human race is within his range; but his general grossness of physique means that his impersonations will always be regarded as flagrant theatre. Iago is capable of real hoaxes; Falstaff, especially in his degenerate *Merry Wives of Windsor* version, can deceive only himself. In some sense Falstaff is the Opera Singer put on stage as a figure of fun: capable of incredible feats of vocal acting, but so obviously a fat sweaty slavering thing that no one can suspend disbelief.

After the premiere of *Mefistofele* in 1868, Boito defended his selection of theme by writing, 'Wherever you find the spirit of negation, there is

Mephistopheles. Job has a Mephistopheles called Satan, Homer has one called Thersites, Shakespeare has one called Falstaff. Mefistopheles is the incarnation of the eternal No to the True, the Beautiful, the Good.'[38] Most of us would have written *Iago* where Boito wrote *Falstaff*, but Boito understood both of Shakespeare's characters as Mephistophelean; it is not entirely accidental that the great baritone Victor Maurel, who created the role of Jago, was also the first Falstaff. There is a moment in Boito's *Mefistofele* where Mephistopheles sings his Credo:

Son lo Spirito
Che nega sempre, tutto;
L'astro, il fior.
Il mio ghingno e la mia bega
Turbano gli ozi al Creator.
Voglio il Nulla e del Creato
La ruina universal,
È atmosfera mia,
È atmosfera mia vital,
Ciò? che chiamasi,
Ciò? che chiamasi peccato,
Morte e Mal.
Rido e avvento questa sillaba:
'No!'
Struggo, tento, ruggo, sibilo:
'No!'
Mordo, invischio,
Struggo, tento, ruggo, sibilo:
Fischio! Fischio! Fischio![39]

I, I am the spirit
that always denies;
both flower and star.
I trouble the Creator's leisure
with my discordant sneer.
What do I crave? the great Nothing
and universal ruin.
I breathe the living oxygen
of what you call death and sin,
evil and sin.
I laugh, and I fling this syllable out:

'No!'
I smash, I tempt, I roar, I hiss:
'No!'
I bite, snare in glue,
I smash, I tempt, I roar, I hiss:
I whistle, whistle, whistle! (my translation)

This aria begins as good Goethe ('Ich bin der Geist der stets verneint': 'I am the spirit that always denies'), but moves disconcertingly into an odd reminiscence of the rhythm of negation in Falstaff's honour monologue:

> honor pricks me on. Yea, but how if honor prick me when I come on? how then? Can honor set a leg? No. Or an arm? No. Or take away the grief of a wound? No. ... What is honor? A word. What is in that word honor? Air. ...Who hath it? He that died a' Wednesday. Doth he feel it? No. Doth he hear it? No. 'Tis insensible then? Yea, to the dead. (*1 Henry IV* 5.1.129–38)

Boito's Mephistopheles sings 'No!' as an isolated note interrupting the aria, if one can use the word *aria* for this bundle of spastic musical gestures; the singer's voice drops almost out of music into speech, as if the 'No!' were a denial of opera, of art, of Mephistopheles himself. When, many years later, Boito wrote the libretto to *Falstaff*, he spliced the honour monologue into the end of the first scene, and Verdi used the same trick of dropping the voice down to a half-spoken 'No', a more casual but still emphatic form of metaphysical dismissal. For Verdi, as for Boito, Falstaff is the devil: the ultimate sad bad man.

Both of Verdi's last operas are temptation-dramas, and the story of their composition is itself a temptation-drama, in which Boito plays the role of Mephistopheles, and Verdi the role of Faust, looking for some excuse to fall.

Did Shakespeare conceive Falstaff in the way that Boito and Verdi did, as a devil, a spirit of denial? Yes and: no. Shakespeare's Falstaff is indeed based on a type, the Vice, the tempter of the old morality play. Tempters are traditionally tricky, omniform, and it's never quite clear whether Falstaff's astonishing histrionic gifts are simply part of his demonic craft, or they represent some magnanimity that spills out of the role of Vice into some true generosity of being. Most of Shakespeare's memorable characters tend to be odd mongrels of two or more types conflated into one.

Let me present the case that Boito was right. Falstaff is quite complacent about his typal nature as a Vice, whose traditional stage accouterment was a wooden dagger. As he tells Prince Hal,

> A king's son! If I do not beat thee out of thy kingdom with a dagger of lath, and drive all thy subjects afore thee like a flock of wild geese, I'll never wear hair on my face more. You, Prince of Wales! (*1 Henry IV* 2.4.136–9)

Obviously Falstaff in a sense is only toying with Satanism, but the debauching of a prince is a grave matter in a monarchical society – even this sort of play-demonic is not necessarily far removed from the real thing.

Falstaff pretends not only that he is a Vice, but that he's surrounded by all manner of subaltern devils: he calls Shallow a 'Vice's dagger become a squire' (*2 Henry IV* 3.2.319–20), and indeed he finds devils wherever he looks:

Falstaff.	Do thou amend thy face, and I'll amend my life. Thou art our admiral [flagship], thou bearest the lantern in the poop, but 'tis the nose of thee. Thou art the Knight of the Burning Lamp.
Bardolph.	Why, Sir John, my face does you no harm.
Falstaff.	No, I'll be sworn, I make as good use of it as many a man doth of a death's-head or a *memento mori*. I never see thy face but I think upon hell-fire and Dives that liv'd in purple; for there he is in his robes, burning, burning. (*1 Henry IV* 3.3.24–33).
Boy.	Do you not remember, 'a [Falstaff] saw a flea stick upon Bardolph's nose, and 'a said it was a black soul burning in hell? (*Henry V* 2.3.40–2)

Falstaff's way of diabolifying his acquaintances is so thorough that everyone starts to regard his henchmen as cartoon devils:

Boy.	I did never know so full a voice issue from so empty a heart; but the saying is true, 'The empty vessel makes the greatest sound.' Bardolph and Nym had ten times more valor than this roaring devil i' th' old play, that every one may pare his nails with a wooden dagger, and they are both hang'd, and so would this [Pistol] be, if he durst steal any thing adventurously. (*Henry V* 4.4.67–74)

And Falstaff's henchmen, solidified into minor demons, start to play Falstaff's own game of attributing diabolical traits to everyone around them: Pistol even refers to silly Slender as Mephostophilus (*The Merry Wives of Windsor* 1.1.130). In one celebrated line, Falstaff boasts that he turns other men into his likes: 'I am not only witty in myself, but the cause that wit is in other men' (*2 Henry IV* 1.2.9–10); and to some extent he is not only hellish in himself, but hell's own plague vector, turning into devils his whole circle of acquaintance.

One of the disturbing features of *Otello* is the continual encroachment of evil, until all is storm: Jago seizes control of Otello's music, the solo ensembles, the choral masses, even the end of Desdemona's willow song. But, in *Falstaff*, Satan's reach is greater still. Open-hearted virtue exists only in the tiny domain of Fenton and Nannetta, a bubble of innocence in a universe of guilt. If Alice Ford and Meg Page evade Falstaff's clumsy attempts to send them to hell as adulteresses, it is because they are already devils: as Verdi wrote on 13 June 1892, Alice is 'full of the devil', the leader of the whole pack.[40] She is such a fun-loving woman that she conspires to throw an old man out of a high window into a river; the correct legal term for this is attempted murder. Indeed the music of their giggle-chatter is at times close to the music of Jago's 'Questa è una ragna' – both Jago and the merry wives spin music-webs to ensnare their victims. Falstaff isn't very good at doing evil, but he is an excellent cause of evil in others: he is an unusual kind of devil, the devil-as-schlimazel. A poor seducer, he's nevertheless a successful tempter, insofar as he presents himself as an irresistible butt for general malice. He converts all Windsor into a giant machine to persecute him.

Similarly, the correct legal term for the action of the fairies in Act 3 is assault and battery. In Shakespeare's time, fairies were considered to be pagan gods, somewhat dwindled in power since the advent of Christianity, but still capable of world-defiling malice: Oberon in *A Midsummer Night's Dream* disrupts the seasons and brings plague. In an undated note from the opera's first rehearsals, Verdi wrote that it was important to avoid the impression that the fairies were 'vestal virgins':[41] they are dress-up devils, but they pinch and poke, inflict real pain. In Shakespeare's play, the degree of obvious torture is up to the director; but in Verdi's opera Falstaff's yelps and shrieks are carefully notated – he bellows as if stung by a whole nest of wasps.

The final scene of Shakespeare's *The Merry Wives of Windsor* has a cleansing, good-natured quality that's mostly absent from the opera. It's odd that Shakespeare chose to end this most bourgeois of his plays with a fairy scene, but the leap into Halloween spookery has its purpose. At one point during the planning of Falstaff's humiliation, Mrs. Ford asks Mrs. Page, 'Shall we tell our husbands?':

> *Mrs. Page.*   Yes, by all means; if it be but to scrape the figures out of your husband's brains. (4.2.213–16).

Figments, crotchets, whims, goblins of jealousy that infest husbands' minds – these must be expelled by *literalizing*. The fairies are like Furies in their pinching and prodding of Falstaff; but they're like Eumenides in that they're spirits of good order; as Pistol (of all people) says,

> Where fires thou find'st unrak'd and hearths unswept,
> There pinch the maids as blue as bilberry;
> Our radiant Queen hates sluts and sluttery. (5.5.44–6)

If Falstaff is all fat, Mrs. Quickly tries to literalize this metaphor too, by rendering him with the fire of a candle:

> With trial-fire torch touch me his finger-end.
> If he be chaste, the flame will back descend
> And turn him to no pain; but if he start,
> It is the flesh of a corrupted heart. (5.5.84–7)

Falstaff almost assents to the theory that only his guiltiness makes him susceptible to pain: 'I was three or four times in the thought they were not fairies, and yet the guiltiness of my mind, the sudden surprise of my powers, drove the grossness of the foppery into a received belief' (5.5.121–5). The fairy scene is a ritual expiation of guilt, a punishment for a premeditated but uncommitted crime: when it's over the crestfallen Falstaff (his very name is an impotence joke) is reassimilated into the community: '*Ford.* Yet be cheerful, knight. Thou shalt eat a posset to-night at my house, where I will desire thee to laugh at my wife, that now laughs at thee' (5.5.170–2).

The opera has some of this quality of forgiveness, but the total effect is far sleeker, more savage. There is a moment where Boito and Verdi write a spoof liturgy:

Le Donne.	Domine fallo casto!
Falstaff.	Ma salvagli l'addomine.
Le Donne.	Domine fallo guasto!
Falstaff.	Ma salvagli l'addomine.[42]

The women.	Make him chaste, O Domine!
Falstaff.	But save my poor abdómen-y.
The women.	Lay him waste, O Domine!
Falstaff.	But save my poor abdómen-y.

The pun on 'Domine'/'addomine' suggests nicely that Falstaff's god is his stomach – earlier in the opera Falstaff said that his abdomen contains a thousand tongues that blazon forth his name, as if speaking and singing were just a matter of eating backwards, that is, belching.

Make him chaste, Lord, but not yet. The music is ecclesiastically solemn, but little cries of 'Pizzica' – 'Pinch him' – keep breaking out in the background, and it is clear that this is only hell's parody of heaven. Any sense of real absolution is undone. Indeed, Verdi's real church music is often disturbing. In the *Requiem* (1874–5), the men of the chorus sing the words 'Rex tremendae majestatis' ('King of fearful majesty') to a great downward smite of a phrase, like a falling club; the phrase-shape echoes a moment in the finale to Verdi's *I masnadieri* (The Robbers, 1847), where a chorus of robbers tell the hero that he cannot leave their band – he has made an unbreakable oath. We have seen that, for Boito, Heaven and Hell speak the same language; and for Verdi, too, they are conjoined – both are modalities of the inexorable, that is, fate.

Verdi's music veers wildly between the inexorable and the declamatory, the too-tight and the too-loose. The ensembles for the merry wives and the grim husbands can be heard as a spiffy retooling of the 5-litre, overhead-cam music-engines of Rossini's first-act buffo finales: precision machines propelled by explosions of chaos. (There may be a smiling homage to Rossini in Act 3 scene 2 of *Falstaff*, when, shortly before the 'Domine fallo casto' prayer, Mr. and Mrs. Ford sing 'Pancia ritronfia! Guancia rigonfia!' to a seeming quotation of the tune to 'Io qui giuro e poi scongiuro', from Mustafà's 'Pappataci' oath in the finale of Rossini's *L'italiana in Algeri*.) Sometimes the orchestra sets a machine in motion over which the voices proceed somewhat inattentively – this is especially noticeable in the opera's opening scene, in which two themes (one a sort of firework that detonates in trails of sparks, the other a skulky rising scale) behave in something like sonata form. Elsewhere, Verdi often parcels out the vocal music into short striking phrases, in a manner that recalls the declamatory practice of Monteverdi at the dawn of opera, but in a more jagged fashion – the individual phrases abut one another without the supple transitions of early opera. Both the orchestra-machine and the collage have a distinctly Modernist feel; perhaps it is no accident that Schoenberg's only comic opera, *Von heute auf morgen* (1930) contains occasional reminiscences of *Falstaff*, translated into a serialist glare. And Stravinsky once said that his two favourite operas were *Rigoletto* and *Falstaff*.[43]

Sometimes the striking vocal phrases harden into epigrams. Falstaff's 'Va, va, vecchio John' ('Old Jack, go thy ways'); his 'Te lo cornifico' ('I'll cuckold him for you'); Quickly's 'Reverenza!' ('Your grace!'), 'Povera donna!' ('Poor woman!') and 'Dalle due alle tre' ('Between two and three' – the time for the assignation of Falstaff and Alice Ford); Ford's 'Il cornuto chi è?' ('Who's wearing the horns now?') – all these music-phrases keep recurring. They are not *Leitmotifs* in the Wagnerian sense: they are stiff chunks, little capable of alteration or development or inter-combination. Instead they become elements of a sophisticated rhetoric of gesture.

Many of these epigrams are simple cadential formulae, and as such operate as forms of gestic punctuation. 'Reverenza!' is at once a curtsey and a colon, a summons to attention before speech; 'Povera donna!' a cluck and an exclamation point; 'Dalle due alle tre' a clock-tick and an ellipsis, like a set of cartoon symbols @#$% for a sexual act too gross to speak out loud. All three are strongly associated with Quickly: we hear them in quick succession in Act 2 scene 1, as she pretends to arrange trysts between Falstaff and the supposedly love-sick pair of wives, Alice and Meg. They constitute part of Quickly's mask as *Mercurio-femmina*, deferential fake bawd; and yet her possession of them is weak. Falstaff instantly takes up 'Dalle due alle tre' as his own favourite melodic bit, and in Act 3 scene 2 he will sing 'Reverenza!' back to Quickly, as he realizes the joke she has played on him. By his own admission Verdi conceived Falstaff and the other characters as types, but their typal quirks are easily transferred among themselves – just as Shakespeare's Falstaff can easily assume the traits of Bardolph (red-faced drunkard) or Pistol (bombastic blusterer) when it suits him. After Verdi's Falstaff tells the thunderstruck Ford (disguised as Fontana) that he's already made plans to cuckold him, the tune-fragment 'Te lo cornifico' keeps replaying in Ford's mind, rapid and incessant. And, after Ford proclaims his little falling-major-second taunt 'Chi è?', Falstaff can throw it back at him when Ford's scheme to marry off Nannetta to Caius goes awry – 'Chi è?' Such epigrams constitute a battery of tiny obses-sions – stick-on mustaches, vampire teeth, Groucho glasses – that the characters can don and doff without effort.

The epigrams provide hard bits of harmony or rhythm on the level of a one-to-four-measure brick. But there are local figures that operate on an even smaller scale. In portraying Falstaff, Verdi was much intrigued by the possibilities of musical corpulence. Shakespeare marbles and farces Falstaff with an amazing battery of similes and metaphors:

> Falstaff sweats to death,
> And lards the lean earth as he walked along. (*1 Henry IV* 2.2.108–9)

Didst thou never see Titan kiss a dish of butter ... that melted at the sweet tale of the sun's? If thou didst, then behold that compound. (*1 Henry IV* 2.4.120–3)

Why dost thou converse with that trunk of humors ... that swoll'n parcel of dropsies, that huge bombard of sack, that stuff'd cloak-bag of guts, that roasted Manningtree ox with the pudding [stuffing] in his belly, that reverent Vice, that grey Iniquity? (*1 Henry IV* 2.4.448–54)

I think the devil will not have me damn'd, lest the oil that's in me should set hell on fire. (*The Merry Wives of Windsor* 5.5.34–5)

Verdi is no less imaginative with musical similes for fat: a theme that spans three octaves (at 'Ho fatto ciò ch'hai detto', – the second theme of the opening 'sonata'); a line with steadily widening intervals ('Se Falstaff s'assottiglia', also Act 1 scene 1 – just after this line the instrumentation fattens with heavy low brass, and the rhythm becomes a ponderous *maestoso* strut); or a great chromatic bloat ('L'acqua mi gonfia', Act 3 scene 1).

Verdi provides nothing like a Falstaff *leitmotif,* but he does provide a characteristic trope: the grace note, which is to Falstaff what the musical Bronx cheer is to Jago. After Quickly tells Falstaff the false news that Alice and Meg crave a sexual rendezvous with him, Falstaff shouts 'Alice è mia!' ('Alice is mine!', Act 2 scene 1) to an earpopping sequence of grace-noted chords. Later in the scene, when the disguised Ford places a bag of gold on the table in order to pay him to seduce his wife ('se voi volete Aiutarmi a portarlo?'), the gold glitters, twitters with grace-notes, in Falstaff's imagination. The grace-note figures represent eager appetite, and a jingly triumph, and a kind of self-insistence. But from another point of view they represent a mocking titter at the ludicrousness of Falstaff's behaviour.

Grace-notes are also among the most insubstantial of musical figurations. Verdi's Falstaff is huge, but nevertheless much lighter than Shakespeare's: a creature of great volume and low density. When Falstaff, in Act 3 scene 1, recollects his swelling-up in the Thames, the music tumesces but deflates instantly, as if a needle popped a balloon, and Falstaff returns to his morose grumbling. In the opera's opening scene, he seems a substantial presence, but he becomes less and less substantial as the opera proceeds, both dramatically and musically, until by the final scene he has given the stage over to other actors. His last sustained effort, the monologue in which he grouses over his dunking, ends in a kind of apotheosis of the trill, as alcohol starts to sing in his blood like a black cricket, and its trilling takes over the world: 'il trillo invade il mondo!' It is an amazing moment, as the trill begins in a few woodwinds and catches fire, conflagrates the whole orchestra. But a trill isn't exactly music: it's a hovering in music's interstices, a loud nothing. In some sense the opera is about Falstaff's vanishing.

Verdi in his old age was much preoccupied with the music of vanishing. In his 1897 *Stabat mater* there is a moment ('Tui nati vulnerati') where the music undergoes a remarkable slithering diminuendo, a chromatic fade, as if Verdi were pronouncing a sentence on the vanity of all earthly things. And I think that *Falstaff* is also an opera of undoing, an opera of emptying.

Shakespeare's Falstaff hears the chimes at midnight. Verdi's Falstaff not only hears them, but counts them aloud: one, two, three, four, five, six, seven strokes, eight, nine, ten, eleven, twelve. Throughout the opera, Boito and Verdi give a lot of attention to counting, from the totalling of the tavern bill in the first scene, to the hour of the assignation, to the talley of the strokes of the midnight bell, when the count is at last complete. The midnight bell is prominent elsewhere in the opera, too: in Act 3 scene 1, Quickly and Alice tell the creepy-crawly tale of Herne the phantom hunter ('Quando il rintocco della mezzanotte') to a tune that suggests the tolling of a bell – and, for a few measures, the two women seem about to embark on, of all things, a fugue. A fugue is the least linear, least clock-bound of musical textures, since it is all overlay of one time-scheme on top of another. There are some moments in *Falstaff* in which time is carefully counted out, one beat after another; but at other moments the clock starts to get confused, go mad.

The opera ends, famously, with a fugue on the words 'Tutto nel mondo è burla' ('The whole world's a joke'): a great fuss over a tiny theme, or much ado about nothing. The terse figure at the head of the fugue consists of a falling minor seventh linked to a falling fifth, as if the first notes of the Westminster carillon were distended and put askew, turned into a sort of heehaw. The fugue balls up time, dismisses it and leaves us on the brink of eternity.

Chapter 3

Individuation as Worship: Wagner and Shakespeare

David Trippett

Shakespeare – Beethoven

In 1864, Shakespeare's tercentenerary year, Richard Wagner divulged a childhood fantasy:

> I remember a dream of my early youth, where I dreamt that Shakespeare was alive, and that I met him and spoke to him, actually, in the flesh; the impression this dream left on me was unforgettable, and turned into a longing to see Beethoven (who was also already dead, however).[1]

Wagner's waking dream, later reiterated to Cosima,[2] hints at the extent of his psychological engagement with the cult of Shakespeare in Germany, one that would see him declare Shakespeare 'a culmination point in civilization'[3] (framed by Dante and Goethe), a figure whose historical greatness offers proof of Homer's existence,[4] and whose universality puts even *Faust* in the shade as a mere 'commentary' on Shakespeare *qua* 'the truest picture of the world [itself]'.[5]

But the veneration was not innocent: 'Shakespeare and I', he mused ambiguously in 1880, 'we could do many things'.[6] What in Freudian circles might be termed Wagner's wish-fulfilment in fantasies and day-dreams projects aspects of his own sense of self-identity, veiled only by the generic forms in which these fantasies recur: childhood dreams; youthful fiction; aesthetic theory; historical reflection. The second station on this progression of Shakespeare appropriation is best illustrated in Wagner's novella 'A Pilgrimage to Beethoven' (1840): an anonymous young composer (not-so-cryptically code-named 'R') ingratiates himself through artistic talent with the revered symphonist, whose aesthetic ideals are curiously similar to those of the later Wagner. Consider the imagined dialogue between master and disciple:

Beethoven: If anyone did compose a truly musical drama, he would be looked upon as a fool, and he would indeed be a fool for not keeping it to himself, but setting it before the world.

R: And what would one have to do ... to create such a musical drama?

Beethoven: Do as Shakespeare did, when he wrote his plays.[7]

Just as some might see this as merely 'a public relations vehicle'[8] or perhaps the transparent fantasy of a 27-year-old wash-out, stranded and increasingly penniless in Paris, so the ventriloquism of Beethoven's legacy as it fuses with Shakespeare's is also a blueprint for what would prevail in *The Artwork of the Future* (1849). For here, less than a decade on, Wagner's fiction became an explicit manifesto. The coupling, in Wagner's mind, sees the one historical genius defined reciprocally in terms of the other, each explicable only by analogy with their equal from a different dimension, symphonist vis-à-vis dramatist and vice versa.[9]

Indeed, Wagner's numerous comments in the Zurich essays linking Shakespeare to Beethoven teeter on the brink of a latent, as yet unfulfilled synthesis. The result of mixing these elemental talents – perhaps quackish alchemy by other standards – lays the ground for Wagner's ideal of the future artist as a sublation of the two (in Lawrence Kramer's gaudy formulation: 'a Shake-toven').[10] Thus, the unstated purpose of Wagner's proposition is precisely to bring 'Wagner', as the artist of the future, into being:

The deed of the one and only Shakespeare, which made him into a universal Man, a god, is still but the deed of solitary Beethoven, [a deed] which allowed him to find the language of the artists of the future: only where these two Prometheus' — Shakespeare and Beethoven — reach out their hands to one another ... there first, in the company of all his fellow artists, will the *Poet* [aka Wagner] also find redemption. ... Who, then, will be the Artist of the Future? Without a doubt, the Poet.[11]

The simplicity of this formulation belies its specificity: 'as in Shakespeare the characters, so in Beethoven the melodies – unmistakable, incomparable, an entire, inexplicable world'.[12] In practical terms, this entails a direct alliance of stage character and musical motive, where Beethoven's *Coriolan* overture – 'the accompaniment to a plastic, almost mimetic scene between C[oriolanus] and his mother and wife in the vicinity of Rome'[13] – for instance, contains two motives corresponding to '[1] the image of the defiant Coriolanus in conflict with [2] his inmost voice, the voice that speaks the more unsilenceably to his pride when issuing from his own mother', as Wagner put it in his programme note.[14] Such semiotic practices between stage and orchestra are of course familiar (from clichéd musical tags in boulevard melodrama to reminiscence motifs in French grand opera), but the specifically literary function of narrating musically what cannot be conveyed comprehensibly by a libretto also displays close ties to Wagner's aspirations towards a technique of *Leitmotive* during the mid-century.

Unfortunately, Wagner's poetic imagination is undermined in this case by factual inaccuracy: Beethoven's programme for *Coriolan* draws on Heinrich von Collin's tragedy of 1804, not Shakespeare's text.[15] (Beethoven strangely declined to compose a Shakespeare work despite being himself an avid reader of the Bard; few sketches remain from his aborted Macbeth opera project).[16] Nevertheless, it is a comparison that cuts into the central thesis of Wagner's second major theoretical essay, *Opera and Drama* (1851), namely an extravagant union of melody and poetry, thereby staging the concept of *Versmelodie* (the theoretical product of such an ideal union) as a commingling of the two men whose heritage Wagner, a sublated Prometheus, seeks to utilize.

The concomitant shift in musical style *Versmelodie* entailed is highlighted retrospectively by a four-bar melody Wagner scribbled in 1882 entitled 'melody composed by Shakespeare' (ex. 1).[17] In mock Elizabethan style, with its simple dance-like rhythmic pattern and pentatonic profile, this is the only instance of Wagner ascribing music directly to Shakespeare, and – lacking a metre and clear bar lines in the manuscript – is most likely his aural recollection of something he mistakenly took to be authentic music written for the plays. Its limited semiotic-expressive capacity (compared to Wagner's mature musical language) speaks to the importance – for Wagner's argument – of Beethoven's music as a worthy counterpart to Shakespeare.

Example 1. Wagner's 'Melody composed by Shakespeare'
(24 January 1882)

But beyond the comparative mindset that saw Shakespeare and Beethoven as two sides of the same coin, Wagner also sought to understand Shakespeare as a historical figure, though this hardly stopped him from further individuating his object of fascination. In his Zurich writings, Wagner's idiosyncratic histories – of art, aesthetics, drama, poetry, theology and civilization, not to mention music – can be breathtaking in their scope and temerity. Shakespeare's role is no exception. Wagner credits him with rescuing the human content of Greek tragedy by means of well-defined central characters that permit a range of perspectives. More emphatically, he argues that Shakespeare condensed the chivalric romance's narrative form into drama insofar as he translated it from recitation into staged performance, thereby embodying its material; crucially, this linked poet and people, form and Volk, by incorporating the people themselves as earthy actors in dynamic interaction with the watching, listening audience:

> Here [Shakespeare] found a stage and actors, who until then had remained hidden from the Poet's eye, as a subterranean stream of the Volk's genuine artwork, flowing secretly, yet flowing constantly.[18]

The new stage also introduced human gestures: sensorily perceptible signals as opposed to acts 'merely figured by the narrative talk of poesy'.[19] But given the size of the open theatres, Wagner projects, this emphasis on ocular communication made for dangerously lop-sided theatre when the 'Schau-spieler'[20] or visually orientated performers 'could produce effect by almost nothing but gesture'. While physical actions were clear enough, their inner motives remained obscured, Wagner avers. (He suspected that historical actors' delivery of Shakespeare's language must have been neither loud nor clear enough, speaking of the plays' 'want of intelligible speech [that rendered them] a monstrous plethora of action'.)[21] This quizzical assessment reflects Wagner's wider dualistic outlook on sensory communication, divided according to the physiognomy of perception: eye and ear. As we shall see, though, it is the monistic impulse to integrate sensory stimuli, to transcend physiological dualism – the eye of hearing, the ear of seeing – that forms the goal of his aesthetic precepts. Shakespeare's subaudible stage, in Wagner's reading, thus merely forms a historical way station en route to this telos.

More critically, Wagner argues that while the historical Shakespeare felt impelled to represent history and the romance dramatically, he committed a singular error whose remedy gives Wagnerian music drama its purpose of 'the definiteness of a universally sentient perception'.[22] Namely, he did not provide 'naturalistic representation' of the scenes through stage directions, and thereby caused 'unparalleled confusion in dramatic art for over two centuries, down to the present day'.[23] The outcome of what, for Wagner, was Shakespeare's failure of *Gesamtkunstwerk* is explained as a recipe for misunderstanding, i.e. the archetypal flaw for an aesthetics of communication: by leaving the staging (scene design, props, backdrop etc.) entirely up to the viewer's imagination, he 'drove people into arbitrary deeds of violence against the living drama'.[24] Had Shakespeare sought to represent scenes 'naturalistically' i.e. in a realist vein, Wagner hypothesizes, he would have sifted and further compressed the romance's material with greater care; noticing that further compression was impossible, however, he would have had to conclude that the 'nature of the romance ... does not really correspond with that of drama'.[25] Such ventriloquism effectively forms a counterpart to Wagner's *Pilgrimage* novella, mentioned earlier. Whether Wagner – in sketching the contours of Shakespeare's aesthetics post facto – merely appropriates the playwright to plot his own modern aesthetics or whether he derives an aesthetic vision more genuinely informed by the historical figure, must remain undecidable within the semiotics of genius and dilettante.

To be sure, Wagner's complaint about ambiguous staging is incidental, merely a means of adding rhetorical clout to his macro-belief that the sensory stimuli of modern art remain un-integrated. After lamenting that Ludwig Tieck's demand about using Shakespeare's original scenery had fallen on deaf ears, and that overly-detailed opera scenery was being used to render scenes 'the most realistic actuality',[26] Wagner reaches his central, self-serving claim about Shakespeare in *Nachmärz* Germany: modern poets are now disillusioned with Shakespearean tragedy because, having read the plays silently as works of literature, comprehending them through their imagination as the 'most perfect poetic unity' ('vollendetste dichterische Einheit'), these poets are now confronted with staged dramas riddled with sensory stimuli, i.e. a thoroughly chaotic experience: 'the actualized picture of [the poet's] imagination only showed him an unsurveyable mass of realisms and actions, out of which his puzzled eye absolutely could not reconstruct it'.[27] The result, voiced as the opinion of Wagner's modern poet, is that the plays should not be performed at all, or should be staged as a 'reflective' form of drama, concerned in the first instance with comprehension rather than sensation, i.e. a euphemism for moribund art.[28]

Over and above this caricatured history of European theatre, how did Wagner first arrive at such an individual evaluation of Shakespeare's plays and their author? We know that he shunned secondary literature, yet read Shakespeare voraciously, reciting a play almost every three months with Cosima from 1869.[29] But what of the composer's first exposure to Shakespeare? After prompting by his uncle Adolf, a well-read and locally respected scholar, the 12-year-old Wagner briefly tried to read Shakespeare's plays in English, apparently reciting Hamlet's monologue to his Dresden school teacher, and completing a metrical translation of Romeo's monologue.[30] While the latter does not survive, Wagner's text for an aborted Shakespearean project, the 'grand tragedy' of *Leubald* (1826–8), does.[31] The plot sees the protagonist – 'a mixture of Hamlet and [Harry] Hotspur'[32] – so disturbed by the ghost of his murdered father, that he is driven to multiple murders in vengeance, his guilt over which ultimately drives him insane. Drawing principally on *Hamlet*, it also mimics aspects of *King Lear* (insanity), *Macbeth* (crippling guilt over a concatenation of murders), *Romeo and Juliet* (lovers unwittingly from opposite sides of a blood feud), and *Richard III* (the ghost of the slain enemy, Roderick, appears along with those of all the other murdered relatives), in what amounts to a totalizing of Shakespeare's canon from a teenager dazzled by the spectacle of his own literary discovery.[33] (Wagner proudly acknowledges the borrowing in *Mein Leben*.) Added to this, the heroine is none other than Adelaïde: the idealized, unattainable female in Friedrich von Matthisson's poem, which Wagner received through Beethoven's Op. 46 setting.

In compounding elements of Shakespeare's plays willy nilly, Wagner's youthful enthusiasm was not anomalous for the period; since the late eighteenth century, plays had been adapted to the intellectual horizons and domestic taste of German audiences.[34] But *Leubald's* fantastical elements (no fewer than 42 characters perish and Wagner calls the majority back as ghosts) nevertheless betrays a certain misconception. He explained in 1874 that as a teenager he used to pronounce the poet's name 'Shar-kes-pay-ar' until he was corrected by a house tutor, from whom he gleaned that the name was in fact 'Schicksper', i.e. an amalgam of *Schicksal* and *Speer*, destiny and spear. Cosima recounts the consequence of his phonemic misstep: 'he had interpreted [Shakespeare's works] as something demonic and fantastic and had even sought a mystical meaning in Falstaff'.[35]

It may be no coincidence, then, that ghostly visions ultimately form the defining conceit by which Wagner seeks to illustrate the integration of Shakespeare with his artistic contrary, Beethoven, in the latter's centennial essay. They reveal, more broadly, the role of Shakespeare in Wagner's convoluted metaphysics as he proceeds to theorize sensory communication. Shakespeare is credited with creating 'real live men' as opposed to the mere 'fictional' characters on stage of Calderón; the former remain only distantly intuited, however, as though falling just short of a right to modern existence: 'we must deem material contact with them as impossible as if we were looking at ghosts'.[36] Wagner draws on the authority of Schopenhauer's physiological dream-theory, whereby seeing a ghost 'is a state of clairvoyance occurring in the waking brain'[37] in which shapes that have no material existence are internal projections by the viewer, deemed to be alive. Shakespeare thus becomes the 'ghost-seer and spirit-raiser' while Beethoven is the audio equivalent, one who 'pierced through [banal forms and conventions] to the innermost essence of music in such a way that from this side he could cast the inner light of the clairvoyant on the outer world in order to show us these forms again in nothing but their inner meaning'.[38]

In a sense, Wagner's convoluted conceit aims to illustrate the romantic cliché that both men, dramatist and symphonist, created from inner compulsion what was real and true, though faintly perceptible, but complicates it by asserting that only by bringing the two together, clairvoyant and apparitionist, does this real art become real enough to be sensibly perceptible:

> Since we have called music the revelation of the most inner vision of the essence of the world, we might term Shakespeare a Beethoven who goes on dreaming though awake. What holds their spheres apart are the formal conditions of the laws of apperception extant in each. The most perfect art-form would therefore have to develop from the boundary points where those respective laws could touch. ... We may call Beethoven — whom we have likened to the clairvoyant sleepwalker — the effective bedrock of Shakespeare the ghost-seer: what brings forth Beethoven's melodies, projects Shakespeare's spirit shapes; and both will blend together into one and the same being, if we allow the musician to enter not only the world of sound, but at the same time that of light. ... Shakespeare's spirit shapes would be brought to sound through the full awaking of the inner organ of music, or equally: Beethoven's motives would inspire the enfeebled sight to see those shapes distinctly, and embodied in those spirit shapes they now would move before our eyes, which have become clairvoyant.[39]

This division of labour into ocular and phonic, Shakespeare's seemingly inaudible stage *vis-à-vis* the Beethovenian symphony, reinforce the separation of channels of communication which represent not just alternate means that ought to achieve parity, but entirely different worlds: sound and light; dream and waking; 'inner life and outer knowledge, time and space'.[40] What – for Wagner – finally cuts across the dualism, conjoining the realities of both worlds in a single impulse, is none other than the (audible) scream of a dreamer – forced awake by the presence of their dream – which must count as more than metaphorical for an aesthetics of opera.[41]

To be sure, Wagner was 13 years old when Beethoven died (though unlike Liszt, he could make no claim of having met the revered composer). It seems that Shakespeare, as the more distant historical agent, one whom Wagner's imagination had to construct, functioned simultaneously as inspiration and pawn, mentor and puppet, in the composer's development. His imagined childhood interlocution with the dramatist 'was my longing finding expression' the composer later reflected – making Wagner arguably the last idealist and first psychologist of Shakespeare reception in Germany.[42]

Das Liebesverbot / The Ban on Love (1836)

Given Wagner's early enthusiasm for, and lifelong attachment to, Shakespeare's literary valency within German theatre, it may seem surprising that he set just one play as an opera. He first planned to adapt *Measure for Measure* in June 1834, while music director of Heinrich Bethmann's travelling theatrical company; two months after drafting a prose sketch, he versified the text, began the music in January 1835 and completed the score on 30 December that year.[43] The opera was only performed complete once in Wagner's lifetime, on 29 March 1836 at the Stadttheater in Magdaburg, after which Wagner was to step down as music director since Bethmann's troupe was going bankrupt. It is a testament to Wagner's charisma that he persuaded the singers and musicians – many of whom had not been paid for months – to cooperate in the first place, but with only ten days of rehearsals the painfully under-prepared cast could make no sense of the opera's complex plot for the Saxon public. Wagner reports that the second night was cancelled after an audience of three turned up and a domestic dispute among cast members turned violent.[44] The work was abandoned until 1922, when a vocal score was published by Breikopf, with a full score from Balling appearing the following year alongside a revival in Munich. The libretto remained unpublished until 1911, when it was incorporated in the *Sämtliche Schriften und Dichtungen* (having been excluded from the *Gesammelte Schriften*, which Wagner himself edited in 1871). Wagner's autograph score has been missing since 1945, after it had been in the possession of one of the opera's more notorious fans, Adolf Hitler. It is a mark of the opera's fringe status, an immature curiosity piece, that *Liebesverbot* will be the last opera to appear in the modern critical edition of Wagner's works.[45]

From the outset Wagner planned to make significant changes to Shakespeare's comedy. He infused it with eroticism and libertine freedoms taken from the first part of Heinrich Laube's trilogy *Das junge Europa: Die Poeten* (a collection of 40 fictional, liberal, occasionally sexually suggestive letters between nine poets) and Wilhelm Heinse's *Ardinghello und die glück-seligen Inseln* (a Künstlerroman [1787] about an artist who establishes a haven for the aesthetic life – albeit erotically charged – on a Greek island), explaining: 'I robbed [the original play] of its prevailing earnestness, and thus remoulded it after the pattern of *Das junge Europa*; free, open sensuality triumphed, of its own sheer strength, over puritanical hypocrisy.'[46] In

Measure for Measure	*Das Liebesverbot*
Duke Vincentio	*(An unnamed King leaves his country for Naples; he does not appear in the opera)*
Lord Angelo (viceroy)	Friedrich (German regent; bass)
Isabella	Isabella (soprano)
Claudio (Isabella's brother)	Claudio (tenor)
Julietta (Claudio's betrothed)	*(exists as Julia; does not appear)*
Mariana (Angelo's betrothed)	Mariana (soprano)
Lucio (a rake; Claudio's friend)	Luzio (leader of the people's revolt; tenor)
Gentleman 1	Antonio (tenor)
Gentleman 2	Angelo (bass)
Elbow (constable)	Brighella (comic servant to Friedrich; character from 16th- and 17th-century commedia dell'arte; buffo bass)
Mrs Overdone (brothel owner)	Danieli (wine shop owner)
Pompey Bum (Overdone's man servant)	Pontius Pilate (Danieli's man servant)
(does not exist)	Dorella (served Isabella as lady's maid before being forced to work in Danieli's wine house).

Table 1.1 The characters in Shakespeare's *Measure for Measure* as compared to those in Wagner's operatic adaptation.

practical terms, Shakespeare's original cast of 22 characters is scaled down to 11; five acts are cut back to two; and the central theme is no longer the scales of justice, but 'free sensuality' ('freie Sinnlichkeit'), where it is 'the avenging power of love'[47] – i.e. the viceroy's own libido – that brings him publicly to justice by exposing his hypocrisy. The locale shifts from Vienna, the Habsbergs' Imperial capital, to Palermo, the deck-chaired capital of Sicily; accordingly, Shakespeare's viceroy, Lord Angelo, is replaced by Friedrich, the German Regent of Sicily, an archetype of Prussian puritanism displaced to southern climes. (The name was selected, we learn, simply in order 'to characterize him as a German.')[48] Table 1.1 correlates the characters between the English play and German opera in full.

The Duke, though extant, does not make an appearance in the opera, bestowing greater agency in the scenario to the role of Isabella, who both instigates the plot to trick Friedrich and leads the call physically to unmask him once she discovers Claudio's stay of execution is not what it seems. Moreover, it was her character, Wagner explained in 1851, that inspired him to adapt the comedy in the first place.[49] Like Shakespeare's play, she swaps identities with the jilted Mariana to trick Angelo/Friedrich, who similarly goes back on his word after he believes he can take Isabella's virginity; but unlike the original, the Regent's deviance is exposed not by the return of the Duke, but by means of 'a revolution', as Wagner put it. While the play reports after the fact on Angelo's sexual rendezvous at night in a Garden, wherein he unwittingly has his way with Mariana instead of the beautiful Isabella, Wagner stages the deceptive erotic encounter within the drunken merriment of the Italian Carnivale, where masks, rather than natural darkness, conceal the two women's identities. Furthermore, Shakespeare's prohibition becomes exaggerated: Friedrich bans not only the brothels, extra- and pre-marital sex, but also alcohol and the said carnival, which a delegate of citizens had implored him to accept. Correspondingly, at the close of the opera, it is not the returning Duke to whom – it seems – Isabella gives her hand, but the leader of the defiant carnival, Luzio, who incites the bloody revolt with the refrain to his carnival song in Act 2: 'Who joins us not in frolic jest / Shall have a dagger in his breast' ['Wer sich nicht freut im Carneval, dem stößt das Messer in die Brust!'] during which an erotic Sicilian dance becomes 'increasingly passionate and wild'.[50] Indeed, so extensive is Wagner's intervention in Shakespeare's play that, in 1922, one linguist summed up *Liebesverbot* frankly as 'a sin against Shakespeare'.[51]

As Wagner's autobiographical accounts about his deliberate reshaping show, however, he understood well enough what he was doing; comments issued jointly with Cosima about the play indicate further that he valued Shakespeare's comedy on its own terms. He was particularly in awe of Isabella and the Duke: 'justice and mercy in their fairest forms; the Duke's transition to mildness, his unspoken love for Isabella (Isabella herself divine …), the two scenes between Angelo and the virgin, the final scene, with its polyphonic construction – how to count up and point out all the many details which enchant and move one?'[52] Although this appreciation was expressed vicariously in 1880, it tallies with the emphasis on Isabella and her exemplary conduct – both dignified and justifiably devious – in the 1836 conception.

There can be no doubt that Wagner's staged, quasi-sexual revolution and draconian prohibitions relate to his view of Restoration censorship and repressive state control as he came of age during the 1830s. Whereas Lord Angelo's proclamation is indirect, gleaned from the dialogue between Overdone and Pompey ('You have not heard of the proclamation, have you?' I, 2), Friedrich's is explicit. Moreover, the latter is not sung but read aloud by Brighello (the only such scripted moment in the whole of Wagner's oeuvre, along with a brief dialogue in Act 2, following the convention in nineteenth-century Italian opera whereby letters are read as speech, but also thereby alluding to traditions of Singspiel and the dialogue opera). In contrast to the rest of Wagner's libretto, the proclamation text has neither rhyme scheme nor regular metre, augmenting the effect of its musical silence:

> In the name of the king, We, Frederick, Viceroy of Sicily, being deeply distracted at the grievous growth of lustful living in this our corrupt and godless city of Palermo, are resolved to bring about a more pure and godly way of life, and to that intent, as well as to the hindrance of further abominations, to cut off and destroy with all severity the original roots of these evils. We do therefore in virtue of our office hereby ordain that that feast of extravagance and vice called Carnival be abolished, and every custom thereof forbidden on pain of death; that all taverns and houses of pleasure be done away with and that every person who shall be taken in drunkenness of lechery be incontinently put to death.[53]

Had the opera not flopped, it is possible Wagner would have come to the notice of Saxon state authorities earlier than 1849. Back in 1836, while the police were concerned about staging the planned comic opera during Easter week, only the title had to be changed – to *Die Novize von Palermo* (The Novice of Palermo) – but as Wagner explains, the presiding magistrate did not bother to read the libretto, and permitted the staging in Magdeburg on the strength of Wagner's assertion that the opera was 'adapted from a very serious Shakespearean play.'[54] A bald lie. The libretto openly incites insurrection. When Isabella realizes that Friedrich's reprieve of the death sentence is duplicitous, she later responds as a female revolutionary: 'Fetch your weapons! Now for vengeance! Overthrow him, the dishonourable tyrant! Luzio, come, avenge me!' ['Greift zu den Waffen! Auf, zur Rache! Stürzt ihn, den schändlichne TyrannenAuf Luzio! Komm' und räche mich.'] Only six years earlier, Auber's *La Muette de Portici* – based on the actual uprising in Naples led by Masaniello in 1647 against Spanish colonialism – galvanized a real uprising in Brussels on 25 August 1830, which led to Belgian independence being declared later that year. Wagner was well aware of this, and his aping of musical and theatrical elements from *La Muette* is surely no coincidence.

Over and above the incitement to overthrow a German ruler by bloody revolution, the word play in lines such as Isabella to Luzio: 'Du wilder Mann, so nimm mich hin' [You rampant man, come take me now!] or the incitement to infidelity 'Jetzt gibt's nicht Weib noch Ehemann' ['there are no more wives or husbands'] proved unpalatable to a more conservatively minded social stratum. One colleague in Leipzig – the influential music director Friedrich Sebald Ringelhardt – whom Wagner approached with the opera, and whose daughter was to sing Mariana, refused to put it on at the Leipzig Stadttheater solely on account of its indecency.[55] There were, however, no repercussions for Wagner after the single performance, for as he explained years later: 'thanks to the unintelligible manner in which it was produced, the story remained a complete mystery to the public'.[56]

The fear of censorship, or more unpleasant forms of state intervention, was not unfounded during the *Vormärz*. In December 1835 the Confederation had issued a decree preventing the circulation within member territories of books by 'Young Germans', a group of youthful, politically liberal writers, including Georg Büchner, Heinrich Heine, Karl Gutzkow, Heinrich Laube, Ludolf Wienbarg and Theodor Wundt. Laube had been exiled from Saxony in 1834 following *Das neue Jahnhundert* (1833), spent nine months in a Prussian prison cell for his association with the Student's League, and earned himself further police surveillance following the publication of *Das junge Europa* (1837); August Heinrich Hoffmann von Fallersleben was stripped of his professorship at Breslau after the second volume of *Unpolitische Lieder* (1841) appeared; and Heine's chief publisher, Julius Campe, was interrogated by police following the publication of *Französische Zustände* (1832), while the author was safely exiled in France.[57] Cooperation between states meant, in short, that large cultural markets were centrally controlled, and loop holes in their regulation could rapidly be closed.

Beyond the Confederation's territorial reach, such fears receded. While in Paris (1839–42), Wagner approached Eugene Scribe to translate *Das Liebesverbot* into French and adapt it for the Parisian stage in 1840 (specifically, for the Théâtre de la Renaissance, which promptly burned down); 'the somewhat frivolous subject matter appeared easily adaptable to the French stage' Wagner judged slyly.[58] In the end, Théophile Marion Dumersan translated three numbers from the opera into French. These were performed to a select audience that included Scribe, the director of the Grand Opéra, Edouard Monnaie, and Meyerbeer's agent, Louis Gouin. Nothing worthwhile came from this auspicious gathering, and Wagner later reflected on his shame at having 'once again seriously concerned myself with this frivolous work of my youth [*Liebesverbot*],'[59] confessing as early as 1843 that 'I could no longer regard myself as its composer'.[60]

Translations and musical setting

Wagner was away from his books, travelling in Bohemia with Theodor Apel, when he first began drafting his scenario so it must remain plausible that he was working from his memory of Shakespeare's comedy, at least initially. We are well informed about which translations of Shakespeare Wagner read when at home. He built up two libraries: one in Dresden, which he was forced in 1849 to cede to Heinrich Brockhaus, the brother of his brother-in-law Friedrich, in exchange for securities against private debts, but which was maintained by the bookseller for posterity; and one at Wahnfried, his residence in Bayreuth. Both are housed at the *Nationalarchiv* in Bayreuth, and confirm that Wagner owned three editions of the celebrated translation of the complete works, including *Maß für Maß*, by August Schlegel and Ludwig Tieck.

This composite edition (it was Wolf Heinrich Graf von Baudissin who actually translated the comedy in question)[61] rapidly assumed canonical status after it was eventually published in 1830–3, just a year before Wagner first drafted the scenario of *Liebesverbot*; Wagner's own editions date from 1851–2,[62] 1863–5, and 1867–71, and it is likely that had he worked meaningfully from a different translation, he would surely have incorporated this into his library. Yvonne Nilges has argued that Wagner used Christoph Martin Wieland's translation, but since this is neither contained in his libraries nor mentioned in his correspondence, the circumstantial evidence must render the claim unsubstantiated. As Kenneth E. Larson points out, moreover, the 1820s and 30s saw an explosion of German translations of, and collaborative projects pertaining to, Shakespeare's works (after collections by C. M. Wieland [1762–6] and J. J. Eschenburg [1775–7, rev. ed. 1798–1805], putatively complete German-language editions appeared from Eduard von Bauerfeld [1825–6]; Johann Wilhelm Otto Benda [1825–6]; Johann Heinrich Voß [1818–29]; and Ernst Ortlepp [1839])[63] leading to 'intense competition' between publishers that signal a daunting range of translations theoretically open to Wagner.[64] All books in his possession relevant to his study of Shakespeare are listed in the Appendix.

Wagner valued Shakespeare in German principally because he could not easily manage the English text, once noting his 'repugnance for the English language'.[65] Cosima reports two bilingual reading sessions – of *Macbeth* and 2 *Henry IV* – wherein Wagner concluded that 'Shakespeare in English [is] vivid and precise, whereas in German it is all nobler, more elegant, even more poetic.'[66] Such comments almost certainly refer to Wagner's Schlegel/Tieck edition at Wahnfried. The translation of *Measure for Measure* contained therein closely observes the iambic pentameter of Shakespeare's original, even to the point of mimicking line breaks. See, for instance, Isabella's chastisement of autocratic rule in Act 2, scene 2:

So you must be the first that gives this sentence,	So muß zuerst von euch solch Urtheil kommen,
And he that suffers. O it is excellent	Und er zuerst es dulden? Ach, 's ist groß
To have a giant's strength, but it is tyrannous	Des Riesen Kraft besitzen; doch tyrannisch,
To use it like a giant. (ll. 112–15)	Dem Riesen gleich sie brauchen.

While the first half of the second line uses two iambs in English, three in German, the latter is immediately balanced by the elision of 'ach' and 'es' which would correspond to a hypothetical ''tis' in English. The suppleness of Shakespeare's formulation (allowing for, but not requiring, greater dynamic and agogic accent on 'O') is set in relief by the German, which arguably places greater emphasis on iambic accent by its preponderance of amphibrachic ('besitzen', 'tyrannisch') and trochaic ('Urtheil', 'kommen', 'dulden', 'Riesen', 'brauchen') words. Put another way, the greater number of monosyllables in the English original of this passage (29, compared to

17 in German) lends greater flexibility to the prosaic delivery. Given the matching eight iambs in the final two lines (ll. 114–15), we can see that the metrical equivalence between the languages is similar enough not to raise undue criticism of the translation. A comparison with Wieland's earlier, less metrical translation of these lines makes this clear: 'So müßt ihr also der erste seyn, der ein solches Urtheil spricht, / und er der erste, der dadurch leidet. O! Es ist vortrefflich, / die Staerke eines Riesen zu haben; aber es ist tyrannisch, / sie wie ein Riese zu gebrauchen.'[67] And it is a mark of the aura that continues to surround the Schlegel/Tieck translation in Germany that one linguist recently dubbed the edition an: 'astonishingly accurate version of Shakespeare's plays'.[68]

Such rigour in poetic metre nevertheless sits uneasily with Wagner's virulent criticism of the same in *Opera and Drama*, as a cage whose restrictions hinder prosaic delivery:

> Just how incapable our language is of any given rhythmically accurate utterance [in Verse], is shown most obviously by that simplest of poetic metres in which she has been accustomed to clothing herself, in order — as modestly as possible — to show herself in at least some sort of rhythmic apparel. We mean so-called *iambs*, through which she tends most frequently to present herself as a five — footed monster to our eyes and — sadly — also to our ears. The unattractiveness of this metre is in and of itself offensive to our feeling as soon as it is performed without pause, as in our spoken plays: but when — as indeed is inevitable — the most severe constraint is put on the living accent of speech, for the sake of this monotonous rhythm, then the hearing of such verses becomes a positive martyrdom; for ... through the mutilation of the speaking accent, the hearer is forcibly compelled to sacrifice his feelings to a painfully fatiguing ride on hobbling iambs, whose clattering trot must ultimately rob him of the last shred of sense and understanding.[69]

As so often with Wagner, the frustration can be read reflexively. His own versification of the adapted scenario from Shakespeare is rigidly metric, with a pervasive (if inconsistent) iambic tetrameter and patchy use of rhyming couplets, likely indebted to Goethe's *Faust* (from the prologue set in heaven onwards). The opening chorus of outraged citizens in *Liebesverbot* – set in Danieli's wine house, where Brighella's men are dismantling pleasure booths of various kinds – is indicative in this respect:

Ihr Galgenvögel, haltet ein,	See here you hangdogs,
ihr Schurken, laßt die Arbeit sein!	You rogues, leave the workers in peace!
Schlagt auf sie los mit kräft'ger Faust,	Beat them off with powerful fists,
bei Rock und Haar die Flegel zaust!	Ruffle their coats and hair with flails!

The strict metre and echoing end-rhyme continue, intermittently, for much of the two acts. Thirty-two years later, Wagner would offer a merciless self-parody where end-rhyme (again, within tetrameter) is grotesquely emphasized in Koethner's reading of the Leges Tabulaturae in *Die Meistersinger*, i.e. monotone chanting leading to the same accented pitches at the rhyme:

Ein jedes Meistergesanges Bar	Each unit of a mastersong
stell' ordentlich ein Gemässe dar	shall present a proper balance
aus unterschiedlichen Gesätzen,	of its different sections,
die keiner soll verletzen…	against which no one shall
(Act 1, scene 3)	offend…

Returning to Wagner's non-ironic use of formulae in *Liebesverbot*, at the end of the first act, he introduces still greater rigidity. Consider again Isabella's entreaty to Angelo/Friedrich, in which she closes all three verses (in tetrameter) with the same rhyming couplet (a schema Wagner would recycle for Tannhäuser's hymn to Venus in Act 1 of *Tannhäuser*):[70]

[Verse 1] O, oeffne der Schwesterliebe dein Herz, / loese durch Gnade meinen Schmerz!
[Verse 2] O, oeffne der Erdenliebe dein Herz, / und loese durch Gnade meinen Schmerz!
[Verse 3] O, so oeffne dem Flehen jetzt den Herz, / loese durch Gnade meinen Schmerz![71]

No such repetition occurs in Shakespeare. Wagner's strophic form supports his musical scheme where Isabella's reiterations function as extended rhyming terminations. Her lines are set to virtuosic, written-out cadenzas in almost parodic imitation of Donizetti; they increase in grandeur, vocal extension, and intervallic leaps with each iteration of the text, offsetting its underlying repetition. Such unmistakable Italianate clichés – cadential dominant minor ninths, articulated arpeggiation, stepwise approach to the sustained peak pitch (B-flat), three vocal caesurae at the cadence points etc. – would never again appear so densely knitted together in a staged Wagner opera.

Indeed, the music for Wagner's Shakespeare setting is explicitly imitative, drawing on conventions of style and form from both French and Italian number operas. Wagner acknowledged the foreign borrowing,[72] and it is no coincidence that his first published essay, a provocatively pro-Italian slingshot entitled *German Opera,* was written in early June 1834 alongside his prose draft of *Liebesverbot.* It appeared on 10 June in Laube's journal *Zeitung für die elegante Welt,* and contextualizes the composer's characterization of a German/Italian dualism in *Liebesverbot.* Carl Maria von Weber's music, representing German opera, is condemned for its sanctimonious search for profundity:

> What splitting of hairs in the declamation, what fussy use of this or that instrument to emphasise a single word! Instead of quickly capturing a feeling with a single bold and telling stroke, he hacks to pieces the impression of the whole with petty details and detailed pettiness ... Oh this unhappy erudition — this source of all German ills![73]

Italian opera, by contrast, is lauded as 'sensuously warm' ('sinnlich-warm'), naturally vivacious and rich in vocal melody.[74] Wagner's choice of musical style in tandem with his revised Sicilian scenario hence present his youthful prejudice against German identity in two, mutually reinforcing guises. His final qualification – in German Opera – makes the role of music clear in what he saw as German hypocrisy over aesthetic and erotic puritanism, respectively caricatured by Weber and – in *Liebesverbot* – Friedrich the 'fool' ['Friedrich ist ein Narr!']: 'Not that I wish French or Italian music to oust our own' the 21 -year-old composer clarified for his native readership, 'that would be a fresh evil to guard against — but we ought to recognise what is true in both, and keep ourselves from all selfish hypocrisy'.[75] This, in short, is the political sting of *Liebesverbot* for German listeners during the Restoration. It seems that, stimulated by Shakespeare's Isabella, Wagner spun the opera's sexual–social narrative out of a perception of hypocritical aesthetic puritanism within German musical style.

While a full musical study is not appropriate here, certain features of the score bear mention. The overture – a genre Wagner would ponder at length in 1841[76] – is a summary apéritif of the opera's themes as per *opéra comique.* It begins with the busy carnival theme, whose opening harmonic gambit (I – I$^{\#5}$ – IVc – IVc^{b6} – I) and bustling character lean heavily on Ferdinand Hérold's *Zampa* (1831), a feverishly popular work in Vienna that Wagner heard there in 1832.[77] More precociously perhaps, Wagner uses two principal themes that assume semiotic value as the polarized cultures of the scenario: the severe proclamation of an austere autocrat, and the forbidden passion and warm sensuality of southern life. The angular intervals, chromaticism and stark sustained unisons of the 'proclamation' theme is characteristic (in the aesthetic sense); it recurs in Act 1 as the ban is first read out, and in the finale as a parodically learned fugato while Friedrich chastises his citizens' licentious appetites; it also pervades Friedrich's extended aria in Act 2 (no. 10). If we recall Wagner's special alliance – 'as in Shakespeare the characters, so in Beethoven the melodies' – the thematic treatment here would seem to offer a literal interpretation, one that would play into Wagner's later refinement of his putative signifying practice as 'melodic moments' wherein the orchestra's 'signposts' are to orientate a listener's feelings.[78]

Within the opera proper, stylistic imitation is all-pervasive. There are cabaletta sections, such as the duet between Isabella and Claudio in Act 2, modelled on Italian opera; the score is more or less through-composed, as per French grand opera, and indeed Wagner's frequent choral tableaux emulate those of Auber's *La Muette de Portici* with its *choeurs dansés* and movements for ballet. The five-part choral writing, doubled by the soloists, in the D-major Act 2 Finale seems specifically to draw on the 'market chorus' from the third act of *La Muette*. Finally, despite Wagner's rapid dumping of the opera, he did recycle the introduction to the first duet between Isabella and Mariana (no. 3), and their ensuing 'Salve Regina' as the music of Catholic Rome from act 3 of *Tannhäuser* (1845). Beyond Wagner's contradictory comments on the music, Thomas Grey's assessment of the 'interminable cadential extensions … [that] almost [give] the impression of a deliberate parody'[79] is representative of the narrowed eyes through which this work is typically viewed. Carl Dahlhaus dubbed it Wagner's *Kapellmeistermusik* (along with *Die Feen* [1833] and *Rienzi* [1842]), excluding it from his discussions of Wagner's *oeuvre*,[80] and Geoffrey's Skelton's laconic dismissal – 'the music … shows … little of the greatness to come' – forms a habitual modern verdict.[81]

Towards transcendent realism

There can be little doubt that Wagner saw parallels between certain works of Shakespeare and his own mature output. Cosima reports their numerous readings of sections from plays, often over several days, and the ensuing conversations, noting, for instance, that Wagner found reflections of *Antony and Cleopatra* in *Tristan und Isolde*: 'inasmuch as [Shakespeare's tragedy] shows a being utterly consumed by love: in *Tristan* time renders it naïve and pure, whereas here it appears in a ghastly, voluptuous setting, yet no less destructively'.[82] That *Romeo and Juliet* may also be implicated here seems obvious. Indeed, the cat's cradle of connections is potentially intricate and extensive: beyond any authorial blessing, we might point to the warring Veronese families in *Romeo and Juliet* as a model of the houses of Colonna and Orsini in *Rienzi* (1842), or, more interpretatively, consider how the comic ban on love from *Liebesverbot* finds a tragic inversion in Alberich's renunciation of love in order to seize the Rheingold, a cosmogonic theft that sets in motion the destructive urges at the centre of the *Ring*. Structurally, Wagner's stratagem in *Tannhäuser* whereby the sensory-erotic pull of the Venusberg's 'magic sights and sounds' is only perceptible to individuals whose 'breast burns with a daring of the senses'[83] perhaps leans on *The Tempest*, in that some characters can hear Ariel's music, while others cannot.[84] Comparative readings like this of Wagner's works emerged even by the early 1860s;[85] the earliest comprehensive study of Shakespearean elements in his plots appeared in the *Bayreuther Blätter* in 1917, tracing correspondences so zealously between different works that at least one contemporary criticized as 'laborious' its delving into 'such minutiae'.[86] Most recently Yvonne Nilges has argued that *A Midsummer Night's Dream* is formatively important for Wagner's *Johannistag* theme within *Die Meistersinger*: a projected escape – from Athens, from Nuremberg – occurs during a certain night within the summer solstice, namely Lysander's plea to Hermia that she leave home and flee with him; and Walter and Eva's planned elopement following the young knight's initial artistic failure (Act 2, scene 2). To regard such parallels as deliberate migration or borrowing may seem risky without further substantiation; accordingly, Nilges also connects imagery between the works: the moon, 'Wahn', midsummer madness.[87] But given Wagner's energetic appetite for literature (if not for literary criticism), and the complex strands of symbolism and narrative archetypes within *Vormärz* drama and *Trauerspiel*, speculation about specific parallels between Shakespeare's plays and Wagner's operas must remain playfully unstable. Moreover, the enduring influence on Wagner of Hellenic theatre and its symbols, with their greater potential for politicization, remind us that while Shakespeare is 'the most enigmatic of them all',[88] his power over the composer forms part of a tapestry of influences, each strand weaving a discernable path among many, Wagner's hyperbole notwithstanding.[89]

Indeed, Wagner's individuation of Shakespeare can profitably be set against a broader German appropriation whose stated purpose was to Germanify the Bard. Tieck asserted in his *Letters on William Shakespeare* (1800) that no Englishman in print had yet understood the dramatist,[90] and in response to Tieck's pioneering, if unfinished, *Book on Shakespeare* (posth. 1920), August Schlegel bluntly remarked: 'I hope you will prove, among other things, that Shakespeare was not an Englishman. How did he possibly come among the frosty, stupid souls on that brutal island?'[91] A few critics balked at such audacity. The dramatist Christian Dietrich Grabbe, for one, vociferated about a 'Shakespeare mania' that was inhibiting emerging German-born dramatists.[92] But within a few decades the aspiration to wrest Shakespeare from Albion found a public platform as one of the principal aims of the Deutsche Shakespeare-Gesellschaft. Addressing the second annual meeting of the society, Hermann Ulrici – a champion of Shakespeare and Philosophy professor at Halle – could state the nationalist position unequivocally, thereby making explicit what had been implicit in the liberalist view of a universal German genius:

> We want to *de*-Anglicize the Englishman Shakespeare, to *Germanize* him, to *Germanize* him in the widest and deepest sense of the word; we want to do everything in our power to *make* him even more and in the truest and fullest sense what he already is — a *German* poet.[93]

Wagner, it seems, had a similar idea, albeit one that formed part of an individualist more than a nationalist agenda. The Shakespeare that Wagner appropriated was very much a product of Idealism, though, as we have seen, Wagner sought to insert him into a discourse about the future of drama based on stage, scenic, even sensory realism (in which Wagner was invested) by arguing that his histories are objective accounts, a 'daguerreotype of historical facts', as he put it in 1851.[94] The climate of stage naturalism and 'poetic realism' (Otto Ludwig's term) simply made these aspects of Shakespeare most laudable for Wagner.

Accordingly, he typically uses the terms 'true' or 'real' in relation to Shakespeare, pointing to a kind of transcendent realism in his conception. The following six observations by Wagner, filtered through Cosima's pen within a five-year period, capture something of this aesthetic:

(i) In Shakespeare everything is spread before us and stays naked and terrifying. Beside it all other poetic works seem like divine lullabies, here it is as if Fate itself had removed its veil to appear before our mortal eyes. (23.1.69)

(ii)   Cleopatra [is] quite incomprehensible and yet so clear, so recognizable, so definite. It is that which distinguishes the true poet, Richard says, the ability to depict everything as it is, without explanation or solution. ... Sh[akespeare] had exploded the whole machinery [of the doctrine of the three unities] and what one sees in him is not the world in a magic mirror, but something so real that one is startled. (4.3.69)

(iii) A true demonstration of how utterly Shakespeare's characters are living persons, and just as incomprehensible, is given in Hamlet's monologue. (9.1.71)

(iv)   Sh[akespeare] is always truthful, he turns out unsympathetic. (19.12.73)

(v)   We pick up *Richard III* and cannot get away from it ... Among other things that interjection — 'Margaret.' 'Richard!' 'Ha!' — is one of those lightning flashes which sharply emphasize the truthfulness of a scene, while making the poet himself even more invincibly elusive. (14.1.74)

(vi)   Shakespeare is the truest picture of the world. (3.9.74)

By the end of his life, however, it seems Wagner finally became frustrated with Shakespeare: 'He is unbearable because he is unfathomable!' So reads the composer's last recorded comment about the dramatist. 'Aeschylus, Sophocles were the products of their culture, but he! And he knew everything.'[95] Perhaps Wagner's frustration speaks to the final envy of one who peered into the concept of genius so self-consciously, who treated Shakespeare's output as a natural object, ripe for systematic, if pleasingly futile scrutiny, noting that his favourite example, Hamlet's monologue, 'is as incomprehensible as Nature herself'.[96] Indeed, his life-long self-identification with Shakespeare, mooted at the outset, arguably plagued him while composing *Götterdämmerung*. 'I am no composer', he protested in 1870, 'I only wanted to learn enough to compose [music for my spoken, Shakespearean tragedy] *Leubald*; and that is how things have remained — it is only the subjects which are different.'[97] It is irrelevant whether we find Wagner's unlikely self-assessment persuasive; that he believed it, and could reflect so from the height of his creative powers, may lead us to reread his words to Cosima as both cryptic individuation and simple worship: '[Shakespeare] is my only spiritual friend'[98] he asserted months before his death, yet he also felt unable to approach the Bard on bended knee: '[I am] not fit to tie Shakespeare's … shoelaces.'[99] This startling clash of arrogance and humility, loftiness and lowliness, perhaps only becomes comprehensible in the context of one of Wagner's own incongruous self-images, namely the artist of the future who once styled himself as Hans Sachs the cobbler.

Appendix : Wagner's Shakespeare Sources in his Libraries

Dresden Library

T. Echtermeyer et al. (ed.)	*Quellen des Shakespeare in Novellen, Maerschen und Sagen*, ed. T. Echtermeyer, L. Henschel, and K. Simrock, 3 vols (Berlin: Finckesche Buchhandlung, 1831)
Schlegel / Tieck (trans.)	*Shakespeare's dramatische Werke uebersetzt von August Wilhelm Schlegel und Ludwig Tieck*, 4th Octave edn., 12 vols (Berlin: G. Reimer, 1851–2)

Wahnfried Library

Michael Bernays,	*Zur Entstehungsgeschichte des Schlegelschen Shakespeare* (Leipzig: Hirzel, 1872)
Friedrich Bodenstedt (ed.),	*William Shakespeare's Sonette in deutscher Nachbildung* (Berlin: n.p., 1862)
—(ed. and trans.),	*Othello, der Mohr von Venedig* (Leipzig: Brockhaus, 1867)
—(ed.),	*William Shakespeare's dramatische Werke*, trans. Friedrich Bodenstedt (Leipzig: F. A. Brockhaus, 1867)
Alexander Dyce (ed.),	*The Works of William Shakespeare*, 2nd ed., 9 vols. (London: Chapman and Hall, 1866–7)
Rudolph Genée,	*Shakespeare: sein Leben und seine Werke* (Hildburghausen: Bibliographisches Institut, 1872)
—	*Geschichte der Shakespeare'schen Dramen in Deutschland* (Leipzig: Engelmann, 1870)
Ernst Ortlepp (trans.),	*Nachträge zu Shakespeares Werken von Schlegel und Tieck* (Stuttgart: Rieger, 1840)

W. Schlegel & L. Tieck,	*Nachträge zu Shakespeares Werken*, trans. Ernst Ortlepp, 4 vols (Stuttgart: Rieger & Co, 1840)
—	*Shakspeare's* [sic] *dramatische Werke*, trans. August Wilhelm Schlegel and Wilhelm Tieck, 6th edition, 12 vols (Berlin: Reimer, 1863–5)
—	*Shakespeare's dramatische Werke / nach der Uebers. V. August Wilhelm Schlegel u. Ludwig Tieck sorgfaeltig revidiert u. theilweise neu bearb.*, ed. H. Ulrici through the Deutsche Shakespeare-Gesellschaft, trans. A. W. Schlegel and L. Tieck, 12 vols (Berlin: Reimer, 1867–71)
William Shakespeare,	*Shakespeare as put forth in 1623: a reprint of William Shakespeares comodies, histories & tragedies / published according to the true originall copies* (London: Booth, 1864)
Karl Simrock,	*Die Quellen des Shakespeare in Novellen, Märchen und Sagen, mit sagengeschichtlichen Nachweisungen*, 2nd ed. (Bonn: Marcus, 1870)
—(trans.)	*Shakespeares Gedichte*, trans. Karl Simrock (Stuttgart: Cotta, 1867)
Ludwig Tieck (ed.),	*Shakespeare's Vorschule*, 2 vols (Leipzig: Brockhaus, 1823–9)

Chapter 4

Britten as Another: Six Notes on a Mystic Writing Pad

Seth Brodsky

First Note

What is Pyramus? (Bottom in *A Midsummer Night's Dream*, 1.2.22)

But first, what is Bottom? He is, in the most restricted sense, a series of words, of inscriptions and sounds – something to be read, then said, then heard.[1] He is, subsequently, a semblance: the shimmer of personhood, a transmogrification of written characters in spiritual character, of what into who (not least, one who transmogrifies). But Bottom is also a program of sorts, a relatively short patch of code designed to write (in mind, in text, on stage) infinite renditions of itself. In addition to Bottom-as-Text and Bottom-as-Character, there is what we might call Bottom-as-Myth, the collection of all Bottoms ever rendered, a Bottom 'consisting of all [his] versions', as Claude Lévi-Strauss once defined myth.[2] For the moment, I am particularly interested in this last Bottom. 'If a myth is made up of all its variants', wrote Lévi-Strauss, 'structural analysis should take all of them into account'. I obviously couldn't do that here, but I might invite the reader into a slightly humbler thought experiment: let's imagine, if not the entirety of all Bottoms, then at least the entirety of all Bottom's-Dream speeches in Shakespeare's *A Midsummer Night's Dream*.[3] Envision thousands – more truthfully, hundreds of thousands – of Bottoms waking up at once on an impossibly deep stage. A *mise-en-abîme* of ex-donkeys: large men, small men, some lying on their left side and some on their right. Some stir suddenly, all blubber and snort and pulmonary pomp; others hairpin out of soundlessness with little twitches and half-yawns. Then comes the first word, a blurry, stereophonic cloud of 'Wwwwhennnnn … '. Then the speech itself, what we might call our mytheme, our minimal unit of mythopoetic replication:

When my cue comes, call me, and I will answer. My next is, 'Most fair Pyramus.' Heigh-ho! Peter Quince! Flute the bellows-mender! Snout the tinker! Starveling! God's my life, stol'n hence, and left me asleep! I have had a most rare vision. I have had a dream, past the wit of man to say what dream it was. Man is but an ass, if he go about [t'] expound this dream. Methought I was – there is no man can tell what. Methought I was, and me-thought I had – but man is but [a patch'd] fool, if he will offer to say what methought I had. The eye of man hath not heard, the ear of man hath not seen, man's hand is not able to taste, his tongue to conceive, nor his heart to report, what my dream was. I will get Peter Quince to write a ballet of this dream. It shall be call'd 'Bottom's Dream', because it hath no bottom; and I will sing it in the latter end of a play, before the Duke. Peradventure, to make it the more gracious, I shall sing it at her death. (*A Midsummer Night's Dream*, 4.1.200–19)

J. Allan Hobson and Robert Stickgold, Harvard professors of psychiatry, are only the latest in a long line of oneirologists trying to collect the entirety of all dreams.[4] But our thought experiment is a bit more complicated technologically, given that it must record not only a 'dream report', but a vast array of 'dream performances', with all their multimedial macro- and micro-details. What mechanism would best capture and document this excessive agglomeration of choreographies, all somatic types, all angles and velocities of neck and head and hand, variants of vocal grain, tempo and accent? We'd need a device with two capacities: infinite storage and infinite re-inscribability. I picture a quasi-transparent, multi-media, completely modular flip-book, instantly rearrangeable according to one or a number of chosen parameters. Given the functionality of a device like the iPad, this kind of mechanism probably isn't too far in the future.

On the other hand, maybe what I'm seeking is closer to Freud's *Wunderblock*, or 'mystic writing pad', a children's toy he described in a short essay from 1925. The toy itself is an analog Etch-a-Sketch with three components: a celluloid covering sheet, a piece of wax paper and, underneath that, a thicker wax slab. You write or draw with a stylus on the celluloid, and the pressure of the stylus creates notations at the point of contact between the three components. But there's a twist:

If we lift the entire covering-sheet — both the celluloid and the waxed paper — off the wax slab, the writing vanishes and, as I have already remarked, does not re-appear again. The surface of the *Wunderblock* is clear of writing and once more capable of receiving impressions. But it is easy to discover that the permanent trace of what was written is retained upon the wax slab itself and is legible in suitable lights. Thus the Pad provides not only a receptive surface that can be used over and over again, like a slate, but also permanent traces of what has been written, like an ordinary paper pad ...[5]

Freud saw in the *Wunderblock* a stunningly apt analogy to his first topography of the psyche. The celluloid represents the system Perception–Consciousness, which is constantly responding to, and being momentarily 'inscribed' with immediate experience. The wax slab represents the system Unconscious, which from the moment of birth is receiving every impression, every experience. We'll come back to this later; for now, accept the *Wunderblock* as a handy device for capturing the radically particular historicity of a performance text, all its read-said-heard-ness, all its inimitable forms of re-writability.[6]

Let's imagine that every new play, Shakespeare's *Dream* included, is a completely fresh *Wunderblock*. In the case of the *Dream*, it begins receiving inscriptions in 1595 or 1596, the number of inscriptions increasing exponentially (with occasional fallow periods) up through June 5, 1960, when Benjamin Britten writes on it again. England: Aldeburgh: Jubilee Hall: the world premiere of Britten's opera on *A Midsummer Night's Dream* – the first and to this day only operatic treatment of the play in its original language.[7] Assuming the opera commenced around 8 p.m., it should now be about 10 p.m.. The third scene of Act 3: Owen Brannigan, an English *buffo* bass for whom Britten created the part of Swallow the lawyer in *Peter Grimes*, rouses himself on an empty stage and sings his monologue.

In many ways, despite the operatic context, Brannigan is just another in the Heraclitean stream of all Bottoms[8]. He is bumbling, sweet-natured and entirely sincere. He stops and starts, trips over words and phrases, mangles quotations from scripture. He is an unremarkable man with remarkable memories, and, like many of us at our most unremarkable, he lacks for remarks. Brannigan-Britten-Bottom is, to follow the speech's spirit of citational misfirings, a man, take him for all in all, we shall definitely look upon his like again.

Paradoxically, though, the Bottom we encounter on June 5th, 1960 at 10 p.m. is also a faithful re-inscription of an old trope, Bottom-as-Ur-Self, or, after Harold Bloom's 1998 book, the Invention-of-the-Human. 'Bottom is Shakespeare's Everyman', Bloom writes, 'a true original, a clown rather than a fool or a jester'.[9] So: the utterly exceptional ordinary guy.

We now lift the *Wunderblock*'s celluloid and wax paper, and peer underneath at the slab. We can trace adjacent grooves in the wax. Here is one from 1849: Charles Knight's exaltation of Bottom as the 'representative of the whole human race'; here is another from 1873, Daniel Wilson's Emersonian claim for Bottom as a 'representative man' and a 'natural genius'.[10] Here is yet a third, from 1904, a kind of re-re-inscription. G. K. Chesterton reads Bottom's character(s), but also inflates Knight's remarks into a marvelous fantasy of the proletarian superior:

> We have all of us known rustics like Bottom the Weaver, men whose faces would be blank with idiocy if we tried for ten days to explain the meaning of the National Debt, but who are yet great men, akin to Sigurd and Hercules, heroes of the morning of the earth, because their words were their own words, their memories their own memories, and their vanity as large and simple as a great hill.[11]

This Bottom-as-Everyman trope is steeped in – not characters, not the dispersing meaning of writing, but character, with all its trappings of presence and personhood. Bottom both is and has subjectivity, he both is and has a face, a voice, a body, a collection of irrefutable experiences. Like many historically durable tropes, this one has an uncanny gift for re-inscribing itself in otherwise distant discourses. There are in fact only a few tweaks in the code needed to imagine Bottom as an invention of popular neuroscientist Steven Pinker, writing in 1997 about 'how the mind works':

> Within moments of awakening from a dream, our memory for its plot is wiped out, presumably to avoid contaminating autobiographical memory with bizarre confabulations. Similarly, our voluntary, waking mental images might be hobbled to keep them from becoming hallucinations or false memories.[12]

A durable trope is a highly modular object, and with the right substitutions, Pinker can be spliced excellently on to/into Knight-Chesterton-Bloom: replace 'clown' with 'research subject'; modify 'own memories' and 'own words' with 'uncontaminated autobiographical memories'; revise 'representative of the whole human race' into 'hero of the morning of the earth' into 'non-hallucinating non-confabulating non-psychotic'. And there we have it: Bottom the Everyman becomes Bottom the Everybrain, a standard-issue cortex which knows better than to confuse dream with reality, hallucination with fact. What is Bottom? He is Himself.

But if we return to the celluloid cover sheet, Aldeburgh 6.5.60/22:00, we also find a stray, not-entirely-welcome mutation in our trope. In the boomy atmosphere of Britten's score, Bottom is, musically speaking, *not* Himself. We have heard His music before this moment. That very evening, we have heard it coming out of the mouths of other singing beings: it is Tytania's music, as she dotes on Bottom in the bower; it is the Fairies' music, as they hail him, sharing handshakes and names; it is the music of Flute's Thisby, at the moment Flute finally stops parroting back Bottom's song and invents his own; indeed, the music to which Bottom wakes up – the only music in his dream-speech which seems new – is an extremely distorted variant of Flute's 'new' song. We have heard some of this music mouthlessly too, and offstage, in the English Opera Group's lithe 27-person orchestra, sunken into a glowing, narrow pit: it is the music of the moon-dappled wood, the resonant aural conversions of half-light against tree-trunk.

This *déjà-entendu* extends further: we have heard this music – Bottom's 'own music', supposedly setting his 'own words' and 'own memories', *his* vanity – before this night. We have heard it in Act 1, scene 5 of Britten's *Turn of the Screw* (when Mrs. Grose sings the words 'Dear God'); Act 2, scene 1 of *Peter Grimes*; Act 2, scene 2 of *Billy Budd*; Variation 'J' in *The Young Person's Guide to the Orchestra*. We have heard it in the first tableau of Stravinsky's *Petrushka* (Petrushka waking in his cell), in the third movement of Ferde Grofé's *Grand Canyon Suite* (notably also redolent of donkey-dom), in Wagner's *Gotterdämmerung* (as Siegfried drinks Hagen's recollection-inducing draught in Act 2, scene 2); in Mahler's Rückert-Lied 'Ich bin der Welt abhanden gekommen' ('I have become lost to the world') and 'Um Mitternacht' ('At midnight'); in a transitional motif in the choral finale to Beethoven's Ninth Symphony (celebrating its everyman 'hero of the morning of the world'); in Olympia the Automaton's wind-up aria 'Les oiseaux dans la charmille' (also known as 'The Doll's Song') in Act 1 of Offenbach's *Les Contes d'Hoffmann*. We have even heard this music in the work of other 'Great Shakespeareans': in the scene where Romeo springs open the Capulets' tomb in Berlioz's *Romeo et Juliette. Symphonie dramatique d'áprès Shakespeare*; and finally, in a perfectly uncanny return, in the famous first four bars of Mendelssohn's *Ein Sommernachtstraum* overture. What is *this* Bottom? A choir of other characters, a resonant polyphony of other voices.

Second Note

On most stages, when Bottom wakes up and can't recall his dream, the audience remembers it for him; it often knows precisely how to behave like a circuit board in a crisis, taking over the charge from Bottom's blown synapses. As he forgets, we become, yet again, Bottom's surrogate remem-berers. But here, as Brannigan stumbles his way through his half-assed anamnesis, something other is at play. There is a vast, supplemental remem-bering agent working through Britten's *Dream*, and we cannot call it 'Bottom', or 'Brannigan', or 'Shakespeare', or even 'Britten'. What is Bottom, besides Bottom? What strange concatenation of others – other characters, other people, other notations – ends up as *this* Bottom? What patchwork *this* weaver?

This essay – indeed, this series – is premised on another concatenation. It is structurally less complicated than the one I introduced above, and far less promiscuous. But perhaps no less strange: let us posit that Britten, or Verdi, or Wagner (or Dryden, or Voltaire, or Lamb) is both Himself and Not-Himself, his own (great) man and another (greater) man by a different name. More specifically: let us posit one person as a function – an author function, in fact – of another person, like one of those writers in Jorge Luis Borges's short stories.[13] This would necessarily be a quasi-reflexive function; that is, it would allow for the possibility that Britten, as an author, 'wrote' (or re-wrote, or mis-wrote) Shakespeare, and yet was in the process also 'written' (re-written, mis-written) by Shakespeare. It would, according the aims of the series editors Peter Holland and Adrian Poole, be a potent – both strong and literally reproductive – function as well. 'What', they ask in their series introduction, 'is a "Great Shakespearean"? Who are the "Great Shakespeareans"?', and their answer is clear: 'those figures who have had the greatest influence on the interpretation, understanding and reception of Shakespeare, both nationally and internationally'; those 'whose own cultural impact has been and continues to be powerful. One of its aims is to widen the sense of who constitute the most important figures in our understanding of Shakespeare's afterlives'.[14]

Britten, a figure of enormous cultural impact on the international musical stage, would certainly count among these figures. He set only three texts of Shakespeare's, of which two are shorter affairs: Sonnet 43, as the last movement of his 1958 *Nocturne* for tenor and chamber orchestra; and a breathless voice-and-piano setting of 'Tell me where is fancy bred?' from Act 2, scene 2 of *The Merchant of Venice*. But sandwiched immodestly between these two works lies a most powerful incarnation of afterliving

Shakespeare. Britten's *Dream* has come to be regarded by many since its première as a singularity: the greatest – the most well-written, the most thoughtfully constructed, the most performed and popular, the truest – Shakespeare opera of the twentieth century, and perhaps the greatest ever in the original language. Noted Shakespearean W. Moelwyn Merchant's 1961 proclamation still enjoys considerable consensus today: 'it is one of the ironies of theatre history that this opera version is the richest and most faithful interpretation of Shakespeare's intentions that the stage has seen in our generation'.[15]

Given the opera's own afterlife and the aims of this series, part of me wanted to set forth here a thesis which toes a certain line. It would be a thesis primarily about Britten *and* and *as* Shakespeare; it would be an attempt to authenticate a filial bond, a family tree, a claim that Britten was a worthy son, inheritor, heir, earner of suffix '-ean'. I wanted to paraphrase Bottom's own question 'What is Pyramus' as 'What is Britten?', and I wanted to paraphrase Bottom's own answer: He, Britten, is not Britten, but Shakespeare the playwright: this will put you out of fear. Freud's *Wunderblock* was to help me in this regard. I would show how, beneath Britten's inscription of 1960, lay a vast, knotty network of earlier inscriptions – interpretations, productions, adaptations – with which it was in conscious and unconscious dialogue. And I would show how, eventually, all inscriptions were impressed upon a slab of Shakespeare's own making, and it was the privilege of a Great Shakespearean like Britten to, well, make a lasting impression, on us but also on the Bard himself.

In the process, however, I found my concept metaphor beginning to overtake my supposed aims. This began with the scene of Bottom's awakening: how would I account for all the other layers of inscriptions, the other *musical* works, written into this passage? How to make room, in this *Wunderblock* model, for the fact that other people's pens – Stravinsky's, Mahler's, Wagner's, Offenbach's, Berlioz's, Mendelssohn's, Beethoven's, a younger Britten's – were being used to scribble on Shakespeare's pad? Britten's Bottom was, if anything, a condensation, a conflation (a confabulation?) of the work of many distinct inscribers, spanning nearly 150 years of Western music history; Shakespeare's text in comparison constituted less a deep back- or under-ground than a scaffolding. This quickly turned into the central question of the endeavour, once I realized that the Bottom's-Dream scene was only one in a vast network of re-written musics. Here was an opera by one of the twentieth century's most textually permeable composers, as far as the music of others was concerned; and a score which featured an opera-within-an-opera. Britten's alley-oop of a solution to

Shakespeare's *Pyramus and Thisby* play, it is one of the most polystylisti-cally virtuosic parodies in existence of its own genre's tradition. Pursuing this course of inquiry with increasing strictness – how many other texts, how many other voices is Britten grooving upon? – I was eventually led to unearth about 200 musical works, passages, moments, all of which Britten, an intensely avid listener and performer, would likely have heard and known. Using the series algorithm – let us posit that Britten is both Himself and Not-Himself – I had come upon an unexpected route, and now had the beginnings of a very different essay. Here was an opera built on the work of another, Shakespeare, but full of the work of *other* others.

It may be that in the hands of certain Great Shakespeareans, Shakespeare becomes an unfathomably elaborate – if not ruse, then at least conceit, something which structures a fantasy with aims quite distinct from the faithful setting of this play or that sonnet. It may be that the truth of Britten's *Dream* is some kind of Borgesian inversion of its semblance, and that Britten did not collect and fastidiously adapt hundreds of previously inscribed musical moments in order to set Shakespeare's *Dream*, but just the opposite: he chose Shakespeare as a means of setting, of re- and mis-writing, of fixing into place decades of memories of these moments from the texts of other artists. 'No one has ever been so many men as this man', writes Borges in 'Everything and Nothing', his short tribute to Shakespeare, 'who like the Egyptian Proteus could exhaust all the guises of reality'.[16]

To some degree Britten's audaciously casual account in *The Observer* of his choice of Shakespeare's play speaks somewhat to this idea: 'There was not time to get a libretto written, so we took one that was ready to hand.'[17] More to the point, perhaps, is Britten's ostentatious placidity about his treatment of the play:

> I do not feel in the least guilty at having cut the play in half. The original Shakespeare will survive. Nor did I find it daunting to be tackling a masterpiece which already has a strong verbal music of its own. Its music and the music I have written for it are at two quite different levels.[18]

Two quite different levels: the *Wunderblock* analogy might be brought back here slightly revised, and in a direction Freud might have appreciated. Let us posit Britten himself in 1960 as a *Wunderblock*. But let us imagine that Shakespeare constitutes not his deep mythic undersurface – the wax scar-tissue bearing four century of accrued inscriptions – but rather the latest inscription on the celluloid surface. Shakespeare's play would constitute that outside stimulus impressing itself on to Britten's consciousness (for everyone to read), but also on to the wax slab of Britten's unconscious, not as immediately visible, and scarred with the memories of thousands of musical works, passages, gestures, transitions, assemblages. Hence Shakespeare's play would be a text inscribed on a profoundly *uneven* surface, one which inevitably pushes and pulls the stylus, forces it to slip innumerable times into the grooves already imprinted underneath – the warps, divots, squirrelling canals, larger shapes and forms, created by another medium.

There are in print a number of wonderful commentaries on Britten's *Dream*, each with their own perspective, all quite attentive to the relationship between Britten's text and Shakespeare's, and any of which could service excellently as an introduction to the opera: Mervyn Cooke performs a fastidious and penetrating analysis of its composition and construction; Philip Brett provides a characteristically provocative but sensitive reading of the opera's psycho-sexual contexts and subtexts; and Daniel Albright applies his thesis of a 'conflict of theaters' to an exploration of the opera's remarkable stylistic multiplicity.[19] The present essay was certainly deeply informed by these authors' work, but my aim and approach are both a bit more idiosyncratic. The remainder of this chapter constitutes less an introduction to Britten's Shakespeare opera than an attempt to take Britten at his word – '[the play's] music and the music I have written for it are at two quite different levels' – and unearth the other opera (or opera of others) which took place while Britten was saying, singing, setting Shakespeare. Every opera is to some extent a 'theater of memory', a vast supplemental remembering agent concatenating different stages, scenarios, characters and authors, all for the sake of the show.[20] But not every opera is a *Dream*, and I'm compelled in this instance to take Freud's famous dictum, that dreams are 'the royal road to the unconscious', quite seriously. To circumvent the *Dream*'s conscious, waking register – to peel back the celluloid of Shakespeare's play – does not of course mean to leave Shakespeare behind. If anything, quite the opposite: at this point, I cannot hear Bottom call for his lines ('When my cue comes') without hearing Brannigan singing Britten singing Mahler-Wagner-Grofé. My own *Wunderblock* is duly impressed.

Third Note

> the spring, the summer,
> The childing autumn, angry winter, change
> Their wonted liveries; and the mazed world,
> By their increase, now knows not which is which.
> And this same progeny of evils comes
> From our debate, from our dissension;
> We are their parents and original. (*A Midsummer Night's Dream*, 2.1.111–17)

Perhaps the deep truth of any Shakespeare play – the sub-cutaneous wax slab, so to speak – is dissension, debate. Give a Shakespeare play a few calendrical cycles, give it enough springs, summers, autumns and winters, and it will prove the parent and original of passionate dis-consensus, it will say, or be said to say, 'I am not what I am'. I am reading with flashes of exhilaration and dysthymia Dorothea Kehler's short essay 'The Critical Backstory and The State of the Art', Chapter One of *A Midsummer Night's Dream: A Critical Guide*, published in 2010 by Continuum Press (who publishes the book you now hold in your hands).[21] In nary 18 pages, Kehler coolly and swiftly tours me past more than 200 different *Dream* interpretations. What astonishes me is how seldom I sense the dissension, how much the very words 'interpret' and 'claim' and 'read' veil a deeply fissured ground always crackling and threatening to break apart. The witching wood of the *Dream* is rooted in a *terra infirma* of readerly isolates ready to quake. The play is light incarnate – no, it is darkness visible; Bottom does not actually sleep with Titania – no, he does; no, he does and it is bestiality; no, he does, and it is a metaphor. Shakespeare is Theseus – no, he is Bottom, no, Quince, no, Hippolyta. The play is not for a wedding – no, it is, but whose? The Earl of Southampton's; the Earl of Southampton's mother; Elizabeth's, and she was present; Elizabeth's, and she was absent; Elizabeth, but her last name was Carey, and she was granddaughter of the lord chamberlain, patron of Shakespeare's company; Carey, *but first* the Earl of Southampton's mother. The *Dream* becomes, in the process, the arena for all manner of couplings, but also *ménages-à-trois*, in which two authors read awry a third and produce an endlessly changing changeling boy, the offspring of parentage partially neoplatonic or proto-Freudian; Chaucerian, Erasmian, Apuleian, della-Mirandolan; Bakhtinian, Lacanian, Derridean, Deleuzian.[22] Perhaps the deepest historical truth of a Shakespeare play is, then, not debate – certainly not a progeny of evils! – but rather something cooler: permutation, serialism, the switching in and out of a given set of figures, names, words, ideas, concepts, until all combinations have been exhausted. In this sense, perhaps the *Dream*'s patron saint, the guardian of its afterlife, is one not mentioned in Kehler's bibliography: Leibniz, whose *Dissertatio de arte combinatoria* (published 70 years after the play) attempted to prove via an 'alphabet of human thought' that 'all propositions are combinations'.[23]

Daniel Albright's chapter on the *Dream* in his 2007 book *Musicking Shakespeare* is not mentioned in Kehler's essay.[24] This is a delightful irony, given that Albright's thesis is that '*A Midsummer Night's Dream* belongs to a class of comic literature that articulates cosmic mechanisms for random distribution – following Italo Calvino, I'll refer to such literature as cosmicomedies.'[25] Albright posits Shakespeare as an idiosyncratic Fortuna, and his play 'a cosmic machine for generating messes' with its own bureaucracy of infernal recombinators: Cupid, Oberon, Puck, the Mechanicals and so on. This process, however chaotic its results, is itself quite strict, algorithmic even; of the lovers Lysander, Demetrius, Hermia, Helena, for instance, Albright asks: 'how many ordered pairs can be extracted from this set? The general rule is $n(n - 1)$ …' And lo, of the 12 possible messes, Shakespeare architects no less than ten – ten venereal pursuits, some motored by love, some by hate, each engendering its own inimitable mishigas. I like Albright's thesis for many reasons, but not least because it reveals a hidden family resemblance between the *Dream*'s reception and its constitution. What Puck is to Bottom, what Oberon to Puck and Cupid to Oberon and Shakespeare to Cupid, are the hundreds of editors and historians and critics and glossers and stagers and scramblers and hackers of Shakespeare's own text – among other things, characters in a marvellous cosmicomedy. (That each character believes he or she is acting independently is, of course, part of what makes the larger 'farce' so utterly compelling.)

Britten would certainly stand among these cosmicomedians. Like most any opera based on another author's text, his *A Midsummer Night's Dream* of 1960 is something of a semi-autonomous creature: a work, *opera*. But it is also *lavoro*, it does work; it is an exorbitantly complex machine for making messes, for wreaking combinatorial havoc on the presumed cohesion and integrity of a pre-existing text. It is difficult to extricate oneself from the second-nature-ness of opera and remember that opera initially emerged in the early seventeenth century as a radical, tormentedly precise form of reading, of pronouncing and hearing and seeing a text, in which every word, every phrase, every punctuation point and phoneme and fricative was made to suffer a transposition, a literal changing-of-place, at the hands of a composite director (composer and librettist) who by any other standards would be considered a monomaniacal tyrant. Opera has always been a matter of deep and systematic tampering, of tempering and tempo-ing the work of another to the limits of its identity. The Oberon-and-Puck coalition, conceived only two or three years before the two Jacopos (Corso and Peri) created the first operatic entertainment in Florence in 1598, could be considered opera's Romulus and Remus: mythic founders, whose incessant cupidic chaotics allegorize a genre's entire history. Some would understandably prefer to maintain the boundaries between critical–theoretical and artistic engagements with a text. But I would issue a plea that the textual tamperings of Britten's opera be placed on a single, supremely elastic band, not only with other musical treatments of the play (from Purcell to Lampe to Mendelssohn to Korngold), but also renowned stagings and filmings of the play by Garrick, Tieck, Vestris, Tree, Reinhardt, Brook, Miller, Hoffmann; and famous interpretations of the play by Kermode and Kott, Bloom, Montrose and Sinfield.[26]

But back to Britten: the construction of the libretto, which Britten accomplished in a matter of weeks with his partner, the tenor Peter Pears, is perhaps the opera's most transparent act of calculated disordering. Britten hacks away half of Shakespeare's text; characters go missing (it is as if Egeus never existed), conversations are excised (Theseus and Hippolyta no longer discourse on the sweet thunder of dog-choruses), lines are re-assigned (it is no longer Puck but the fairies who pronounce that 'The man shall have his mare again, and all shall be well').

More strictly cosmicomic are Britten and Pears's intensive re-sequencing and re-segmenting of the play [Figure 4.1]. Shakespeare's opening scene is now transposed into the middle of the opera's last act; the mechanicals first appear after, rather than before, Demetrius and Helena rush on stage; Titania's first and second scenes with Bottom are smushed together, while Oberon's initial consultation with Puck is split in two in order to frame Lysander and Hermia's elopement planning session – which is no longer interrupted by a distraught Helena. The larger architecture of the play is redefined: act-wise, Britten wants five (better for Shakespeare plays) to go into three (better for operas), which produces a good number of dramaturgical-tectonic shifts. The opera's second act largely preserves the sequence and structure of the play's third act; the opera's third act sutures together the play's fourth and fifth, but begins with Titania being roused by Oberon rather than aroused by Bottom. The opera's first act, unquestionably one of Britten's most virtuosic feats on the musical stage, wildly scrambles the chrono-logic of Shakespeare's first two acts. It now

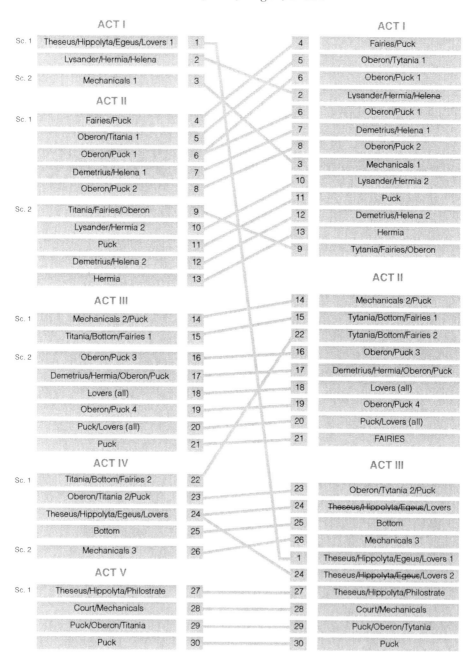

Figure 4.1 Play vs. Libretto

begins, ends and middles entirely in Fairyland – yet another transposition. No Athens, no Peter Quince's house; it is in the wood that the lovers first rendezvous and the mechanicals first rehearse, and in which they are from the beginning only partly welcome guests. Britten's first act belongs rather to the wood's natural citizens, who consecrate its opening and closing moments with their own strange species of sylvan singing; the act begins with Shakespeare's Act 2, scene 1 ('Over hill, over dale') and ends not with lonesome Hermia petrified by creepy-crawlies, but with Titania's ensomnulation-by-fairy-roundel and Oberon's creepy-scheming.

With the addition of music – if such a complicated operation can be called addition – Fortuna's wheel begins to spin more wildly [Figure 4.2].

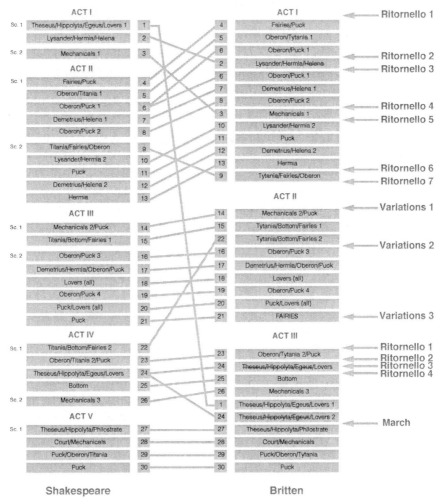

Figure 4.2 Musical Punctuations

Britten builds into Shakespeare's now redistributed scenarios an entire paratextual network of punctuations in the form of musical interludes. First, two acts into one, and four scenes into seven: the four scenes from the first two acts of Shakespeare's play, now the first Act of Britten's opera, are woven into place by a seven-fold *ritornello*, literally a 'little return', a pliant tissue of string music which continuously re-calibrates itself with each re-instantiation. Next, two into one, parsed into fours: Britten's second Act (Shakespeare's Acts 3 and 4) is limned and bisected by a slow, ever-developing sequence of four beguiling chords; though they retreat into the deep background for much of the act, they exert a constant influence on the onstage periodicities, bracketing encounters, dialogues, events, as if everything in Fairyland were naturally recalculated in base-four. Finally, a more motley segmentation: Britten's last Act preserves the division between Shakespeare's Acts 4 and 5 by inserting an extended march, material-izing in a hush out of the morning dew and swelling into noonday sun and cymbal crash; but Britten also parses Shakespeare's fourth Act with another set of four *ritornelli*, assembled out of wispy-cloudy string lines and skewed, dampened horn-calls. These interluding musics are meticulously interstitial, but they also have the effect of pitching Shakespeare's fourth Act into the distance, as if their own offstage atmospherics had pulled the text with them.

This re-scaffolding is mild combinatory, however, compared with the musical scoring – an appropriately *Wunderblock*-y metaphor – of Shakespeare's text. It is in this register where all of Shakespeare's individual characters, groups, places, events, are inscribed into a deeper cosmicomedy. Now, when Oberon and Tytania disagree, they do so in different keys; when Puck carries out his fly-by love-juicings, he is enveloped in themes and timbres which first emerged alongside Oberon; the lovers perpetually permute each other's melodies, and so on and so on and so on. Every bar of Britten's 3,952-measure paratext de- and re-coordinates the play's imagi-nation according to a tireless transpositional will. Now every character or character-group, every interaction, scenario and scene, is harmonized (constantly and dissonantly) with multiple networks of primarily sonic logic: networks of key, harmony, tessitura (range), tempo, timbre, melody, gesture, texture. The result is, among other things, one of the most graciously decipherable semiospheres in opera history. Here fairies, it turns out, do have high, unsexed voices; their words are sung to parochial warm-up exercises by pre-pubescent boys. Oberon, on the other hand, is a super-kinky man-child, and we know this not only by the androgyne call of the counter-tenor, but by the ambiguous, celesta-coated harmonies and solo string lines that accompany his nearly every word. The lovers, snagged in desire's Möbius-strip metonymies, are represented by palpitating chords and fidgety, modular 12-tone themes which, in a running joke, are all just slight rearrangements of one another; the lovers, so convinced of each others' irreplaceability, sing literally substitutable lines. Meanwhile, the mechanicals bumble and fret, at home in the world but klutzy on its stages; Britten's score crowds them with hives of *staccatissimi*, forcing them to wobble around a terrain made almost entirely out of oom-pahs – the pub is never too far away. In its surveillant semaphoring of consensual communicative details, the opera could carouse easily with cartoons and kiddy shows, an unlikely stop on the way from Carl Stalling's Warner Brothers scores of the 1940s through the glinty make-believe music in Mister Roger's Neighborhood circa 1970. (Perhaps it was this eager, almost appeasing tone, as much as any aristocratic preciosity, that moved W. H. Auden to delicately opine of the opera, 'Dreadful. Pure Kensington!'[27])

These sonic networks still don't quite capture the radical re-writing of Shakespeare's play at the hands of an opera composer, however; and so imagine the following thought experiment. Peter Brook, as notoriously demanding a Shakespeare director as ever there was, is rehearsing his epic *Dream* production with the Royal Shakespeare Company in 1970. Alan Howard is in the middle of Oberon's 'I know a bank' speech, when Brook interrupts and holds out a stopwatch.[28] Better yet, he flicks on a metronome, foists up a conductor's baton and magically summons a 27-person instrumental ensemble. The word 'eglantine' ('… Quite over-canopied with luscious woodbine, / With sweet musk-roses and with eglantine … '), Brook decides, shall be enunciated differently. How, exactly, Howard asks? It must be at least 12 seconds long, but not equally parsed among the three syllables. The first 'e' must last roughly half the word's entire duration; it must begin in the middle register of the voice, spring open quickly, doodle slightly upward while gradually losing speed, and come to a long frozen point, about 1.5 seconds of stilled tone; then the voice must drop an octave, pronounce the 'glan' in less than a half-second, and then sit down plush on 'tine' and there remain for a good four seconds, all the while getting quieter and quieter. The initial springing-open must be synchronized perfectly with the springing-open of a fanciful meta-instrument, a harpsichord, harp, cello and two muted horns acting as one single mechanism. The instruments will imitate my gesture then, Howard wants to know? No, responds Brook; the instruments will mime only obliquely; in fact, they will behave like a resonance chamber of sorts, feigning the quiver of the elements as your voice vibrates them – a near-replication (save the surreal inclusion of

modern brass) of the continuo groups which defined the sound of seventeenth century music, beginning just a few years after Shakespeare's play
was first rendered. Finally: the whole word must be sung, Alan. It must be
sung to these notes – D–E–F–G, then F#–G–A–A–B, then a low G, twice –
and be sung by a man. But this man must sing in falsetto. And it must be
the purest, most finely wrought, most tintinnabulous falsetto in the world;
in fact, it must be sung by a specific man, by the great counter-tenor Alfred
Deller – sorry, Alan, I've got to let you go!

All these forms of tampering and tempering and tempo-ing certainly
make a mess of Shakespeare's play – but it is a meticulous, intricate,
calculated mess, hardly the result of a series of literal 'mechanisms for
random distribution'. Shakespeare plays Fortuna with his play's contents
and constituents; Britten plays Fortuna with Shakespeare's play. Here,
though, taking into account the wax-slab metaphor, I would posit a third
cosmicomic register: Britten's memory, in the form of his musical unconscious, plays Fortuna with 'him' – that is, with the calculating–composing
ego who consciously divides, distributes, coordinates, constructs, evaluates,
revises according to a series of motives he himself can understand and
articulate. This unconscious register – comprising the hundreds of musical
moments from other works – finds itself in parable-form in the scene of
Bottom's dream. Bottom's strange quasi-anamnesis is Britten's opera in
microcosm, one man's dream is the other's *Dream*: a free-associative play
of and through memories of others, memories of others' memories. These
memories are not libretto-like, not 'ready to hand' like Shakespeare's play.
Rather, they remember both Bottom and Britten against and despite their
intentions; one opens his mouth to sing his music, another presses his pen
to write his music, and out come the musics of others.

Fourth Note

Unknown Britten? You'd think we knew all about a composer that
famous, but in fact there's lots of material around we don't know. NMC
Records has pioneered British new music for 20 years, so this is a good
time for a recording as unusual as this.

This is Doundou Tchil, the alias author of the blog 'Classical Iconoclast',
writing about one kind of unknown Britten: unearthed Britten, dug-up
Britten, *new* Britten, *more* Britten, where 'unknown' is said with a smack of
the lips.[29] The recording under review here was released by NMC in 2009,

and contains unpublished material – 'valuable because [it] shows how [Britten's] compositional process operated', and, in the case of 'Movements for a Clarinet Concerto' recomposed *but not completed* by Colin Matthews out of fragments, 'an excellent way to hear what might have been and isn't lost'.[30]

One could call this kind of unknown an archeological unknown, at work in what art historian Whitney Davis calls 'the defining material conditions of the archeological situation – that strata of different ages are materially separate and some of their past realities have been utterly destroyed'.[31] The NMC recording, down to its choice of cover art, operates according to precisely this logic. *Up to a point*: past realities have been destroyed, but 'Unknown Britten' signifies, in the end, exactly the opposite of what it says: purchase, enjoy, archive, but remember to file under 'some of their past realities have been utterly destroyed'.

To talk about Britten's unconscious is to access quite a different 'unknown' – *das Unbewusste*, that level of mind which one technically knows, but does not *think*.[32] Davis points out that psychoanalysis 'is a version of impossible archeology, a not-archeology', in that archeology's 'defining material conditions … are precisely the conditions psychoanalysis must imagine to be violated in a cognitive or psychic domain: all contents of the mind, of different antiquity, are supposedly preserved, though perhaps in a revised or negative form, all at once in the same stratum – namely, the present time of the psychoanalysis itself.'[33]

So far as I know, Britten never experienced such a time. But beginning in his thirties, he became an object of intense psychoanalytic scrutiny, from Hans Keller's astoundingly detailed 1940s 'case studies' of Britten and his opera characters, through Philip Brett's 'Britten and Grimes' of 1977 and Humphrey Carpenter's 1993 biography, on to recent unpublished work by J. P. E. Harper-Scott.[34] In any case, if we take Davis seriously here, we're in a curious predicament in 2011 *vis-à-vis* a composer like Britten, and indeed many dead artists about whose psyches we wish to inquire – among them, it ought not go without saying, Shakespeare. We have, often in text-form, a trace, a semblance, a promise of psychoanalytic time, but made available to us as an archeological artifact. Here, in an artwork, in a material form, is something psyche-like: a potentially infinite collection of different antiquities, a documentation of all kinds of time, their subject-ed coexistence and simultaneity. And yet – this material has lost its psyche. The work is inconsolably cut off from its own head, it is a *gran torso*, perhaps even less: perhaps only a body-part, on to which a once-active psyche converted thoughts into somatic symptoms. Or, to put it more simply: a work as a fixed contradiction, artifact-like and psyche-like at once.

In the first section of this essay, I tried to listen in on a scene from Britten's *Dream* – the scene of 'Bottom's Dream' – and to ask: where have we heard this before? And I suggested two types of answer, each situated at a different register. On the one hand, this experience of *déja-entendu* is framed by the experience of the work itself, the *hic-et-nunc* of a night at *this* opera, in which Britten's score unfolds as a quite literal form of working memory. One could call such listenings-in *intratextual*: where have we heard this music before, here, this night, in this opera? On the other hand, I proposed an alternate elsewhere for the music of 'Bottom's Dream', and, correspondingly, another kind of listening-in one might call *intertextual*: where, in the works of others, on other nights, on other stages, have we heard this music before?

To take one example of an intratextual listening-in: Where, when and how, has Britten literally heard this before? Tytania, late in Act 1 of the opera, flanked by obedient fairies and preparing for bedtime, sings to an ecstatic plummeting flourish the words 'Sing me now asleep; Then to your offices and let me rest.' Below, in the pit, a family of violins, violas, cellos and double basses creates an elaborate, meticulous diaphony of soft slip-sliding chords. Each chord is a major triad, a glowing concordance of three notes which announces confidently, 'You are here'; but the triads themselves are not immediately relatable, each materializes as a syntactic surprise – and, as if to register its precariousness, each chord is articulated in *tremolo* fashion, with a quick, minuscule shivering motion from the players' bows.

Consensus seems to be that Britten composed the opera in sequence, and if this is the case, then he heard this moment at least five times before. Where? In Act 1 of the same opera. When? At the very beginning of the opera, and then, in extended passages beginning around bars 269, 407, 582 and 833. How? By making it: by playing it at the piano, by conducting it with an orchestra, by fixing it with ink on paper, by meticulously re-calibrating its multiple variables upon each iteration.

Materially speaking, virtually all of the 3,952 measures of Britten's *Dream* are composed this way. One hears music – and it is always a very specific music, an aggregation of wonderfully particular details of colour, harmony, melody, rhythm, gesture – and then it vanishes, replaced by another cunningly specific aggregation of different sounds. And *then* this vanished music comes back; often enough, it is only upon its return, only retrospectively, that one notices this music to constitute something like a kind, a type. And in all but two cases, when *some kind* of music comes back, it comes back changed.

Operating on this principle – one of the most basic of Wagnerian and post-Wagnerian opera – I was able to identify eighty types of music. (Others might be able to identify more, or argue for less.) I'm less concerned here with the number of types than the fact and nature of their differentiation. They tend to correlate highly with the major differentiations in Shakespeare's play – characters (20), communities (4), places (2) – but *also* with other, more fluid signifieds: actions (flying, boasting, doting), physical things (clock-bells, trees, tongs and bones, flutes), emotional and physical states (fear, anger, confusion, somnambulation), etc. These so-called types exhibit a remarkable modularity and plasticity; they might be better conceived as constellations, whose individual coordinates (alternately 'features', 'attributes', 'entities', etc.) comprise a traditional host of musical parameters (pitch, rhythm, timbre, tempo), but also particular sounding actions (flutter-tonguing, tremolandi); sounding bodies (simple: celesta, trumpet; complex: melodic unison + repeated chords); words and word-chains; classes of utterance (commands, questions, echoes, retorts, spells). In Figure 4.3 I've arranged these 80 types in the form of a tree-diagram.

I've assigned each type an associated action; when Puck appears, for instance, he is nearly always doing one of two things – scrambling (from one place to another; one person into another) or impersonating – and the accompanying music works hard to illustrate those actions with a kind of iconizing zeal native to opera's first century.

The coordinates or features out of which these types are assembled also function, of course, as signifiers: they signify not only the temporally and spatially proximate signifieds they accompany (onstage performers and the characters/actions/states they endeavour to depict) but also each other as well. This reflexivity permits potentially unceasing processes of association and disassociation; that is, an entire constellation or any one of its coordinates can each be easily circumscribed and subject to a variety of revisionary processes (i.e., omission, foregrounding and backgrounding, displacement and replacement, transposition). As the opera continues, these processes operate constantly, not least on each other: constellations are fused with others, or else teased apart, reduced, transformed until virtually unrecognizable.

What emerges – again, Britten's opera is not remarkable in this sense – is a quite sophisticated intratext, a tissue of independent threads, a network of interconnected nodes. And this tissue or network constitutes a contingent totality, one which seems to develop its own working memory, and which tests yours, which says: when you hear music, you will feel compelled to ask 'Where and when and how have I heard this music before?', and your

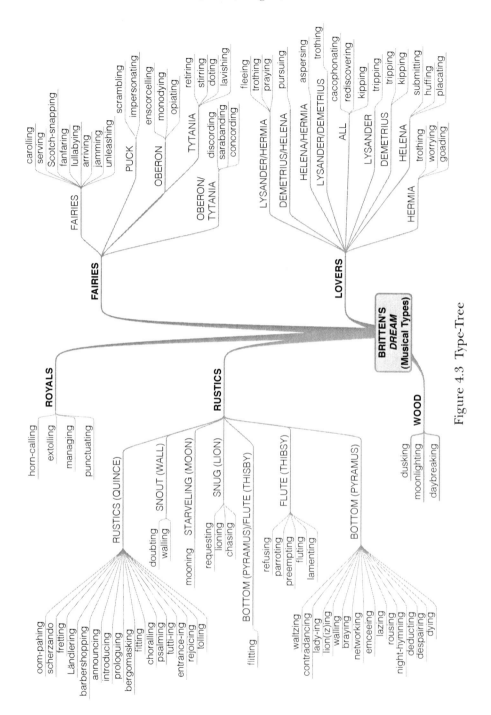

Figure 4.3 Type-Tree

answer will be, 'Here, in this contingent totality, in this opera'. A graph of the opera according to type [Figure 4.4] reveals the intensity of this memory game, which increases noticeably with each act: the x-axis represents the course of the opera from left to right, while the y-axis represents the musical types 1–80 in chronological order of appearance.

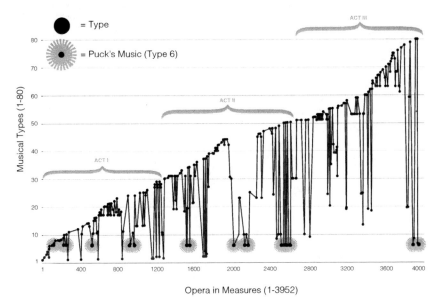

Figure 4.4 Graph 1

I have highlighted the appearances of 'type 6' music – Puck's hallmark trumpet-and-drum constellation – in order to show how the disorientations he inflicts on the play's dramaturgy are also disorientations for the listening subject. As the opera unfolds, Britten submits these musical types to constant processes of fusion, splicing, reduction and so on. We begin to hear multiple types simultaneously, and the opera enters into an increasingly reverberant echo-chamber; sometimes this simultaneity functions explicitly (as when Tytania sings her doting music dissonantly against music in Oberon's key), while at other moments it operates in a looser, more freely associative way (Tytania's triple-time coloratura scales resonating with the triple-time coloratura scales of Helena as she dotes on Demetrius). In Figure 4.5, the larger outlined gray circles represent only the 'echoes' I've been able to document so far; there are doubtless more.

I've highlighted two types nestled in the middle of Britten's Act 2; type 40 (Bottom and the fairies in a meet-and-greet: 'I cry your worship's mercy,

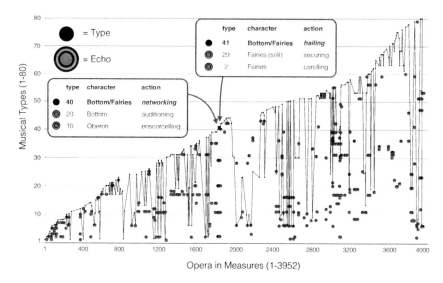

Figure 4.5 Graph 2

heartily: I beseech your Worship's name.') carries echoes of types 20 (Bottom auditioning for the role of Pyramus) and 10 (Oberon's 'enscorcelling' music). Meanwhile, type 41 (the Fairies addressing Bottom with 'Hail, mortal!') echoes types 29 (as the fairies securing Tytania's sleep: 'Never harm, / Nor spell nor charm, / Come our lovely lady nigh; / So, good night, with lullaby.') and type 2 (the fairies' first appearance, to the words 'Over hill, over dale').

By the time you reach the middle of Act 3 [Figure 4.6], and the scene which opened this essay, you can hear a intratextual showpiece composed completely out of *other kinds* of music, in which you must say of its entirety: I have heard this before, elsewhere, otherwise, out of the mouths of other characters, in the depiction of other actions, in the midst of other scenarios and states, with other pitches, timbres, tempi, etc.

Britten is scrupulous here, yet again besting the most exacting commands of a Peter Brook: Bottom's monologue will be parsed in 11 segments, each allotted its own constellation of tempi, instrumental combination and colour, gestural, rhythmic, harmonic and melodic specifications, etc. The scene will begin slowly, above a deep, stark low pedal in the basses and solo trombone; the orchestra's two clarinets will limn a mellow arc 'very sweetly', gradually nestling into a trill in the lower *chalumeau* regions; later, after Bottom exclaims 'Starveling!', the instrumentarium will suddenly shift to the remarkable sound of two flutes and bow-less strings, each

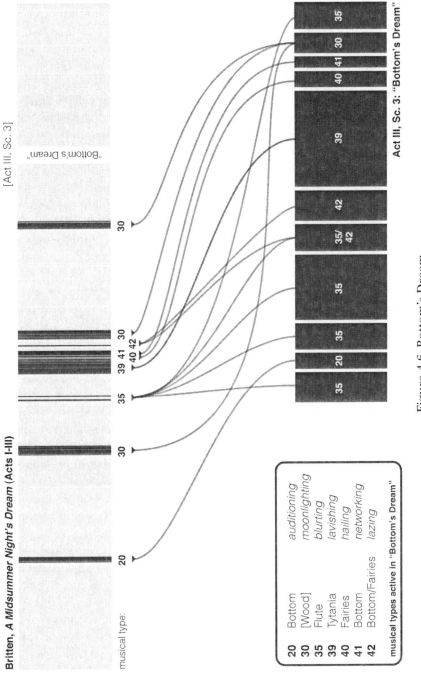

Figure 4.6 Bottom's Dream

plucking in such a way as to emit a special muted bell-sound, while Bottom wordlessly 'hunts around' in six-beat groups at the speed of roughly 178 dotted-quarter notes per second. In less than five minutes, Bottom will re- and mis-write musical 'types' 20, 30, 35, 39, 40, 41 and 42, and along with them correlated actions of 'auditioning' (Bottom first tries out as Pyramus), 'moonlighting' (Britten's music for the wood at the beginning of the second act), 'blurting' (Flute, as he rejects Bottom's Thisby-music and invents his own), 'lavishing' (Tytania smothers the newly donkey-ed Bottom with amorous attention), 'hailing' (the fairies nod to Bottom and 'do him courtesies'), 'networking' (Bottom politely requests the fairies' names) and 'lazing' (Bottom requests honey bags, chin-scratches, tongs and bones from the fairies).

In the process, Bottom becomes an operatic enactment of one of Freud's more robust postulates about the unconscious: namely, that were we to admit its existence, 'we would have to say: all the acts and manifestations which I notice in myself and do not know how to link up with the rest of my mental life must be judged as if they belonged to someone else: they are to be explained by a mental life ascribed to this other person'.[35] It is not surprising that Bottom's speech reaches its highpoint in a fantasy of another writing his own dream. (Here, it is no longer Shakespeare who is Quince, but Britten himself.)

Now, to return to the end of Tytania's aria late in Act 1 from an intertextual perspective: where, when, and how *else* has Britten heard this music before, beyond the first and last bars of his *Dream*, beyond the working memory of his work? For one, in Purcell's *Dido and Aeneas* – very near the end of Nahum Tate's libretto (Dido: 'Thy hand, Belinda, darkness shades me, / On thy bosom *let me rest* …'), and beginning four and a half bars after figure 33 in the score arrangement Britten made, rehearsed, and conducted in May 1951, and again, in a revised version, in September 1959, just as he was beginning work on *Midsummer*. In the arrangement, Britten transposed the score down a step, so one needs to listen to an untransposed version to get the full effect.[36]

This is perhaps not a transparent instance, if ever there could be, of *das Unbewusste*, 'the Other's discourse' does not simply mean 'some other's music'. It's a pretty funny, probably quite *conscious* joke on Britten's part: when a queen in an Englishman's opera sings the request LET ME REST, one simply has no choice, she sings it to a specific musico–technical complex (in this case, a '9–8 melodic suspension' over a 'phrygian cadence'). Admittedly, it is a joke not without a certain psychopathological frisson: the Queen of Carthage returns as the Queen of the Faeries;

instead of commanding her sister to watch as she throws herself on a sword on the docks, she commands silver-wingèd sprites to secure a glowing grove's perimeters, lullaby her with a roundel and prepare her for an entirely unforeseen night of bestial seduction. The scenario is fastidiously estranged, musically as well: not harpsichord and viola da gamba and theorbo, also not harp and cello (as in Britten's *Dido* arrangement), but rather a chamber orchestra of modern strings supplemented by the pearly punctuations of a glockenspiel; not idiomatic arpeggios but rather tapered *glissandi* with the occasional harmonic; not languid chromatic recitative but ethereal coloratura arioso.

As far as I know, this is the only moment one could traditionally define as an actual quote in an opera famously saturated with the music of others, with 'acts and manifestations which *could* be heard as if they *once* belonged to someone else'. But I'm interested less in that fact on its own than in what kind of work is undertaken with such other music, and how this work may actually put a composer in precisely the position of Bottom the Weaver when he recounts his dream – the position, as Harold Bloom puts it, of the idiot questioner: 'Who wrote my poem?'[37] Indeed, this work might be understood as analogous to what Freud called dream-work, that collection of revisionary processes by which one kind of text (the latent dream-thoughts) is transformed into another (the manifest dream-content).[38] Contrary to many subsequent interpreters of his dream theories, Freud himself considered the essence of a dream to lie not in its latent content but in the transformational processes of dream-work. This work – algorithmic, modular, encrypting, unconscious – was to be the object of dream analysis, the very reason one might engage an analyst. Who is, in traditional analytic practice, a listener. 'The fully unconscious', psychoanalyst Jacques-Alain Miller claims, 'depends on the listener. If the listener is not there, how do you know the unconscious exists?'[39]

Fifth Note

In 1963, the musicologist and critic Eric Roseberry decides (unsolicitedly) to play Quince to Britten's Bottom, in-listening analyst to Britten's dream-recounting analysand. Roseberry writes the composer about a remarkable moment at the beginning of the opera's second Act: as the curtain opens, the orchestra unfolds a series of four pristine, euphonious, cosmically spacious chords, each unified by its own precise instrumental colour, each capped with a fermata and cradled in a *pianissimo*. Where, Roseberry wants to know, has he heard these chords before? Where has Britten heard them before? What, in the meantime, has happened to them? You, reader, have already heard *about* them: they are the chords which accompany Bottom's announcement that he will have Quince 'write a ballade of this dream: it shall be called Bottom's dream, because it hath no bottom … '. Technically, these chords comprise 'type 30'; by the time Bottom sings those lines, the opera's listener will have heard the chords three times, first wordlessly, then as Tytania exclaims to Bottom 'O, how I love thee! how I dote on thee!', and then again, as the fairies (displacing Puck) issue their benediction on the sleeping lovers ('On the ground, sleep sound … ').

Roseberry hears back from Britten, and then decides to recount their correspondence in the British new music journal *Tempo*, recollecting how he had 'accidentally stumbled (aurally, be it noted) upon the remarkable fact that the four chords used in Act II of the Dream were almost identical with those used in the setting of Keats's "Sonnet to Sleep" in the Serenade', a cycle of songs for tenor, horn, and strings Britten composed in 1942.[40] This seems reasonable enough, given that 'the poetic element in each piece is concerned with the properties of sleep (inducing a healing forgetfulness on the one hand, a fantastic change of identities on the other)'. 'I fully expected to learn', Roseberry continues, 'that the composer had consciously borrowed from the earlier work, reversing the order of the first two chords (adding a B to the D major chord) and magically re-spacing and re-scoring them.'

Britten surprises him: 'He expressed amazement at the similarity of the chords separated by nearly twenty years – which, he assured me, was purely subconscious. But what he found interesting was that whereas in the opera he had found it necessary consciously to use all the 12 semitones to create a four chord "theme" (dramatically to make each chord sound a surprise, structurally as a basis for many variations), in the Serenade he had unconsciously arrived at the same chord series by a more instinctive technical process … .'[41]

Roseberry maintains a scrupulously respectful pose *vis-à-vis* Britten, and closes his note with a kind of *Tempo*-typical chummy Anglophone awe: 'Technical considerations apart, the close harmonic identity of the two passages discloses a remarkably precise and consistent musical response to the same poetic idea. And one is left marvelling at the quality of sheer inspiration, defying analytical comment.'[42]

There are some nice details in this little note. The correspondence is real, imminently symbolizable, articulate and manifold. It is a complex correspondence, or more aptly a correspondence-*complex*: a seldom-found-together-ness of otherwise perfectly generic categories. Roseberry identifies at least four: 'Britten', 'Four-chord progression', 'Great English

Authors' and 'Sleep'; we might add to these a few others which are strongly implied: 'very slow', 'tonally distant' and 'triadic'. Roseberry then supplies a concise, cogent analytic account of the displacements and substitutions needed to recuperate this correspondent text: under 'Britten' substitute '1942' for '1960'; under 'Great English Authors' substitute 'Keats' for 'Shakespeare'; under 'Sleep' substitute 'healing forgetfulness' for 'fantastic identity change'; under '4-Chord Progression' substitute the string of three-note chords 'C#/D/Eb/C' for 'D/C#/Eb/C.' Here things get a bit complicated: remember to add an extra note (B-natural) to the second (D major) chord; respell the notes of the third chord (which changes the way they look on the page, but not the way they sound); get rid of the top note in that last chord (so that there are only two rather than three notes in it) … aaaand *voilà* [Figure 4.7].

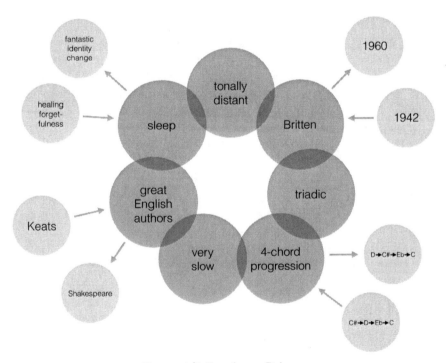

Figure 4.7 Roseberry-Britten

Of course, you must also remember to re-score the whole affair: the sound of four violas and solo cello must be replaced with, respectively, a complete string orchestra; then muted brass instruments (trombone, trumpet, two horns); then a small chorus of wind instruments (bassoons, clarinets, oboes, flutes); and finally an exquisite concoction of suspended cymbal (struck with a soft stick), vibraphone, two harps and harpsichord. Complicated, but not mystifying: this is less a matter of turning wine into blood than putting the heads of asses on to the heads of weavers. So far, the old switch-a-roo.

The curious moment in this fantasy emerges when Roseberry goes looking for the *subject* of this act of switching. The subject is Britten, specifically Britten's consciousness. But Britten's consciousness is not where it ought be. So the subject must be Britten's – 'subconscious'? His 'unconscious instinct'? But this is not a subject, or at least not a subject enough for Roseberry. So he gracefully plugs his ear, fogs up his speculating gaze, and agrees to sympathetically forget what he had tried to help his interlocutor recall. This sympathetic forgetting cannot, however, be entirely accomplished; the correspondence remains recalcitrantly in mind, and so Roseberry must situate its uncanny return in the register of the mystical: sheer inspiration. Britten, meanwhile, does not actually vanish as a subject. But he becomes – or is called upon by Roseberry to play – a subject of a different kind, in this case not one who produces a text but one who regulates a discourse, who subliminally invalidates an act of recollection with a delicate paternal interdiction. So he *is* a switching agent after all: a Keatsian 'soft embalmer ... Shutting with careful fingers and benign / Our gloom-pleased eyes, embower'd from the light ...'.[43]

It's understandable why Roseberry shrinks in the face of remembering *this* music in *that* music. It pulls the listener into that precarious territory native to both puns and etymologies. 'Not surprisingly', writes Jonathan Culler,

> in both the realm of puns — relations between signs in a language at a particular moment — and the realm of etymology — relations between signs from different periods — there is no dearth of people anxious to control relations, to enforce a distinction between real and false connections, true etymologies and folk etymologies, puns and valid conceptual relations.[44]

To open a single musical moment on to the entirety of its potential history of resemblances summons a semiotic vortex before the listener, an invitation to a kind of madness. It was one of Samuel Johnson's more merciless charges against Shakespeare that puns – Johnson called them quibbles – made the bard literally go insane:

... he follows [a quibble] at all adventures; it is sure to lead him out of his way, and sure to engulf him in the mire ... A quibble, poor and barren as it is, gave him such delight, that he was content to purchase it by the sacrifice of reason, propriety, and truth. A quibble was to him the fatal Cleopatra for which he lost the world, and was content to lose it.[45]

(Mark Twain issued a similar complaint when he claimed that 'Middletown' could be derived from 'Moses' by dropping -oses and adding -iddletown.) Forgetting is an excellent defense against the mire of affinities, a regulon delimiting the imagination's power to mend, to turn anything into anything else.

But I wish Roseberry had followed his quibble's adventures a bit further, and so I – who have no soft-embalming Britten to check me – will. Because it is precisely at a moment like this, in the multiple resonances of these chords, their proliferating inscriptions, that we find Britten's *Dream* most resembling a 'royal road to the unconscious'. It is a road (or a line in a wax slab) we can go down by listening – not simply the way a music analyst might, but the way a psychoanalyst would, that is, listening for the others enunciated in a subject's own enunciations.

At the beginning of the second act of *A Midsummer Night's Dream*, in front of a mostly empty stage (Tytania is sleeping in one corner), we are dealing with the presentation by a hidden orchestra of a sequence of distinct, homophonic, timbrally homogeneous but also timbrally segregated block chords, one per measure. (That is, each chord uses only its own orchestral family: the first chord employs only the sound of strings, the second only the sound of brass, etc.) They are performed in a deliberate way, 'very slow' (quarter note = 50), almost didactically, as if to communicate that they are not just chords, but *merely* chords, that they *lack* something and are awaiting a sculptor who will come along and 'set free' their latent figuration.[46] They are also triadic chords, but weirdly so: they are missing a syntax, or at least, if they *have* a syntax, it is also latent; instead, each follows on the next with the unknowing action of an echo – the pseudo-voice released by inanimate objects. The syntax is, of course, the 'aggregate', the collection of all 12 equal-tempered tones; Roseberry and Britten are both desperately keen to point this out. But this doesn't mean these chords are intended to sound or signify 'aggregate'. Just the opposite, one could argue: these chords are aurally obvious *and* auratically inscrutable, too hard to have content. They keep signification at bay. This is of course ideally suited to scenarios involving enchanted midsummer woods after midnight, in which anything could and will happen.

Something similar – more similar than Moses and Middletown – happens in the 'Interview' passage from *Billy Budd*, Britten's otherwise very different opera from four years earlier. It is the moment when Edward Fairfax Vere, Captain of the HMS Indomitable, must relay to his foretopman, the 'welkin-eyed' Billy Budd, that he will be hanged come morning. He suffers a crisis of conscience, and sings these words: 'Beauty, handsomeness, goodness, it is for me to destroy you. I am the messenger of death. How can he pardon? How receive me?' He then exits swiftly and we again hear the presentation by a hidden orchestra in front of a now-empty stage (no Tytania) of a sequence of distinct, homophonic, timbrally homogeneous but also timbrally segregated block chords, one per measure, performed very slow ('Largo'), involving triads in often distant keys.[47] It is night – probably quite late, perhaps even after midnight; we're at sea rather in the forest, but we are still lost to the world, nowhere near home. More importantly, we are in the sonic hub of something unwitnessable. 'Beyond the communication of the sentence', writes Melville in his short story,

> what took place at this interview was never known ... the twain briefly closeted in that state-room, each radically sharing in the rarer qualities of our nature — so rare indeed as to be all but incredible to average minds however much cultivated ...

So: we cannot see it, we cannot know it, but the revelation (in this case, that one is fated to die) is audible.

We might reconfigure Roseberry's correspondence–complex thus: 'Britten', 'triadic', 'tonally distant', and 'very slow' are preserved; 'Sleep' is modified to accommodate harder forms of embalming; '4-chord progression' is altered to 'multi-chord, one-chord-per-measure progression'; 'Great English Authors' is excised and replaced with a number of different categories: 'timbrally segregated orchestral groupings', '(mostly) bare opera stage', and 'audible but invisible midnight revelation'.

Now Hector Berlioz's *Romeo et Juliette, Symphonie dramatique d'après la tragédie de Shakespeare*, is suddenly at hand. Specifically, at Fig. 71 in the astonishing sixth movement, 'Romeo at the tomb of the Capulets', where Romeo, having broken into the crypt, confronts what he believes to be the corpse of Juliette. At least one *could think* that's what's going on here: without Berlioz's explanatory note one doesn't exactly know, and Berlioz was famously unapologetic about this not-knowing:

> The general public lacks imagination; pieces that appeal exclusively to the imagination are therefore lost on the general public. The following

instrumental scene is of that kind, and in my view it should be omitted whenever this symphony is not performed before an élite audience ... gifted with a high degree of poetic feeling. That is to say that it should be left out ninety-nine times out of a hundred.

This sounds more than a little like Melville's tantalizing non-description of the interview between Vere and Budd, not least in its implicit meta-voyeurism: only you and I know that no-one knows exactly what's going on here. More to the point: we can preserve everything in our corre-spondence–complex except 'Britten', for which we might simply substitute, in an uncanny return, 'Shakespeare'. The words '(mostly) bare opera stage' must be qualified, but not much: Berlioz, like Britten 1960 and Britten 1956, is interested in staging an imageless action on a proscenium otherwise infested with an evening's worth of visual representations. The music is a mystery, quite literally: an opening of inner eyes coincident with the closing of outer ones. So let us amend the category to reflect this switch-up between ear and eye – to something like 'visible music illustrating invisible images'.

We could at this point sharpen 'Shakespeare' by adding 'A Midsummer Night's Dream', and we would conjure the first four chords of Mendelssohn's famous overture from 1826, about which Liszt wrote, 'One thinks only of the wind chords at the beginning and end! Do they not resemble slowly drooping and rising eyelids, between which is depicted a charming dream-world of the most lovely contrasts?'[48]

Of course! Mendelssohn! What were we thinking? How did we not see the enchanted forest for the trees? Was Britten dealing with any greater precursor when it came to providing Shakespeare's comedy with music? We would, of course, have to soften '(Big) sleep' once again; 'timbrally segre-gated orchestral groupings' must also be buffered, given that Mendelssohn presents only one – marvelous – timbral shift, from winds to strings, the key of E major to the key of E minor. And 'tonally distant' must be, if not displaced, then heavily qualified: we're dealing by most accounts with a quite standard harmonic progression. On the other hand, we can now bring back '4-chord progression'.

We might even try our hand at a Roseberryan account of what Britten actually did to produce his own sequence *from* Mendelssohn's. Was it a series of logical operations? A series of, say, literal transpositions, in which the height of the pitches is changed, but their contour and internal relationship are preserved? Or perhaps Britten performed a combination of logically consistent, generalizable displacements (play this progression backwards, then upside down, then slightly higher) (and arbitrary, radically context-dependent displacements (this three-note chord should have its top note raised a bit and its second note lowered a bit; this chord should have an extra note, and so on). Indeed, Britten's preliminary sketches for these chords preserve a much closer resemblance to Mendelssohn's own sequence; Britten clearly wanted to send and simultaneously scramble his message here.[49]

More importantly: perhaps 'Mendelssohn' himself – or, here, 'itself' – constituted something *like* an operation for Britten. If one can retrograde the opening chords of Mendelssohn's overture, why can't one 'Mendelssohn' the moment in Berlioz's *Roméo et Juliette* when Roméo stands before Juliet's tomb? Or vice-versa? The conscious or pre-conscious intention to misprise, to literally mistake, a specific text may utilize – or simply produce – *another* intertext, itself open to misreading.

Along these lines: Why is the *appropriate* scoring of the first of Britten's four chords (a Db major chord to be exact) a bed of strings? Is there a precedent for a Db major chord *exactly* like this – slow, full, low, oceanic, prefatory, *pianissimo*, bowed? Is this, for instance, Anton von Bruckner's chord, from the opening of the *Adagio* third movement of his Eighth Symphony from 1892?[50] Almost. In Bruckner's score, the chord's top note doesn't materialize for a few seconds, when the first violins enter throatily on their lowest strings with a tremulous figure; Britten's chord has no figuration at all – in its first iteration. But, as Roseberry mentioned, Britten treats these four chords as a kind of repeating cycle (in musical terms, a passacaglia – one of Purcell's favoured techniques), and submits them to a series of variations which continue for some five minutes. When Britten presents the *second* iteration of the strings' chord, there is a figure: a solo cello ascends in chasmic leaps from a low bass note into the mid-upper register, where Bruckner's chord begins its figure. Then, in the third iteration of Britten's chord, he goes full-Austrian – at least as far as he will go: 'fourth string', 'more flowing', *espressivo, crescendo, tenuto*. If Mendelssohn is present here as a cohesive 4-chord unit – in which each chord is nonetheless instantly 'translated' – then Bruckner is presented demurely, in the auratic glow of a single instant which, memory-like, assembles itself gradually from broken, talismanic fragments.

We might return to this first chord of Britten's. In its first instantiation, it insinuates Bruckner; in its second, it seems to speak it – but also misspeak it, adding something else to the mix, a leaping cello figure. Is this cello figure anything *other* than *not-Bruckner*? It leaps up at specific intervals (a major sixth, then a perfect fifth), and, reaching its upper note, lands there squarely, edges up just a bit, then down just a bit more, and then descends in a three-link chain of equal intervals – perfect fifths, the same intervals to which the cello is tuned, and which resound boomily in the tuning sessions preceding most any orchestra concert. This is not exactly what happens at the slow, soft, prefatory and, yes, Austrian beginning of Alban Berg's famous *Violin Concerto* from 1935. But it could be a conflation of a number of adjacent moments: Britten's solo cello is Berg's solo *violin*, playing its chromatic turn, but also simultaneously Berg's background clarinets, harp and bassoon playing their rising and falling chains of open fifths. Or perhaps Britten's cello and strings conflate this prefatory moment with the very end of Berg's *Concerto*, where we hear an arpeggiated fan of open fifths in violins and basses, glinting through a luminescent, hazily haloed major chord with an added note as it swells and ebbs. It turns out that the third chord in Britten's four-chord cycle is a transposition of the chord which ends Berg's concerto. And the last chord in Britten's cycle shares key components of Berg's orchestration at this closing moment: the washed-out shimmer of metallophones, the plucked harps, the ambiguous *laissez vibrer* ('let vibrate') direction which leaves the sound to freeze and fade in mid-air.

A hypothesis forms: the unfurling of the first four chords of Britten's Act 2 constitutes (or perhaps even stages) a musical anamnesis. A Db major chord acts as madeleine; this amorphous, unfigured orb of harmony gently rattles awake the sound – quite literally, the sympathetic strings – of Bruckner's gargantuan symphonic edifice; associations of Austrian orchestra adagiana beckon forth Berg from Bruckner, and the clasping-closed of Berg's Violin Concerto, whose last sonority crystallizes into the second of Britten's four chords; the last of these chords intercepts another feature of Berg's chord (its orchestration); the subsequent return of the Db chord intercepts another feature of Bruckner's chord (its figuration), and so on. Berg's concerto, it should be added, is a virtuoso effort in deep punning: Berg composed the work in a quite strict and continuous 12-tone style, but such that traditional tonal sounds would emerge virtually every- and anywhere; as if seemingly by accident, one constantly hears phantoms of an older grammar, of Mahler and Brahms and – Bruckner. Britten's own four-chord sequence, built as it is out of tonal sounds, accomplishes the same effect: taken together, the chords employ all 12 equal-tempered tones, or rather, they materialize 'coincidentally' out of a 12-tone collection. This classically Bergian constructive premise was already institutionalized in contemporary music by the late 1950s; Britten would surely have enjoyed and practised it consciously. What I find more striking is how, in the midst of this conscious, relatively abstract compositional decision, the actual sound – indeed, the very materiality – of Berg's score would infiltrate and fill out the details of Britten's composing work.

I should stress again that I have no idea whether this is 'what actually happened'. I can't write to Britten, but if I could, I doubt it would help. Would it help to know that Britten fantasized about studying with Berg in Vienna? That he attended the 1936 Barcelona world première of Berg's concerto, and recorded in his diary that he found the performance 'just shattering'; 'a very moving experience [of] a very great work ...'? That a few months later he confided 'I become very extravagant & bought the full score of Berg's miraculous Violin concerto. My God what a sublime work'; and that before the year was through, recorded after another performance, 'It is a grand work – & has an extremely moving effect on me like no other stuff. It is so vital and intellectually emotional?'[51] Perhaps. It may be, however, that such subject-validated scripts – letters, diaries, interviews – quickly turn into purloined letters, making us go hunting for something hiding in plain sight (or plain earshot): an overdetermined, modular, idiosyncratic constellation of affinities between otherwise generic categories.

In the context of such a constellation, one might also de-prioritize Britten's emotional testimony on Berg's score, and concentrate for a moment on the score's inscription: 'To the memory of an angel', specifically the 18-year old Manon Gropius, daughter of Walter Gropius and Alma Mahler – the latter to whom Britten dedicated his 1958 orchestral song-cycle *Nocturne*, setting eight poems about sleep, the last being Shakespeare's Sonnet 43, a verse consumed with heavy-lidded insight, and which begins, 'When most I wink, then do mine eyes best see'.[52]

So let us wedge a sixteenth coordinate – 'the death of an angel' – into this constellation, and pose it a larger question [Figure 4.8]. What does it suggest about what Britten – or rather, *it*, Britten's unconscious, 'Unknown Britten' – may have been thinking, hearing and remembering in the moments when it precipitated these four chords at the beginning of Act 2 of his *Dream?*[53]

It was certainly thinking of night (midnight) and of sleep, of a sleepy music but also of music as an actual sleep-aid, something to raise the stage's curtains while lowering the curtains of the eyes. It was thinking of what could be spoken without words, heard but not seen, heard with eyes and seen with ears, like the wordless interview between Vere and Budd or the wordless tomb scene between Berlioz's Romeo and Juliet. It was thinking of Great English Authors, but not only of Shakespeare plays. Also Shakespeare's sonnets ('When most I wink'), and also sonnets of Keats ('O soft embalmer

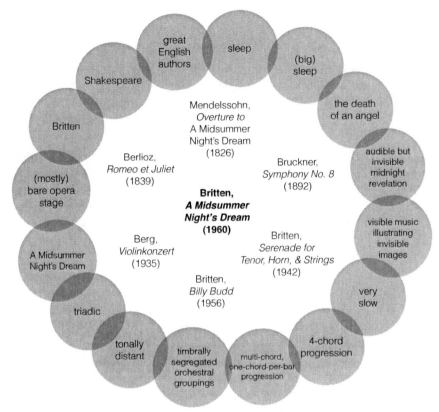

Figure 4.8 Final Constellation

of the still midnight'), and with them an especially Keatsian form of sleep, less late sixteenth century and more early nineteenth century, more 'half in love with easeful Death'. Perhaps Britten's fairies were partially modelled on a vision of Keats himself, and were, themselves, about to die: young, welkin-eyed, adolescent, full of handsomeness and goodness, and about to die, and Britten was Vere, messenger of death come to tell them so, or Romeo, ready to spring them from their tomb before the fateful moment. Unknown Britten was thinking of the *Dream*-work of other composers: of Mendelssohn's overture, written only a few years after Keats's sonnet by a composer fascinated by the British Romantics. But it was also thinking of Bruckner's music, and of a midsummer forest located in the Austrian Alps more than the Athenian hills, a forest as slow and chasmic as a late nineteenth-century symphonic *adagio*. It was thinking of Berg's music, of a work in memory of an angel but also of a fastidious endeavour in magical thinking, an impossible attempt from *entre les deux guerres* to conjure the souvenirs of a musical language's former life. Perhaps tonality itself became a proxy-precursor. Tonality: a dead nineteenth-century fairy, hovering between Mendelssohnian and Keatsian sleep. Tonality plays a remarkably similar role in Berg's concerto, whose most explicit precursor was no less than J. S. Bach (it is his cantata chorale 'Es ist genug' ['It is enough'] that constitutes the very bones of Berg's score). But that is another story.[54]

At the same time, Britten's unconscious was thinking a complex of quite irreducible, in many ways arbitrary sonic quiddities – fermata-covered chords hanging in air, syntax-stretching triads, pristine colorations that split the orchestra back into its unbroken, pre-symphonic consorts. Endless pathways are opened up by this split between contiguous senses and contiguous sounds. The hypothetical 16-module constellation I've gathered up here is in this regard analogous to the 'verbariums' of the kind Freud assembled in analysing the dreams of certain of his patients (the 'Rat Man' and 'Wolf Man' in particular): both are networks whose logic, like that of so many dreams, knows nothing of the waking boundaries between the lexical and semantic, material and meaning, even as it wantonly disregards their contractual agreements in other cases.[55]

In his 1915 essay on the unconscious, Freud outlined four distinct characteristics of the 'system Ucs.': 'exemption from mutual contradiction, primary process (mobility of cathexes), timelessness, and replacement of external by psychical reality'.[56] The hypothetical unconscious of the first four chords of Act 2 of Britten's *Dream* exhibit a strikingly similar set of characteristics: it can be 1596 and 1892 and 1935 and 1826 in any order, or all at once; fairies can be alive, then dead, then suddenly alive again; harmony can be tonal and post-tonal; the first bars of a symphonic movement can produce the last bars of a concerto; a comedy can also be a tragedy, or a love sonnet, and so on. But all these *Dream*-thoughts (names, words, concepts, objects, scenarios) are not themselves the equivalent of Act 2's opening bars, any more than a dreamer's unconscious is his dream. There is here another agent, engaged not only in acts of free assemblage, but also in a strategic process of recombination and substitution remarkably consonant with Freud's account of dream-work – that is, 'under some kind of necessity to combine all the sources which have acted as stimuli for the dream into a single unity'.[57] Here, Britten's unconscious is not given entirely free reign, but rather forced to engage with a will to displace and distort and condense, which leaves no 'dream thought' untouched. Here Britten is a transformer, a translator, an alchemist concocting formulae for Germanicizing English fantasies of Ancient Greece; for Keatsifying Shakespeare; for Brucknerizing and Bergolating and Berliozing Mendelssohn; for deliberately confusing his earliest precursor with those who came after him, such that they will show him to be old, so that Britten – who came *even later* – will now have the chance to render him young as the dawning day.

Considered from the perspective of dream-work, one might do well to consider this constellation, and especially the music it involves, for what it does not present. There are in these four chords at least six 'spots of time', as Wordsworth might have called them: six windows into other historical moments in works Britten would have known, as a composer, a conductor, a pianist, a listener, a student, a memory. Such that Britten's own moment could become a seventh spot of time, it could not reproduce any of these moments exactly. Each is produced, but not reproduced; presented, but also absented. But only from the standpoint of fidelity are these 'other' moments mis-memories. From the standpoint of what Harold Bloom would call the anxious artwork – as an achieved anxiety in response to 'what would end one as a poet' – one can regard these botched memories as successful. How successful? Here we might recall Britten's initial response to Roseberry: 'He expressed amazement at the similarity of the chords.'

It is no secret that, as long as there has been music, there has been the phenomenon of *this* music showing up in *that* music. The real question may not be – may not ever have been – is this music that music, but rather: by what rules – under whose law, under whose adjudication – is any transformation deemed adequate? A simple start at an answer would be: when the composer appears amazed at the similarity, when the composer's own memory mis-speaks itself so well that it cannot recognize itself. In this sense, perhaps we ought stellify Bottom the Weaver as Freud did Oedipus the King, and speak of a Bottom complex: a complex whereby dream-work, *Traumarbeit*, and its attendant processes of distortion, condensation, displacement and secondary revision manifest as scrupulously crafted malapropisms, dogberryisms, mondegreens. Such a complex, in its incessantly recombinant otherwise-ing of the recollected, would come in extremely handy for an artist, after all. It would constitute an algorithm for misprision, an amnestic script – essentially, a form of non-repetition compulsion.[58] Certainly Shakespeare had this complex himself, and exhibited it beautifully by using Bottom to forget and mis-remember Paul's first letter to the Corinthians, now returned to him as a character in his own play: 'The eye of man hath not heard, the ear of man hath not seen, man's hand is not able to taste, his tongue to conceive, nor his heart to report, what my dream was.'[59] If this is really true, then can he say anything about it at all? Only one thing: that this misprision is his, and shall bear his name.[60]

Sixth Note

'Its music and the music I have written for it are at two quite different levels.' Britten's attempt to 'transpose' Shakespeare's play to another register may be a defensive manœuvre, but it also invites the possibility of an entire mode of listening. After all, if Shakespeare's play is playing, not least on an audible level, always simultaneously with Britten's score – and if we accept Britten's designation of both 'levels' as *music* – then we're thrown into one of the most gloriously native of musical scenarios: polyphony, the cognition of multiple independent lines or threads of sonic activity, each possessed by its own cohesion, each participating in a constant contrapuntal game of serendipitous synchronies and clamorous blurs of noise and nonsense.

What kind of polyphony might this be? A chorale? A canon? I'm compelled to venture that Britten's *Dream* presents something like a fugue. An outrageous, hyperbolic fugue, to be sure: a three-hour, four-thousand-measure fugue, composed of at least 20 subjects (each character representing a subject or figural sequence to be imitated) and 80 voices (each of the opera's types would constitute its own line or track). One might conceptualize this as a virtual polyphony, less analogous to standard musical definitions than their literary metonyms. That is, a Bach fugue would be a less appropriate comparison than the 'Sirens' chapter in Joyce's *Ulysses*, where voices and subjects operate according to a diachronic, one-thing-after-another logic; they come and go, and when they return they carry with them the memory of how they used to be and the surprise of how they have changed in the meantime. For instance, Puck first appears in Britten's opera in measure 71 of Act 1, breaking into the fairies' song with a raucous teenage shout of 'How now, spirits?' The musical type changes accordingly: in place of a spritely unison chant against harps and harpsichord, we hear a swift, dry, trebly coupling of trumpet and snare-drum, snares removed to give it a more toy-like sound, as if a father had complained about the racket. In the roughly 50 measures that follow, the two instruments remain locked into a single, hyper-agile rhythmic tread, unfolding a series of unevenly metered statements (some in groups of five beats, others in groups of seven, nine, ten, or twelve), each interrupted by the fairies' monotone introduction. Each time Puck's music returns it is 'more or less' the same – a hopped-up bugle-and-drum march, mimicking the overtone scales of unvalved brass tubes – but little details are altered: melodic segments are extended or compressed, note-sequences reversed, new figurations added. It is a music of constant minor mutation, shapeshifting when one is not hearing.

A less whimsical question: on what level, in what media are these polyphonies active? The polyphonies of Britten's *Dream* would clearly exist on planes beyond the merely audible. Here are not only sounding counterpoints, but also polysemies, counterpoints of sign, of psychic register, of textual segment, of author and authorial voice, of fictional and mythic character. To take the Puck music again as an example: each of its varied modules between bars 71 and 123 has its own specific intertextual echo, its own spot of time; here is where the minor mutations matter. The first module conjures the iconic horn theme from Richard Strauss's 1895 tone-poem *Till Eulenspiegels lustige Streiche* ('Till Eulenspiegel's Merry Pranks'); the second module Bela Bartók's 1945 *Concerto for Orchestra*, specifically the trumpets-and-snareless-snare-drum segment in the second movement's 'Giuoco delle coppie' ('Game of couples'). The third and fourth modules rewrite Igor Stravinsky: respectively, his 1918 work for ensemble and narrator *L'Histoire du Soldat*, movements 1 ('Marche du soldat') and 4 ('Petit concert'); and the opening of the third tableau of the 1911 ballet *Petrushka*, when the puppet ballerina captivates the clown with a cornet-and-military-drum duet. Puck was already in Shakespeare's time an 'emblem of hybridity', as Jonathan Gil Harris calls him.[61] In Britten's opera Puck is a hyper-hybrid, a meta-shapeshifter whose polyphony of times and texts suggests a transcontinental Frankenstein of sweeter and more diminutive disposition – part Elizabethan hobgoblin, part concertante virtuoso, part Russian circus puppet, part Faustian foot soldier of the Great War, part German folk hero (and, via Strauss's own intertextual dialogues with Wagner, part anti-Siegfried).[62]

Unlike the four chords at the beginning of Britten's Act 2, Puck's music is rampant, its many variants infiltrating hundreds of bars of the opera, and fusing often with the music of other characters, each embedded in their own intertextual constellations. One of the more compelling cross-pollinations comes near the end of Act 1, when Puck, on Oberon's orders, squeezes the love-juice on Lysander's eyes ('Churl, upon thy eyes I throw / All the power this charm doth owe.'). As Puck intones his mock spell, we hear a monstrous mashup of his music (type 6) and Oberon's (type 11), such that the accompanying instrumentalists themselves seem flustered: the trumpeter's tongue furiously flutters a lyrical melody originally scored for viola or cello; the celesta player's hands, normally operating in lullaby-mode, suddenly have to sweep the keyboard in manic septuplet rhythms. Another intertext is produced in this pseudo-séance: the jittery horror-scene climax to the slow third movement of Bartók's 1936 *Music for Strings, Percussion, and Celesta*.

Bartók's score – a score Britten admired immensely – could be said to constitute a central character in Britten's opera, arguably as central as Puck. Certainly it 'pops up' as frequently; its remarkably specific sound-world permeates more measures of the opera than the words of Oberon. But the logic which controls Bartók's presence here is obscure and askew, strangely indifferent to the logic of Shakespeare's play, the why-and-wherefore of its plot, imagery, characters, places. Extended passages from Bartók's first movement fugue are often minimally rewritten as the music for the Athenian lovers, particularly Lysander and Hermia; middle sections from the second movement provide the scaffolding for fairies' opening song, which returns late in Act 1 as well. A crucial moment late in Bartók's finale, when the work 'remembers' its own first movement, rematerializes in Tytania's roundel-request – the same music which simultaneously produces the quote from Purcell's *Dido*. And the famous string *glissandi* in Bartók's third movement – operating in his characteristic 'night music' vein – could be said to form the skeleton of the *ritornelli* (type 1) which provide the structure of Britten's Act 1.

There are many works – Wagner's *Tristan und Isolde*, Tchaikovsky's *Nutcracker*, Britten's own *Turn of the Screw* – which also striate the temporal fabric of Britten's score. But in the case of Wagner (an opera with lovers 'ill met by moonlight'), Tchaikovsky (a ballet with visions of fairies), and Britten's *Turn* (another opera featuring a kinky man-child tied to the sound of a celesta), the connections are validated by waking sense. In the case of Bartók's *Music*, however, we see a connection validated less by sense than sound, less by a making-sense than a making-sound. One can always venture a hypothesis in such cases; for instance, one can imagine that Britten, in the process of freely imagining the kind of night-time he wanted for his wood, found himself thinking of (or more exactly, found himself being thought by) Bartók's night-music in general, with its iconic fusion of gossamer melodic lines, creeping chromaticism, and tremulous, seismographic insect gestures. This preoccupation found its way to his ear, then his pen, and then, eventually, expanded into a reservoir of rewritable musical material – not a single passage, but a series of passages from an entire four-movement work; in the play of associations which developed, Bartók's score ceased operating primarily as an allusive signifying agent, and became a kind of raw, rhizomatic material, growing its own semi-auton-omous networks of tissue in quite disparate, seemingly random spots.[63]

To return to Britten's *ritornelli*: in their orchestration (strings), structure (the refrain for the opening act) and antiquated tonal inflections, they resonate ambitiously – not with the *very* first opera, but with the first 'great' opera, Claudio Monteverdi's *L'Orfeo, Favola in musica* of 1607, whose own string *ritornelli* similarly segment its own first act. They also introduce another fairy-like figure simultaneously mistress and product of nature: Music herself, as manipulative of birds, breezes, plants and lovers as Tytania or Oberon.[64] But Britten's *ritornelli*, taken as their own network, are the product of another nocturnal mis-hearing too, far richer than the third movement of Bartók's *Music for Strings*: a passage in the middle of Maurice Ravel and Colette's 1925 opera *L'Enfant et les sortilèges*, when the opera's naughty child, previously locked in his room, suddenly finds himself in his beloved moonlit garden. There are striking musical resonances: Britten's music preserves Ravel's creeping, sluggish *glissandi*; his wayward tonal shifts, in which unrelated chords are melted together to form quasi-atonal melodic lines; and the droning, gothic sound of parallel open fifths – an absolute no-no in the parochial world of proper counter-point, but apparently legion in such extra-curricular territory as this. As in the case of the four chords at the beginning of Britten's Act 2, however, these musical features are part of a larger web of signifying entities. Not just *glissando* and *parallel fifth* and *tonally distant chord*, but also *night* and *tree* and *enchanted grove* and *young boy*: under Britten's aegis, these floating intermedial modules flock together to transpose Shakespeare's wood with at least two fugal subjects: a space where a young fairy might not just flit about freely in service to a benevolent queen, but (as in Colette's libretto) find peace from an angry, reprimanding mother; where the woods would harbour not only fairies but lovelorn dragonflies, coloratura nightingales, widower bats and crippled squirrels; in which the trees would not merely sway, but, bleeding sap, shame the child who lacerated them thus: 'Ah, my wound … my wound … The wound you inflicted but yesterday in my side with the knife you stole … .'[65] Given the essential role of silent young boys in Britten's work (the operas *Peter Grimes* and *Death in Venice* in particular), I am tempted to suggest that the bark-branding rascal from Ravel and Colette's opera is an ideal oneiric substitution: he becomes the 'changeling boy', equally voiceless in Shakespeare's play, who initiates the fierce custody battles between Tytania and Oberon and, in doing so, turns the wood on its head and initiates the cosmicomedy itself. To whom does this ciphering boy belong? Britten, Shakespeare, Ravel, Colette? That custody battle, played out on an intertextual register, is its own cosmicomic game of $n(n-1)$.

Any discussion of intertextual polyphony in Britten's *Dream* would have to address the famous 'opera within an opera', with which Britten transposes Shakespeare's 'Pyramus and Thisby' skit on to the musical stage. Here the opera has been remarkably well-served with commentary, the most extensive being Albright's.[66] For my purposes, I would point out that (by my count) Britten's rendition of 'Pyramus' employs – quotes, paraphrases, parodies, mangles, has its way with – passages out of at least 21 works from the extended operatic canon. [Figure 4.9; the operas are designated by darker rectangles.][67] Three of Mozart's late operas; three of Britten's own; another appearance by Purcell's *Dido* ('Remember me!' recast as 'Thus Thisby ends!'). As Pyramus and Thisby 'kiss' (the) Wall (played by Snout), we hear a music-box diminution of the bone-crunching dissonance at the end of Richard Strauss's *Salome*, when Salome kisses the severed head of John the Baptist. Britten makes the Italians into Shakespeare's central polyphones here, however, with two operas each by Rossini and Donizetti and one by Bellini.[68] The operas of Giuseppe Verdi ring in with no less than seven soundings. Among the more notable instances: Renato's warning to the King ('Alla vita che t'arride') in *Un Ballo in maschera* is now warped into Peter Quince's MC turn to the Athenian court ('Gentles, perchance you wonder at this show')[69]; Pyramus (actually Bottom), 'at Ninny's tomb', serenades the moon to music remarkably resonant with Act 1, scene 1 of Verdi's *Simon Boccanegra*, in which Amelia (actually Maria) also serenades the moon. A more remarkable feat of character-counterpoint comes in Britten's 'night' aria for Pyramus, which confabulates deftly Banco's two 'night' arias from Verdi's *Macbeth*. Pyramus, immune to his inner thesaurus, pumps out the bloated lines 'O grim-look'd night! O night with hue so black! / O night, which ever art when day is not! / O night, O night! alack, alack, alack … .' But Britten's perfectly calibrated musical accompaniment references more desperate models (Banco in Verdi's Act 1, scene 2: 'Oh what an awful night! / Mourning voices were heard / in the blind air, voices of death'; Banco in Act 2, scene 1: 'How the gloom falls / more and more darkly from heaven! / It was on a night like this / that they stabbed my lord Duncan.') There is something especially vertiginous about this intertextual convolution: an opera within an opera within an opera, setting words of Shakespeare to music which had previously set words adapted from another play by – Shakespeare.[70] Bottom, both himself and not-himself, Pyramus and not-Pyramus, is now also Banquo and not-Banquo in a play quite literally 'merry and tragical'.

Save the few instance of Britten-quoting-Britten (*Peter Grimes*, *Albert Herring*, *Paul Bunyan*), most of the operatic interlocutors on parade here call out from other centuries. A notable exception is Stravinsky, whose 1951 opera *The Rake's Progress* (with a remarkable libretto by W. H. Auden) appears to have provided Britten with the sound and style of his recitative sections. When the Athenian hecklers get going (and they never

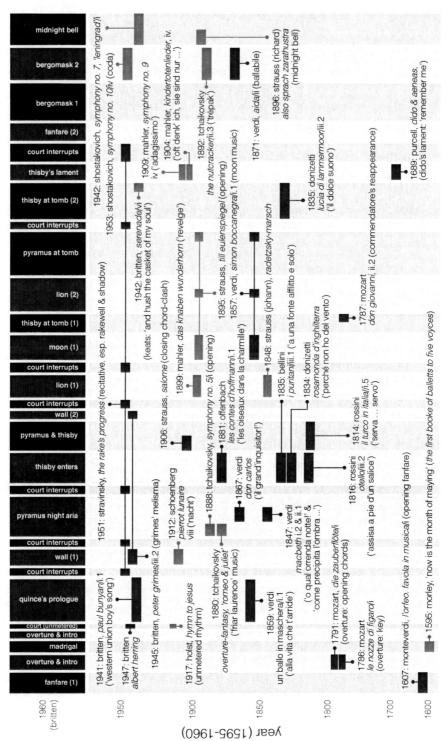

Figure 4.9 Operas within an Opera (Britten, mm. 3410–3842)

miss a chance), Britten punctures his mock-number opera with stylized
eighteenth-century recitative – crunchy keyboard interjections, rhythmi-
cally frayed and often confused about the key they're supposed to be in. It
is a rare confluence of gesture, sonority and context in twentieth-century
opera and, in 1960 at least, hard to find outside of *The Rake*'s recitative
dialogues between Tom Rakewell and Nick Shadow.[71]

The Rake has become known as a *locus classicus* of intertextual reference,
a cosmicomedy of styles alternately considered proto-postmodern and
hopelessly reactionary, radically forward-looking and a bitter autopsy of
the entire opera genre.[72] Britten appears to have sided with the latter
assessment, and in a letter to George and Marion Harewood shortly
after *The Rake*'s premiere in September 1951, he seethed with (arguably
premature) disapproval about the ethos and *techné* of Stravinsky and
Auden's new creation:

> I feel miserably disappointed (I have done since I first saw the libretto
> & first few pages of the score) that easily the greatest composer alive
> should have such an irresponsible & perverse view of opera (of the voice
> & of the setting of words & of characterisation in particular). Of course
> I am sure it will contain lots of beautiful music, & it will be throughout
> original & distinguished, but I'm not yet convinced that it helps opera to
> keep alive one little bit — & I feel Auden to be largely to blame, being
> the cleverer & more sophisticated of the two. What these two could have
> produced ... ! But the subject seems quite wrong for them both.[73]

It is strange to read these words coming from the composer of the
Pyramus skit, which so cunningly and mercilessly undoes the onion-skin
around opera's golden age; 'in the Pyramus skit', writes Albright, 'Britten
is not just making a joke about opera but declaring that opera is itself a
joke'.[74] I am inclined to agree, but wonder if the joke is less on eighteenth-
and nineteenth-century opera than on Stravinsky's own 'irresponsible &
perverse view of opera'. Indeed, one might venture the hypothesis that
Britten's opera within an opera is itself a parody of *The Rake*, and a rather
astonishing one at that – an act of fastidious, cold-eyed diminishment
and compaction, a half-stern, half-frivolous putting-in-its-place in which
the model's actual music is relegated to the seams, to the flimsy glue of
recitativo secco barely holding this rickety claptrap together. Of course,
Shakespeare did something to this effect already in his own play within
a play – alternately a travesty of Ovid's Pyramus-and-Thisbe story in Book
4 of the *Metamorphoses*, of Arthur Golding's 1567 translation of the same,

possibly even a diminishment-and-compaction of Shakespeare's own *Romeo and Juliet*.[75] It's possible, however, that Stravinsky's music is a MacGuffin here, and that the real object of Britten's vitriol is Stravinsky's librettist Auden, whose close friendship and intensely productive collaboration with Britten came to a bitter end by the early 1940s.[76] Here, perhaps, is yet another perspective on Britten-as-Great-Shakespearean: Britten-as-anti-Audenite, as the composer who, having lost Auden to 'the greatest composer alive', collaborated with the greatest unintentional librettist of all time, one utterly compliant, literally 'ready to hand'.

Notes

Notes on Introduction

1 Mason, Edward Tuckerman, *The Othello of Tommaso Salvini*. New York and London: G. P. Putnam's Sons, 1890: 107.
2 Rosen, David and Andrew Porter (eds), *Verdi's Macbeth: A Sourcebook*. New York: Norton, 1984: 110.

Notes on Chapter 1

1 'With her Romeo, as Juliet lies dead / Have done with Letourner, whose French is so banal, / With Berlioz alone Shakespeare is truly read / The translator is as great as the original.' See *New Berlioz Edition* [hereafter *NBE*], ed. Hugh Macdonald et al., 26 vols (Kassel: Bärenreiter, 1967–2004), XXVI: 189.
2 F. E. Halliday, *A Shakespeare Companion* (London: Duckworth, 1952), 65.
3 In Chapter LIX of his *Mémoires*, Berlioz wrote of Shakespeare: 'C'est toi qui es notre père ...' ('It is thou who art our father ...'). In this article, all translations, unless otherwise indicated, are my own. See Berlioz, *Mémoires*, ed. Pierre Citron (Paris: Flammarion, 1991), 543 (the best current edition). Because other editions exist in French and in translation, passages from the *Mémoires* are here cited by chapter number only.
4 I cite the last page of the *Voyage en Dauphiné* that concludes the *Mémoires*.
5 See Berlioz, 'Aperçu sur la musique classique et la musique romantique,' in *Le Correspondant* (22 October 1830), reprinted in Berlioz, *Critique musicale* [hereafter *CM*], ed. H. Robert Cohen, Yves Gérard, Anne Bongrain, Marie-Hélène Coudroy-Saghaï et al., 6 vols [of a projected ten] (Paris: Buchet/Chastel, 1996–2007), I: 67.
6 Berlioz spoke of Shakespeare *and* Goethe as 'les muets confidents de mes tourments, les explicateurs de ma vie' – 'the silent confidents of my suffering, the interpreters of my life'. See Hector Berlioz, *Correspondance générale* [hereafter *CG*], ed. Pierre Citron et al., 8 vols (Paris: Flammarion, 1972–2003), I: 208.
7 Different from all contemporary editions, including the anonymous version published by Mme Vergne, in 1828, and the version by Benjamin Laroche, in 1839–40 (versions to be considered below), this seems to be Berlioz's own translation of *Macbeth*, 5.4.24–8.

8 The English text of the Mme Vergne edition does indeed have 'full', not 'foul'.

9 See *CG* VII: 379n.

10 See *CG* VII: 151.

11 See *CG* V: 669.

12 Jacques Barzun, *Berlioz and the Romantic Century*, 2 vols (Boston, MA: Little, Brown and Company, 1950; 3rd ed., New York: Columbia University Press, 1969).

13 Paul Scudo, *Revue des deux mondes* (15 July 1856), reprinted in Scudo, *Critique et Littérature musicales* (Paris: Hachette, 1859), 117. Scudo paraphrases Beaumarchais' Figaro in Act 5, scene 3 of *Le Mariage de Figaro*: 'il fallait un calculateur, ce fut un danseur qui l'obtint'.

14 *CG* IV: 565.

15 On Berlioz the writer see Katherine Kolb, 'Hector Berlioz', in *European Writers: The Romantic Century*, vol. 6 (New York: Scribner's, 1985), 771–812; various essays including one by Katherine Kolb (who uses the phrase 'comic masterpiece') in *The Cambridge Companion to Berlioz*, ed. Peter Bloom (Cambridge: Cambridge University Press, 2000); *Berlioz écrivain* (Paris: Ministère des Affaires étrangères, 2003); and *Hector Berlioz: Homme de lettres*, ed. Georges Zaragoza (Neuilly-lès-Dijon: Éditions du Murmure, 2006).

16 See A. W. R. James, 'Berlioz the poet?', in *Hector Berlioz: Les Troyens*, ed. Ian Kemp (Cambridge: Cambridge University Press, 1988), 67–75.

17 I have slightly modified the translation in the excellent edition of *The Memoirs of Hector Berlioz*, trans. and ed. David Cairns (New York: Knopf, 2002).

18 *CG* VIII: 19.

19 *CG* VIII: 25.

20 See *The British Theatre, or A Collection of Plays which are acted in Paris / printed under the authority of the managers, from the acting copy / HAMLET, / Prince of Denmark* (Paris: Mme Vergne, 1827).

21 See, for example, *CG* I: 539; *CG* II: 129; *CG* VII: 218.

22 *CG* V: 702 (28 July 1859).

23 *CG* VI: 406.

24 The Guizot revision – *Shakespeare. Œuvres complètes. Traduites de l'anglais par Letourneur*. Nouvelle édition, revue et corrigée par F. Guizot et A.P. [Amédée Pichot]. Précédée d'une notice biographique et littéraire sur Shakespeare par F. Guizot, 13 vols (Paris: Ladvocat, 1821) – essentially replaced words now considered stilted with words now considered common.

25 See David Cairns, *Berlioz: The Making of an Artist 1803–1832* (London: Deutsch, 1989), 14: 243.

26 Among other sources, the essay is found in Hugo, *Préface de Cromwell*, in Hugo, *Œuvres completes*, ed. Jacques Seebacher et al. (Paris: Laffont, 1985), vol. 5.

27 On the Garrick generation, see Todd Borlik, ' "Painting of a sorrow": Visual Culture and the Performance of Stasis in David Garrick's *Hamlet*', *Shakespeare Bulletin*, 25 (2007): 3–32. See also Peter Raby, 'Shakespeare in Paris, 1827', in *The Musical Voyager: Berlioz in Europe*, ed. David Charlton and Katharine Ellis (Frankfurt am Main: Peter Lang, 2007), 208–23.

28 Cited by Raby, 214.

29 According to the *Revue britannique*, cited by Joseph-Léopold Borgerhoff, *Le Théâtre Anglais à Paris sous la Restauration* (Paris: Hachette, 1913), 153 n1.

[30] From Janin's obituary for Harriet, in the *Journal des débats* of 20 March 1854. Berlioz cited much of this in Chapter LIX of the *Mémoires*.

[31] Cited in Borgerhoff, *Le Théâtre anglais*, 91: 'La douceur de ses paroles, les modulations incertaines de son chant, tout à fait de ce tableau un ensemble parfait.'

[32] Moreau is quoted by John R. Elliott, Jr., 'The Shakespeare Berlioz Saw', *Music and Letters*, 57 (1976): 76.

[33] *Gazette musicale* (7 December 1834): 391. This unsigned article, a review of Cesare Pugni's ballet-pantomime 'La Dernière Heure d'un condamné' performed at the Théâtre-Nautique, immediately preceded by a review signed by Berlioz, is not included in *CM*, but its description of Smithson's private life could only have been known to Berlioz. In Julien Tiersot, *Hector Berlioz et la société de son temps* (Paris: Hachette, 1904), 54–8, the review is indeed attributed to Berlioz.

[34] For this reason, in an article treating Berlioz's engagement with *Othello*, Katherine Kolb assumes that Berlioz did not see the play in 1827. See Kolb, 'Berlioz's *Othello*', in *The Musical Voyager*, 241–62, esp. 249.

[35] *CG* VIII: 59–60. The lampooning occured in *Les Brioches à la mode*, with a Smithson character called 'Miss Qui Sonne'. See Sylvie Vielledent, *1830 aux théatres* (Paris: Honoré Champion, 2009), 75.

[36] Harriet, born on 18 March 1800, was three-and-a-half years older than Berlioz. As Juliet ('not yet fourteen') according to Shakespeare, she was, in 1827, thirteen years 'too old'. In the Mme Vergne edition of *Romeo and Juliet* we find 'not yet eighteen'.

[37] *La Quotidienne* (14 March 1836), cited in *CG* II: 289n.

[38] *CG* IV: 468.

[39] *CG* IV: 500.

[40] See, for example, *Galerie de Shakspeare, dessins pour ses œuvres dramatiques, graves à l'eau forte d'après Retzsch* (Paris: Audot, 1828.)

[41] Another *Pensées de Shakespeare* (Besançon: Metoyer, 1801) is also found at the Bibliothèque de l'Arsenal. This is a collection of 190 Shakespearean 'maxims' in 46 pages, none identified by the name of the play or character.

[42] *The Beauties of Shakspeare, regularly selected from each play*, ed. William Dodd (Paris: Baudry's European Library, 1839). The original edition appeared in 1752.

[43] Chateaubriand, *Essais sur la littérature anglaise* (Paris: Gosselin, 1839), I: 285.

[44] *CG* III: 207.

[45] *CG* III: 433 (to Michel Wielhorski, 1 June 1847).

[46] *CG* III: 547 (to Duc, 26 May 1848).

[47] *CM* I: 57 (6 October 1829) (from 3.1.70–3). The passage as quoted conforms to the 1827 English version published in Paris by Mme Vergne.

[48] *CM* IV: 194.

[49] *CG* I: 506.

[50] *Journal des débats* (6 March 1857), reprinted in Berlioz's third collection of articles, *À travers chants*, of 1862. I refer to the Léon Guichard's edition (Paris: Gründ, 1971), 253.

[51] *CM* I: 279 (18 October 1840).

[52] *CM* I: 70–2.

53 *CG* VII: 345.

54 *CG* III: 106 (15 June 1843).

55 The feuilleton is reprinted in *Les Soirées de l'orchestre* of 1853. I refer to Léon Guichard's edition (Paris: Gründ, 1968), 162.

56 Berlioz has paraphrased the Guizot translation.

57 The quotation is from *L'Art poétique*, Canto I, 183–6: if you fear public censure of your poetry (I paraphrase), be yourself its most severe critic. See Anselm Gerhard, 'De Boileau à Berlioz: Affinités sélectives', in *La Note bleue*, ed. Jacqueline Waeber (Bern: Peter Lang, 2006), 200–10.

58 *CG* V: 679.

59 *CG* VII: 58 (3 or 4 May 1864), citing *Hamlet*, 2.2.435–9.

60 *CM* IV: 383.

61 *CG* IV: 660.

62 *CG* VI: 72 (2 December 1859).

63 *À travers chants*, 302.

64 *CG* VI: 75.

65 *CG* VII: 102.

66 *CM* II: 59 (12 February 1835). Beethoven marked his second movement Allegretto, quarter note = 76, but later worried that the movement would be played too fast. See Gustav Nottebohm, *Beethoveniana* (Leipzig: Rieter-Biedermann, 1871), 21–2.

67 *Journal des débats* (13 March 1861). The article appears again as the penultimate chapter of *À travers chants*, 363–5.

68 *CM* IV: 185.

69 *CM* IV: 188.

70 *CG* III: 662. Berlioz uses this expression elsewhere as well, as in his letter to the Princess Wittgenstein of September 1855 (*CG* V: 140).

71 *Journal des débats* (19 June 1858); the article is reprinted in Berlioz's *Les Grotesques de la musique* [1859], ed. Léon Guichard (Paris: Gründ, 1969), 205.

72 *Œuvres complètes de Shakspeare*, trans. Francisque Michel, vol. 1 (Paris: H. Delloye, 1839), 85.

73 See, for example, *Roméo et Juliette*, trans. Victor Bougry, in Shakespeare, *Œuvres complètes*, vol. 1, ed. Michel Grivelet et al. (Paris: Laffont, 1995), 657; and *Roméo et Juliette*, trans. Jean-Michel Déprats, in Shakespeare, *Tragédies*, vol. 1, ed. Déprats (Paris: Gallimard, 2002), 417.

74 *Mémoires*, Chapter XXIX.

75 See *CG* III: 526. Berlioz again cites the expression – from *Othello* (5.2.235) – in Chapter LVII of the *Mémoires*.

76 *CG* II: 62.

77 *CM* I: 226–7.

78 The anecdote comes from Anton Schindler, Beethoven's not always reliable amanuensis. See Schindler, *Beethoven As I Knew Him*, ed. Donald MacArdle, trans. Constance Jolly (New York: Norton, 1966), 406.

79 *CG* VIII: 438.

80 The feuilleton of 3 July 1857 was taken over into *Les Grotesques de la musique*, here 209.

81   *CG* VI: 339; *CG* VII: 64.

82   *CG* VII: 138–9.

83   *CG* V: 402.

84   See Maurice Charney, 'Shakespeare's Unpoetic Poetry', in *Studies in English Literature, 1500–1900*, 13/2 (Spring 1973): 199–207, here 200.

85   *Journal des débats*, 24 October 1861; *À travers chants*, 235–6. Berlioz here extrapolates from *King Lear* (2.4.380 – 'Who stocked my servant' – to the end of the scene).

86   *CM* II: 82.

87   *CM* IV: 325 (17 May 1840).

88   *CG* IV: 404.

89   *CG* V: 669.

90   *CG* III: 583.

91   *CG* V: 448.

92   *Les Grotesques de la musique*, 252. Berlioz cites this passage elsewhere, in English, e.g. 24 March 1857; 21 September 1862. On 19 November 1848 (*CM* VI: 449) he had put it the other way round: 'le beau est horrible, l'horrible est beau'.

93   *CG* VI: 343.

94   *CG* V: 42–3.

95   *CG* V: 646.

96   *CG* V: 686.

97   *CG* V: 362–3.

98   *CG* V: 660.

99   *CG* VI: 51 (28 October 1859).

100 *CG* VI: 60–1.

101 *CG* VI: 85.

102 *CG* I: 351. To Ferrand in October 1830, he said the same thing: 'À sa taille élancée, à son vol capricieux, à sa grâce enivrante, à son génie musical, j'ai reconnu l'*Ariel* de Shakespeare' (*CG* I : 366). After his first concerts in Paris, in 1832, Frédéric Chopin was dubbed the 'Ariel du piano'.

103 *Les Soirées de l'orchestre*, 341.

104 The feuilleton of 24 September 1857 was taken over into *Les Grotesques de la musique*, here, 145–6.

105 *CM* I: 189 (11 March 1834).

106 *CM* II: 59 (12 February 1835). This analysis was taken over into *À travers chants*.

107 *CM* II: 59 (11 February 1838).

108 *CG* IV: 266 (14 January 1853).

109 On the Haydn (Hob. XXVIa: 34.4), see Katalin Komlós, 'Viola's Willow Song: She Never Told Her Love', *Musical Times*, 140 (1999): 36–41.

110 *CM* I: 210.

111 *CG* II: 68 (19 January 1833).

112 *Journal des débats* (5 October 1854); reprinted in *Les Grotesques de la musique*, 257.

113 *CG* IV: 593.

114 *CG* VI: 92–3.

115 See Katherine Kolb, 'The Berlioz-Wagner Dialogue', in *Hector Berlioz: Ein Franzose in Deutschland*, ed. Matthias Brzoska, Hermann Hofer, and Nicole Strohmann (Laaber: Laaber-Verlag, 2005), 310. Wagner did of course love

Shakespeare, and said at the end of his life, echoing Berlioz, that Shakespeare had been 'my only kindred spirit' ('meine einziger Geistes-Freund'). See Cosima Wagner, *Die Tagebücher*, ed. Martin Gregor-Dellin and Dietrich Mack (Munich: R. Piper, 1977), II: 948.

[116] *CG* VII: 376.

[117] *CM* I: 348 (*Richard III*, 5.4.7).

[118] *CM* VI: 200.

[119] *CG* VI: 337.

[120] *CM* I: 270.

[121] *Les Soirées de l'orchestre*, 452. Berlioz goes on to quote in English a long passage from *1 Henry IV* (5.1.129–41), then supplying a French translation. My translation slightly alters what is found in Berlioz, *Evenings with the Orchestra*, trans. and ed. Jacques Barzun (Chicago, IL: University of Chicago Press, 1999), 360.

[122] *CG* VII: 282.

[123] *Journal des débats* (25 April 1850): 1–2.

[124] *CG* VIII: 297.

[125] The article was taken over into *Les Grotesques de la musique*, 212.

[126] *CG* VII: 445.

[127] *Journal des débats* (8 September 1857).

[128] *CM* V: 538 (25 August 1844).

[129] *CG* VII: 37 (28 February 1864).

[130] Jean Boorsh writes these words of Victor Hugo, in 'Hugo's Fraternal Genius', *Yale French Studies*, 33 (1964): 67.

[131] From the song in Cole Porter's *Kiss Me, Kate*.

[132] *CM* III: 238 (a review of Georges Onslow's *Guise ou les États de Blois*).

[133] See Ann Slater, *Shakespeare the Director* (Totowa, NJ: Barnes and Noble, 1982).

[134] See D. Kern Holoman, 'Performing Berlioz', in *The Cambridge Companion to Berlioz*, 173.

[135] See *CG* II: 265.

[136] See Berlioz, *Grand Traité d'instrumentation et d'orchestration modernes*, ed. Peter Bloom (Kassel: Bärenreiter, 2003) [*NBE*, vol. 24], 490.

[137] Meredith Skura, *Shakespeare the Actor and the Purposes of Playing* (Chicago, IL: University of Chicago Press, 1993), 137.

[138] Samuel Taylor Coleridge, Lectures and Notes on Shakespeare and Other English Poets (London: George Bell and Sons, 1904), 350.

[139] See Xavier Eyma and Arthur de Lucy, *Écrivains et artistes vivants français et étrangers*, vol. 2 (Paris: Librairie universelle, 1840), 71.

[140] *CG* VIII: 522.

[141] *CG* VII: 213.

[142] *CG* VII: 214.

[143] *CG* VII: 309.

[144] *CG* VII: 317.

[145] *CG* VII: 635.

[146] Stephen Heller, *Lettres d'un musicien romantique à Paris*, ed. Jean-Jacques Eigeldinger (Paris: Flammarion, 1981), 252 (to Eduard Hanslick, 1 February 1879).

[147] August Barbier, *Souvenirs personnels et Silhouettes contemporaines* (Paris: Dentu, 1883), 232.

[148] *Les Soirées de l'orchestre*, 340.

[149] See (among other sources) Hugo, *Actes et Paroles*, in Hugo, *Œuvres completes*, ed. Seebacher et al., vol. 4: 561.

[150] The other members were Léon Carvalho, director of the Théâtre-Lyrique, Édouard Alexandre, the organ manufacturer, Nogent-Saint-Laurent, the lawyer, and Bressant, the actor. See *CG* VII: 168.

[151] Letter of 16 April 1864, cited by Bernard Leuilliot, ed., Hugo, *William Shakespeare* (Paris: Flammarion, 1973), 21.

[152] See Hugo to Paul Meurice, 2 May 1864, in *Œuvres complètes de Victor Hugo, Correspondance*, vol. II (Paris: Albin Michel, 1950), 471. A detailed accounting of the anniversary banquet may be found in Jean-Marc Hovasse, *Victor Hugo* (Paris: Fayard, 2008), II: 884–93.

[153] *CG* VII: 52. This letter must be dated 'after 16 April 1864' and was probably written on the 21st, since it took several days for the news of the cancellation to make the rounds.

[154] At the marriage of Pirithous, King of the Lapiths in Thessaly, a battle took place between the Centaurs and the Lapiths. Jouvin transforms the verb 'lapider' ('to stone') into 'lapither'. I follow suit.

[155] In his obituary of Berlioz for the *Revue des deux mondes* (15 April 1869), Henri Blaze de Bury wrote, 'J'ai vu des Anglais le consulter sur leur poète.'

[156] *CG* VI: 464. The Shakespeare quotation (Lorenzo, in *The Merchant of Venice*, 5.1.83–5) occurs shortly after the passage ('In such a night as this'; 5.1.1–24) upon which Berlioz built the main text of the love duet in Act 4 of *Les Troyens*.

[157] *CG* V: 379 (to his sister, 26 October 1856).

[158] *CG* I: 213.

[159] See *CG* I: 167 (a letter of 10 January 1829, misdated here as 1828).

[160] *CG* II: 63 (7 January 1833).

[161] *CG* II: 69.

[162] *CG* III: 459.

[163] Hugh Macdonald, *Berlioz* (London: Dent, 1982), 12.

[164] Jacques Barzun, *From Dawn to Decadence: 500 Years of Western Cultural Life* (New York: HarperCollins, 2000), 517.

[165] In a review of an opéra comique, Berlioz makes a triple pun on Chaix (the singer François-Amédée Chaix, the inventor of the railroad timetable Napoléon Chaix, and the first syllable of 'Shakespeare') and 'pires' – the sound of the second syllable of 'Shakespeare' and the word in French for 'worse' (*CM* VI: 149).

[166] See David Cairns, 'The Reboul-Berlioz Collection', in *Berlioz Studies*, ed. Peter Bloom (Cambridge: Cambridge University Press, 1992), 11.

[167] 'Villemain', in *Nouvelle Biographie universelle*, vol. 45 (Paris: Firmin Didot, 1866), col. 196.

[168] Nicola Vaccai (1790–1848), the middling Italian opera composer whom a modern scholar (Julian Budden in *Grove Music Online*) calls 'an honourable failure' and in whose *Giulietta e Romeo* Berlioz found 'neither colour nor passion' (*À travers chants*, 356).

169 *Théâtre Anglais, / ou / Collection / des pièces anglaises / jouées à Paris, publiées avec l'autorisation des directeurs / et entièrement conformes à la representation. / Anglais-Français. / Roméo et Juliette. / Prix: 3 fr. / À Paris, / chez Mme Vergne, Libraire-Éditeur, / Place de l'Odéon, n° 14 / Au théâtre, à la porte du foyer; / Et chez les Marchands de nouveautés. / 1827.* This copy, formerly at the Bibliothèque de l'Arsenal, is now held in the Département des Arts du spectacle at the Bibliothèque nationale de France (8-RE–8373). Another copy is at the Folger Shakespeare Library (PR2831 1827 Sh.Col.). In addition to Thomas Otway's *Venise sauvée*, Mme Vergne also brought out the two other non-Shakespeare plays given in Paris by Harriet Smithson's company, Nicolas Rowe's *Jane Shore* and James Sheridan Knowles's *Virginius*.

170 *CG* V: 379.

171 *CG* II: 240.

172 *CG* V: 126.

173 *CG* VII: 139.

174 Margaret Gilman, *Othello in French* (Paris: E. Champion, 1925), 114.

175 In the *Opinion Nationale* of 5 January 1862, Hector Malot accused Didier et Cie of hastily publishing a second edition of Guizot in order to compete with F.-V. Hugo. 'Un professeur' then wrote a defence of Didier et Cie. See *Shakspeare* [*sic*] *et ses traducteurs: MM. Guizot et François-V. Hugo* (Paris: Didier et Cie, 1862).

176 *CG* VIII: 521; *CG* VII: 279, 288.

177 Lacroix, *Histoire de l'influence de Shakespeare sur le théâtre français* (Bruxelles: Lesigne, 1856), 292–340.

178 See Gilman, *Othello*, 191–3; and Helen Bailey, *Hamlet in France* (Geneva: Droz, 1964), 161–2.

179 See Barry-Vincent Daniels, 'Shakespeare à la romantique', *Revue d'histoire du théâtre*, 106 (1975): 133, quoting *Le Globe* of 28 October 1829: '[…] chaque fois qu'il revient à sa terrible question: "le mouchoir?" ils ont osé rire du mot […].'

180 See Berlioz, *Benvenuto Cellini: Dossier de presse parisienne (1838)*, ed. Peter Bloom (Heilbron: Musik-Edition Lucie Galland, 1995), ix.

181 On this subject see in particular John Pemble, *Shakespeare Goes to Paris* (London: Hambledon and London, 2005), Chapter 4.

182 *Œuvres complètes de W. Shakespeare*, trans. François-Victor Hugo, vol. 1 (Paris: Pagnerre, 1865), 34.

183 *CM* V: 376–7. As noted above, 'Despair and die' from *Richard III* was one of Berlioz's favourite expressions.

184 See *NBE*, vol. 5. Gérard de Nerval's new translation of *Faust* Part I was announced in the *Journal de l'imprimerie et de la librairie* on 28 November 1827, but carries the date of 1828. See Gérard de Nerval, *Les Deux Faust de Goethe*, ed. Fernand Baldensperger (Paris: Honoré Champion, 1932), x.

185 The meaning of 'Miching mallecho' is hardly settled. Attached to the song of the flea, 'miching', for Berlioz, may have meant 'munching'. See Jane Crawford, 'Hamlet, III.ii.146,' *The Review of English Studies*, 18 (February 1967): 40–5.

186 Rainer Schmusch, 'Shakespeare and the Genesis of Programme Music: The Mottoes of Berlioz's *Huit Scènes de Faust*', in *The Musical Voyager*, 224–40.

187 See Hugh Macdonald, 'Berlioz's Lost *Roméo et Juliette*', in *Berlioz: Scenes from*

the Life and Work, ed. Peter Bloom (Rochester: University of Rochester, 2008), 125–37.

[188] In a letter to Ferrand of 16 April 1830 (*CG* I: 319) that features a first sketch of the programme of the *Symphonie fantastique*.

[189] The line should read 'How if, when I am laid into the tomb', but Berlioz quotes 'correctly' from the Mme Vergne edition of 1827 (98).

[190] *CG* I: 270.

[191] *CG* I: 267 (12 August 1829).

[192] Katherine Kolb, 'Berlioz's *Othello*', in *The Musical Voyager*.

[193] The autograph manuscript of the *Fantastique* itself bears witness to Berlioz's first reading of *Lear* in the form of a quotation from the play (4.1.36–7) in the Guizot translation: 'Nous sommes aux dieux ce que sont les mouches / aux folâtres enfans/ ils nous tuent pour s'amuser. / (Roi Lear / Shakespeare).'

[194] *CG* VI: 432 (18 April 1863).

[195] *CG* VI: 436 (26 April 1863).

[196] *CG* V: 610 – referring, clearly, to *Lear*, Act 1 scene 1, although the king enters to a 'sennet', or trumpet call. Berlioz adds: 'I intended to evoke his madness only towards the middle of the Allegro, when the basses take up the theme from the Introduction in the middle of the storm' (mm. 340–410).

[197] See *NBE*, 7: ix.

[198] *NBE*, 7: 234–5 (original libretto; my translation).

[199] The quotation is in the Mme Vergne translation except for the word *songes*, which replaces Mme Vergne's *rêves*.

[200] *NBE*, 7: 235.

[201] *NBE*, 7: 239.

[202] *CG* IV: 723–4.

[203] *NBE*, 7: 239.

[204] *CG* III: 492, citing Hamlet's praise of Horatio's reserve in the second scene with the players: 'Give me that man / That is not passion's slave, and I will wear him / In my heart's core, ay, in my heart of heart' (3.2.71–3).

[205] *CG* II: 184.

[206] Bourgault-Ducoudray's recollections (published in 1886) are cited in Michael Rose, *Berlioz Remembered* (London: Faber & Faber, 2001), 242.

[207] The article, by J.-A. David, is cited in *CG* II: 225n.

[208] Barzun, I: 301.

[209] See his essay on *Romeo and Juliet* in *À travers chants*, 353.

[210] *CG* I: 418.

[211] *CM* IV: 277 (15 March 1840).

[212] *CM* IV: 24 (17 February 1839).

[213] *NBE*, 18: 2.

[214] *CG* V: 478.

[215] See Ian Kemp, '*Romeo and Juliet* and *Roméo et Juliette*', in *Berlioz Studies*, 37–79.

[216] *CG* VII: 326 (4 November 1865, to Estelle Fornier). The translation appears to be Berlioz's own.

[217] See Jean-Pierre Bartoli, 'Beethoven, Shakespeare, and Berlioz's *Scène d'amour*', in *Berlioz: Scenes from the Life and Work*, 138–60.

218 *NBE*, 18: 253.

219 Daniel Albright, *Berlioz's Semi-Operas* (Rochester, NY: University of Rochester Press, 2001), esp. 73–7.

220 *CG* V: 667 (10 March 1859).

221 *CM* VI: 212 (30 August 1846). Berlioz paraphrases Shakespeare's 'My bounty is as boundless as the sea, / My love as deep' (2.2.133–4).

222 *Journal des débats* (13 September 1859), reprinted in *À travers chants*, 349–60.

223 *À travers chants*, 359. 'O potent poison' is not said in *Romeo and Juliet*; Berlioz is thinking of *Hamlet*: 'O, I die, Horatio, / The potent poison quite o'er-crows my spirit' (5.2.353–4).

224 See Heather Hadlock, 'Berlioz, Ophelia, and Feminist Hermeneutics', in *Berlioz: Past, Present, Future*, ed. Peter Bloom (Rochester, NY: University of Rochester Press, 2003), 123–34.

225 Julian Rushton, *The Music of Berlioz* (Oxford: Oxford University Press, 2001), 280.

226 *CG* V: 77 (30 April 1855). Berlioz is thinking of *3 Henry VI*, where, to his son the Duke of Gloucester, who will become Richard III, Henry says, before Gloucester stabs him: 'Teeth hadst thou in thy head when thou wast born, / To signify thou cam'st to bite the world' (5.6.53–4).

227 *CG* V: 363.

228 See the 'Dix-huitième Lettre' in Voltaire, *Lettres philosophiques*, ed. Raymond Naves (Paris: Garnier frères, 1964), 104–9. Were Voltaire to utter such views at the current time, Berlioz wrote in 1837, one would 'laugh in his face' (*CM* III: 265).

229 *CG* V: 357.

230 *CG* V: 316.

231 The sketch for the love duet is reproduced in Catherine Massip, *Le Livre de musique* (Paris: Bibliothèque nationale de France, 2007), 99.

232 See James, 'Berlioz the poet?', 72.

233 See Camille Slights, 'In Defense of Jessica: The Runaway Daughter in *The Merchant of Venice*', *Shakespeare Quarterly*, 31 (1980): 359.

234 Laroche, *Œuvres dramatiques de Shakspeare*, 1: vii: 'les types de tout amour, de tout charme et de toute pureté. [...] ces types suaves et poétiques.'

235 *CG* VI: 174.

236 *CG* VI: 319 (to the Princess Wittgenstein).

237 *CG* VII: 139.

238 *Mémoires*, Postface.

239 Andrew Porter wrote a review of a performance of the work in *The New Yorker* (17 December 1979), 171–2.

240 See Skura, *Shakespeare the Actor*, 156–7.

241 *CG* VI: 320 (to the Princess Wittgenstein, 22 July 1862).

242 *CG* II: 68 (19 January 1833).

243 See *NBE*, 3: 299–300.

244 See Peter Bloom, 'Un épisode (politique) de la vie de Berlioz', in *Musique, esthétique et société en France au XIXe siècle*, ed. Damien Colas, Florence Gétreau, and Malou Haine (Wavre: Margada, 2007), 231.

245 Victor Hugo as cited by Pemble, *Shakespeare Goes to Paris*, 15.

246 Jonathan Bate, *Shakespeare and the English Romantic Imagination* (Oxford:

Clarendon Press, 1986), 247, quoting David Cairns's translation of this passage from Chapter XLIX of the *Mémoires* (which I have slightly modified). By 'us' Berlioz refers to Harriet Smithson and himself. In the Latin quotation from Psalm 129, Berlioz scrupulously omits the word 'Domine'.

247 Philarète Chasles, 'Le Théâtre anglais à Paris', *Revue Contemporaine*, 20 (June 1855): 339–53, here, 341 ('Nous avons renoncé à Shakespeare et à ses pompes').

248 *Mémoires*, Chapter LVI.

Notes on Chapter 2

1 David Rosen and Andrew Porter (eds), *Verdi's Macbeth: A Sourcebook*, (New York: W. W. Norton & Company, 1984), 119. An extremely valuable reference book, hereafter Rosen and Porter.

2 Rosen and Porter, xiii.

3 Frank Kermode (ed.), *Four Centuries of Shakespearean Criticism*, (New York: Avon Library, 1965), 73. Translator uncredited.

4 Victor Hugo, *La Préface de Cromwell*, ed. Maurice Souriau (Paris: Bloivin, n.d.), 22–3. Translated by me.

5 Kermode, *Four Centuries of Shakespearean Criticism*, 536–7.

6 Rosen and Porter, 346–8; August Wilhelm Schlegel, *Sämmtliche Werke* VI, ed. Eduard Böcking (Hildesheim: Georg Olms, 1971), 254–6.

7 Rosen and Porter, 8.

8 Rosen and Porter, 54.

9 Francis Toye, *Giuseppe Verdi* (New York: Vintage Books, 1959), 250–1.

10 Julian Budden, *The Operas of Verdi*, 3 vols (New York: Oxford University Press, 1973–81), 1: 212, 217.

11 Budden, *Verdi*, 3: 505.

12 Rosen and Porter, 56.

13 Verdi, *Ernani*, from http://www.giuseppeverdi.it/stampabile.asp?IDCategoria= 162&IDSezione=581&ID=19851 (my translation).

14 Verdi, *Attila*, from http://www.giuseppeverdi.it/ing/page.asp?IDCategoria=162 &IDSezione=581&ID=19844 (my translation).

15 Gary Schmidgall, *Shakespeare and Opera* (New York: Oxford University Press, 1990), 14.

16 Verdi *Macbeth*, from http://www.giuseppeverdi.it/page.asp?IDCategoria=162&I DSezione=581&ID=19898, as are all subsequent quotations from the libretto of *Macbeth;* all translations from this libretto are mine.

17 Marjorie Garber, 'Shakespeare's "New Gorgon"', in *The Medusa Reader*, ed. Marjorie Garber and Nancy J. Vickers (New York: Routledge, 2003), 249–57.

18 Letter of 7 Jan. 1847, in Rosen and Porter, 30–1.

19 Rosen and Porter, 40.

20 Rosen and Porter, 51.

21 Rosen and Porter, 110.

22 Rosen and Porter, 84.

23 Jonas Barish, 'Madness, Hallucination, and Sleepwalking', in Rosen and Porter, 154.

[24] Jane Bernstein, '"Bewitched, bothered and bewildered": Lady Macbeth, sleep-walking and the demonic in Verdi's Scottish opera', *Cambridge Opera Journal* 14, 1 & 2 (2002): 36, 45.

[25] Letter of 3 Feb. 1865, Rosen and Porter, 97.

[26] Boito, *Nerone,* 17 from http://dante.di.unipi.it/ricerca/libretti/neroneb.html (translated by me).

[27] Gide, *Les caves du Vatican,* 698, from http://fr.wikisource.org/wiki/Page:NRF_11. djvu/698.

[28] Letter to Count Arrivabene, 20 March 1879, from http://www.magiadellopera. com/pdf/aavv_pdf/BOITO%20ARRIGO.pdf, 15 (translated by me).

[29] *Arrigo Boito,* 208–9, http://www.magiadellopera.com/pdf/aavv_pdf/ BOITO%20ARRIGO.pdf (translated by me).

[30] *Amleto,* 20, from http://www.librettidopera.it/zpdf/amleto.pdf (translated by me).

[31] W. H. Auden, *The Dyer's Hand* (New York: Random House, 1962), 258.

[32] Verdi, *Otello,* from http://www.giuseppeverdi.it/page.asp?IDCategoria=162&ID Sezione=581&ID=19930#AT2S1. All subsequent passages from the libretto are from this text, and all translations by me.

[33] James Hepokoski, *Guiseppe Verdi: Otello* (Cambridge: Cambridge University Press, 1987), 185.

[34] Letter of 15 August 1880, *The Verdi-Boito Correspondence,* ed. Marcello Conati and Mario Medici, tr. William Weaver (Chicago, IL: University of Chicago Press, 1994), 4.

[35] Letter of 18 October 1880, *Verdi-Boito Correspondence,* 7.

[36] James Hepokoski, *Giuseppe Verdi: Falstaff* (Cambridge: Cambridge University Press, 1983), 20.

[37] *I copialettere di Giuseppe Verdi,* ed. Gaetano Cesari and Alessandro Luzio (Milan, 1913), 712, translated by me.

[38] http://www.magiadellopera.com/pdf/aavv_pdf/BOITO%20ARRIGO.pdf, p.13.

[39] Boito, *Mefistofele,* http://opera.stanford.edu/Boito/Mefistofele/atto1.html (translated by me).

[40] Hepokoski, *Falstaff,* 117.

[41] Hepokoski, *Falstaff,* 126.

[42] Verdi, *Falstaff,* from http://www.giuseppeverdi.it/stampabile.asp?IDCategoria= 162&IDSezione=581&ID=20353. All quotations from the libretto are from this source; all translations are mine.

[43] Igor Stravinsky and Robert Craft, *Conversations with Igor Stravinsky* (Berkeley, CA: University of California Press, 1980), 75.

Notes on Chapter 3

[1] Wagner to Eliza Willie, 9 September 1864, Starnberg, *Richard Wagner: Sämtliche Briefe,* ed. Gertrud Strobel, Werner Wolf (vols. 1–5), Hans-Joachim Bauer and Johannes Forner (vols. 6–8), Klaus Burmeister and Johannes Former (vol.

9), Andreas Mielke (vol. 10), Martin Dürrer (vols. 11–13, 16), and Andreas Mielke (vols. 14–15). Leipzig: Deutscher Verlag für Musik 1967–2000 (vols. 1–9); Wiesbaden, Leipzig and Paris: Breitkopf & Härtel, 2000– (vols. 10–), 16: 296–7. Hereafter *SB*. All translations are mine unless otherwise indicated.

2   *Cosima Wagner: Die Tagebücher*, 2 vols (Munich and Zurich: R. Piper & Co. Verlag, 1976–7); Eng. trans. Geoffrey Skelton, *Cosima Wagner's Diaries*, ed. Martin Gregor-Dellin and Dietrich Mack, 2 vols. (London: Collins, 1978). I use Skelton's excellent translation throughout, but cite only the entry dates for ease of reference between editions: 26 May 1871. Hereafter, *CT*.

3   *CT*, 21 July 1877.

4   *CT*, 28 November 1870.

5   'Shakespeare is the truest picture of the world. *Faust* is a commentary on that picture, a commentary on the Shakespeare.' *CT*, 3 September, 1874.

6   *CT*, 8 September 1880.

7   *Richard Wagner: Sämtliche Schriften und Dichtungen*, ed. Richard Sternfeld, 16 vols (Leipzig: Breitkopf & Härtel, and C. F. W. Siegel, 1911 [vols. 1–12], 1914 [vols. 13–16]), 1: 109. Hereafter *SSD*. Cf. Eng. trans. William Ashton Ellis, *Richard Wagner's Prose Works* (Lincoln, NE, and London: University of Nebraska Press, 1995), 7: 40. Hereafter *PW*.

8   Nicholas Vazsonyi, *Richard Wagner: Self-Promotion and the Making of a Brand* (Cambridge: Cambridge University Press, 2010), 32.

9   'We cannot but become aware that, of these worlds, the one completely covers the other, so that each is contained in each, no matter how remote their spheres may seem.' *SSD* 9: 107. Cf. *PW* 5: 107.

10 Lawrence Kramer, 'The strange case of Beethoven's "Coriolan": romantic aesthetics, modern subjectivity, and the cult of Shakespeare', *Musical Quarterly* 79 (1995): 256–80, here 257.

11 *SSD* 3: 110, 161. Cf. *PW* 1: 141, 195.

12 *CT*, 31 July 1870. See also *CT*, 4 December 1880.

13 Wagner to Hans von Bülow, 30 January 1852, Zurich, *SB* 4: 275.

14 *SSD* 9: 107. Cf. 5: 108.

15 Wagner's letter to Hans von Bülow indicates the extent to which Wagner bent reality to his will: 'I almost prefer *his* poem of Coriolanus to Shakespeare's, at least with regard to its artistic conception, since it has a graphic unity and succinctness which almost allows the subject-matter to achieve the sensuality of myth.' Wagner to Hans von Bülow, 30 January 1852, Zurich, *SB* 4: 276.

16 H. von Collin was to be the librettist, and Beethoven was to base the opera on Shakespeare's play this time. His sketches for the planned opera date from 1809–11. The overture for the opera has been recreated in a highly speculative realization by Albert Willem Holsbergen using themes from the Ghost trio. See http://www.nytimes.com/2001/08/23/arts/beethoven-s-macbeth-bubbles-to-the-surface.html [accessed 6 July 2011].

17 'Melodie comp. v. Shakespeare' entered in Cosima's diary on 24 January 1882. See Hs 220 in the Nationalarchiv, Bayreuth.

18 *SSD* 4: 9. Cf. *PW* 2: 127.

19 *SSD* 4: 9. Cf. *PW* 2: 127.

20 Ibid., Wagner's articulation plays on the German compound 'Schauspieler'

('actor'), namely 'schauen' ('to look') and 'spielen' ('to play'). He draws authority from the term's suspected etymology, which, in hobbling translation, turns an actor into a *visual*-player, not dissimilar to the 'strolling players' who performed plays in Tudor England, and whose identity continued into the nineteenth century, even gaining mention in such realist literature as Thomas Hardy's *Far from the Madding Crowd* (1874).

21 *SSD* 4: 9. Cf. *PW* 2: 128.

22 *SSD* 4: 11. Cf. *PW* 2: 129.

23 *SSD* 4: 12. Cf. *PW* 2: 130.

24 *SSD* 4: 12. Cf. *PW* 2: 130.

25 *SSD* 4: 17. Cf. *PW* 2: 136.

26 '[O]n the more recent English stage, people translated Shakespeare's scenes into the most realistic actuality; wonders of mechanism were invented for the rapid change of the most elabourate stage scenery: marches of troops and mimicry of battles were presented with astonishing exactitude. This was copied in larger German theatres.' *SSD* 4: 19. Cf. *PW* 2: 47.

27 *SSD* 4: 19. Cf. *PW* 2: 139.

28 It is unclear exactly what Wagner means by *reflektierten Gestaltung des Dramas* (*SSD* 4: 19). He explains that the modern poet turns 'more or less involuntarily to the reflective form of drama in order to actualize in a practical way his fantasy [*Phantasiebild*]'. This relates to the Aristotelian doctrine of unity within the *Poetics*, and was recognized in the mid-century as pseudo-antique drama, Wagner explains. His use of the adjective 'reflective' elsewhere in *Opera and Drama* relates it, negatively, to process of conscious cognition, which – for Wagner – precludes the proper reception of art.

29 Cosima's diary records the details between 1869–82. While some, such as Tony Palmer, reject the doctored text as invalid evidence for the Wagners' opinions, its detailing and partly verifiable list of events (from visits to communal readings, composition to concerts) remains largely undisputed as a record of fact. Palmer flaps ad absurdum: 'we don't know precisely what … Wagner said to Cosima as he was pulling off her knickers. We know what Cosima would *like* us to think they said to each other. … If we are to believe her, they discussed Schopenhauer and the finer points of vegetarianism while having sex. … The point is that to rely on what appear to be "the facts" in reconstructing historical truths is a blind alley for the dumb. You have to face the fact that you are dealing with fiction.' Tony Palmer, 'Forward' *Wagner & Cinema*, ed. Jeongwon Joe & Sander L. Gilman (Bloomington and Indianapolis: University of Indiana Press, 2010), xi–xii.

30 Wagner's uncle translated into Germany both Augustine Skottowe, *The Life of Shakespeare: Enquiries into the Originality of his Plots and Characters*, 2 vols (London: Paternoster-Row, 1824) and Anna Jameson, *Characteristic of the Women: Moral, Poetical, and Historical* (London: Saunders and Otley, 1832).

31 See WWV 1 in *Wagner Werk-Verzeichnis*, ed. John Deathridge, Martin Geck, and Egon Voss (Mainz, London, New York, Tokyo: Schott, 1986), 63–4.

32 Wagner, *My Life*, trans. Andrew Gray, ed. Mary Whittall (Cambridge, New York, Melbourne: Cambridge University Press, 1983), 26. Hereafter, *ML*.

33 *ML*, 25–6.

[34] See Werner Habicht, 'Shakespeare and the German imagination: cult, controversy, and performance', in *Shakespeare: World Views* (Newark, DE: University of Delaware Press, 1996), 87–101.

[35] *CT*, 14 June 1874.

[36] *SSD* 5: 108. Cf. *PW* 5: 109.

[37] *SSD* 9: 109. Cf. *PW* 5: 110. The text of Schopenhauer's on which Wagner is drawing is the 'Essay on Spirit Seeing' in *Parerga and Paralipomena: Short Philosophical Essays*, trans. E. F. J. Payne, 2 vols. (Oxford: Oxford Univ. Press, 2000), 1: 225–310.

[38] *SSD* 9: 79. Cf. *PW* 5: 78–9.

[39] *SSD* 5: 108, 110. Cf. *PW* 5: 108, 110–11.

[40] *SSD* 9: 68–9. Cf. *PW* 5: 67–9.

[41] Ibid.

[42] *CT*, 26 May 1871.

[43] See WWV 38, in *Wagner Werk-Verzeichnis*, 131–43, here 140.

[44] *ML*, 119.

[45] At the time of writing, Klaus Döge is in the process of editing the first act of *Das Liebesverbot* for a critical edition in the Wagner *Sämtliche Werke* series published by Schott, which is due to appear in the coming years. See the SW newsletter from 2010: http://www.adwmainz.de/fileadmin/adwmainz/MuKo_Berichte/JB_2010/Wagner-10-HP.pdf [accessed 24 June 2011].

[46] *SSD* 1: 10. Cf. *PW* 1: 10. Wagner gives an account of his intention towards *Measure for Measure* in all three of his autobiographies, from 1843, 1851, and 1865. In addition to that just quoted, see also *SSD* 4: 254–5 and *ML*, 83ff..

[47] *ML*, 83.

[48] *ML*, 113.

[49] 'It was Isabella who inspired me: she who leaves her novitiate in the nunnery to beg for mercy for her brother from a hardhearted governor... [her] chaste soul urges on the stony judge such cogent reasons for pardoning the offence, her growing feeling knows to present these reasons with such a gorgeous warmth that the stern protector of morals is himself seized with passionate love for the glorious woman.' *SSD* 4: 254. Cf. *PW* 1: 295.

[50] 'Der Tanzist nach jedem Verse immer feuriger und wilder geworden.' Act 2, Finale (no. 11), *Das Liebesverbot*, vocal score (Wiesbaden: Breitkopf & Härtel, 1922), 511.

[51] Edgar Istel, 'Wagner and Shakespeare' *Musical Quarterly* 8 (1922): 498.

[52] *CT*, 3 May 1880.

[53] 'Wir—tief entwürdigt durch das gräuliche Überhandnehmen abscheulicher Lüderlichkeiten und Lasterhaftigkeiten in unserer gottlosen und verderbten Stadt, fühlen uns zur Wiederherstellung eines reineren und gottgefälligeren Wandels, sowie zur Verhütung größerer Ausschweifungen bewogen, mit exemplarischer Strenge den Grund und die Wurzel des Übels zu vertilgen. Wir befehlen Kraft der uns übertragenen Gewalt hiermit: 'Der Carnival, dieses üppige und lasterhafte Fest, ist aufgehoben, und bei Todesstrafe jede Gebräuchlichkeit desselben verboten; alle Wirtschaften und Belustigungörter sollen, aufgehoben und geräumt warden, und jedes Vergehen des Trunkes, sowie des Liebe, werde fortan mit dem Tode bestraft.' Wagner, *Das Liebesverbot*, vocal score (Wiesbaden: Breitkopf & Härtel, 1922), 36.

54 *ML*, 118.
55 Ibid.
56 Ibid., (translation modified).
57 For a study of political censorship during the *Vormärz* and the means by which authors sought to resist its encroachment, see Katy Heady, *Literature and Censorship in Restoration Germany: Repression and Rhetoric* (Rochester NY: Camden House, 2009).
58 *SSD* 1: 14. Cf. *PW* 1: 14.
59 *ML*, 182.
60 *SSD* 1: 16. Cf. PW 1: 16–17.
61 Kenneth E. Larson, 'The origins of the "Schlegel-Tieck" Shakespeare in the 1820s' *The German Quarterly* 60 (1987): 30ff.
62 Curt von Westernhagen, *Richard Wagners Dresdener Bibliothek: 1842 bis 1849* (Wiesbaden: F. A. Brockhaus, 1966), 103. The earliest edition of the Schlegel/Tieck translation in Wagner's possession is something of a mystery because the extant 1851–2 edition must have been added to Wagner's Dresden library only after the composer sold it to Heinrich Brockhaus in 1849. Given Brockhaus's desire to maintain the integrity of the collection, a likely scenario is that he replaced an earlier Schlegel/Tieck edition of Shakespeare, which Wagner owned, and which had somehow been detached from the library, with a later edition, that of 1851–2. Notes corroborating this hypothesis exist in the Bayreuth archives, though for the moment no proof has come to light either way.
63 A useful summary is given in Larson, 'The origin of the 'Schlegel-Tieck' Shakespeare,' 19–23.
64 Ibid., 20.
65 *CT*, 14 November 1878.
66 Ibid.. See also *CT*, 6 February 1881.
67 Christoph Martin Wieland, *Wielands Gesammelte Schriften*, ed. by the German commission of the Royal Prussian Academy of Sciences, 28 vols. (Berlin: Wiedmannsche Buchandlung, 1909-), II.1: 264.
68 Peter Wenzel's statement leans on evidence from a survey of German translations: 'in a recent linguistic study of the reliability of five German Shakespeare translations, Schlegel still comes off better than two of the modern translators.' See 'German Shakespeare Translation: The State of the Art,' in *Images of Shakespeare: Proceedings of the Third Congress of the International Shakespeare Association,* ed. Werner Habicht, D. J. Palmer, and Roger Pringel (Newark, Del.: Univ. of Delaware Press, 1988), 314–23, here 315.
69 *SSD* 4: 105–6. Cf. *PW* 2: 242.
70 Tannhäuser's verse concludes with the lines: 'Aus deinem Reiche muss ich fliehn! / O Koenigin! Goettin, lass' mich ziehn!' three times, where each verse (in rhyming couplets) rises by a semitone.
71 Act 1, Finale (no. 6), *Das Liebesverbot* vocal score (Wiesbaden: Breiftkopf & Härel, 1922), 251–62. Friedrich's pithy interjections also exaggerate the poetic metre with their rhyming couplets and musically dotted rhythms ('Die Schwesterliebe ehre ich, / doch Gnade hab' ich nicht fuer dich.' ['I honour your sisterly love,/but I can offer you no mercy.']).

[72] 'I took no trouble whatsoever to avoid sounding French and Italian.' *SSD* 1: 11. Cf. *PW* 1: 10–11.

[73] *SSD* 12: 2. Cf. *PW* 8: 56.

[74] *SSD* 12: 1. Cf. *PW* 8: 55.

[75] *SSD* 12: 3. Cf. *PW* 8: 57–8.

[76] Wagner's essay 'De L'Ouverture' was published in the *Gazette et revue musicale* (10, 14, 17 January 1841). See *SSD* 1: 194–206. Cf. *PW* 7: 153–65.

[77] For further consideration of his, see Thomas S. Grey, '*Meister* Richard's apprenticeship: the early operas (1833–1840)' in *The Cambridge Companion to Richard* Wagner, ed. Thomas S. Grey (Cambridge: Cambridge Univ. Press, 2008), 18–46, here 28. For Wagner's view of *Zampa* in Vienna, see *ML*, 62–3.

[78] *SSD* 4: 200. Cf. *PW* 2: 346.

[79] Thomas S. Grey, 'Richard Wagner and the Legacy of French Grand Opera,' *The Cambridge Companion to Grand Opera*, ed. David Charlton (Cambridge and New York: Cambridge Univ. Press, 2003), 321–43, here 324.

[80] Carl Dahlhaus, *Nineteenth-Century Music*, trans. J. Bradford Robinson (Berkeley and Los Angeles: Univ. of California Press, 1991), 177.

[81] Geoffrey Skelton, 'Das Liebesverbot. International Youth Festival Meeting' *The Musical Times* 114 (1973): 805.

[82] *CT*, 1 March 1869.

[83] *SSD* 5: 177. Cf. *PW* 3: 230.

[84] Alonso is at once deaf to the sound ('I heard nothing' I, 2: 310), and sensible to it ('What harmony is this?' III, 3: 18), depending on Ariel's whim. Despite Caliban's earthy singing and corrective chastisement of Stephano and Trinculo ('That's not the tune' III, 2: 117), he never truly sees or hears Ariel, reporting only the spirit's torment of him: 'the isle is full of noises,/Sounds, and sweet airs, that give delight and hurt not./Sometimes a thousand twanging instruments/Will hum about mine ears; and sometimes voices' (III, 2: 127–30). Only Prospero, by his own order, sees Ariel as s/he is: 'Be subject to/No sight but thine and mine, invisible/To every eye-ball else.' (III, 2: 302–4).

[85] One of the earliest was Eduard Kulke, 'Semele und Lohengrin: eine Parallele,' *Anregungen für Kunst, Leben und Wissenschaft* 6 (1861): 41–6, 77–90.

[86] Carl Meinck, 'Shakespeare und Wagner. Zusamenhänge, Vergleichungen, Parallelen' *Bayreuther Blätter* 39 (1917): 120ff. Regarding this study, Edgar Istel remarks dismissively: 'there is no particular sense in seeking after disconnected reminiscences ... I regret my inability, by reason of artistic scruples, to join in this sort of research-work; the decisive factor is not the words, which are often a mere furtive echo, but the spirit.' Istel 'Wagner and Shakespeare' *Musical Quarterly* 8 (1922): 495–509, here 503–4.

[87] Yvonne Nilges, *Richard Wagners Shakespeare* (Würzburg: Königshausen & Neumann, 2007), 138–69.

[88] *CT*, 8 March 1881.

[89] For a thoroughgoing study of Hellenic influences on Wagner, and Wagner's appropriation of his Hellenic sources, see Daniel Foster, *Wagner's* Ring *Cycle and the Greeks* (Cambridge: Cambridge Univ. Press, 2010).

[90] Cited in Roger Paulin, *Ludwig Tieck: a Literary Biography* (Oxford: Clarendon Press, 1985), 242.

91 Karl von Holtei, *Briefe an Ludwig Tieck* (Breslau, 1864), 3: 227.
92 Christian Ditrich Grabbe, 'Über die Shakespearo-Manie,' *Werke und Briefe.*
   Historisch-kritische Gesamtausgabe, ed. Alfred Bergman, 6 vols., (Goettingen:
   Emsdetten, 1966), 4: 29–56.
93 'Wir wollen den Engländer Shakespeare gleichsam *ent*englisiren, wir wollen
   ihn *verdeutschen*, verdeutschen im weitesten und tiefsten Sinne des Worts, d.
   h. wir wollen nach Kräften dazu beitragen, dass er das, was er bereits ist, ein
   deutscher Dichter, immer mehr im wahrsten und vollsten Sinne des Worts *werde*.'
   Hermann Ulrici, 'Jahresbericht', *Shakespeare Jahrbuch* 2 (1867): 1–15, here 3.
94 'das Daguerreotyp des geschichtlichen Tatsachen.' *SSD* 4: 23. Cf. *PW* 2: 143.
95 *CT*, 27 March 1882.
96 *CT*, 9 January 1871. See also Wagner's comment on *Henry IV*: 'all of it the simple
   truth, like Nature herself.' *CT*, 5 February 1881.
97 *CT*, 31 January 1870.
98 *CT*, 27 May 1882.
99 *CT*, 13 September 1881.

Notes on Chapter 4

1 See Wes Folkerth, *The Sound of Shakespeare* (London: Routledge, 2002), 91–8 for
  a particularly interesting account of 'Bottom's ear' (as opposed to ears). For a
  larger, groundbreaking approach to the sound and soundscape of Shakespeare's
  plays, see Bruce R. Smith, *The Acoustic World of Early Modern England: Attending
  to the O-Factor* (Chicago, IL: University of Chicago Press, 1999), particularly Ch.
  8, 'Within the Wooden O', 206–45.
2 I am referring here to the structuralist conception of myth; see Claude
  Levi-Strauss, 'The Structural Study of Myth', in *Structural Anthropology*, trans.
  Clair Jacobson and Brooke Grundfest Shoepf (New York: Basic Books, 1963),
  vol. 1: 217–18. The complete passage is worth citing here:

  > Thus, our method eliminates a problem which has been so far one of the
  > main obstacles to the progress of mythological studies, namely, the quest
  > for the *true* version, or the *earlier* one. On the contrary, we define the
  > myth as consisting of all its versions; to put it otherwise: a myth remains
  > the same as long as it is felt as such … An important consequence
  > follows. If a myth is made up of all its variants, structural analysis should
  > take all of them into account …

3 Happily, one of the most thorough and wide-ranging accounts of the theatrical
  afterlife of any Shakespeare play concerns the *Dream*. See Gary Jay Williams, *Our
  Moonlight Revels: A Midsummer Night's Dream in the Theatre* (Iowa: University of
  Iowa Press, 1997).
4 To my knowledge, the most extensive dream-collection remains the work of
  Calvin S. Hall, a professor at Case Western Reserve University, who over four
  decades beginning in the mid–1940s managed to collect over 50,000 dream
  reports. See C. S. Hall and R. van de Castle, *The Content Analysis of Dreams* (New
  York: Appleton-Century-Crofts, 1966).

[5] Sigmund Freud, 'A note upon the "mystic writing-pad"' (1925), in *The Standard Edition of the Complete Psychological Works*, ed. and trans. James Strachey, 24 vols (London: Hogarth Press, 1961), 19: 227–32.

[6] For an interesting exploration of Freud's *Wunderblock*, and his model of the psyche, from the perspective of media theory, see Thomas Elsaesser, 'Freud as media theorist: mystic writing-pads and the matter of memory', *Screen* 50.1 (Spring 2009): 101–13.

[7] Admittedly, this claim must be qualified; Shakespeare's play has had a quite complicated (cosmicomic?) musical afterlife. There is a famous masque (Henry Purcell's *The Fairy Queen* of 1692); there are 'operatized' versions (Garrick's intensely abbreviated adaptations of 1755–63, with music written and/or collected by John Christopher Smith, and Frederick Reynold's versions of 1816 and 1833); there are mini-operas based entirely on the 'Pyramus and Thisbe' skit (Richard Leveridge's now lost treatment from 1716, and John Frederic Lampe's marvellously cheeky 'mock-opera' from 1745); there are actual operas, largely from the nineteenth century (Franz von Suppé, 1844; Ambroise Thomas, 1850). And there is of course the play's musical 'long tail': the vast collection of incidental music for the comedy, which would have included (now lost) music for its original production; the iconic score of Felix Mendelssohn (1826, 1842) and its bizarre adaptation by Eric Wolfgang Korngold for Max Reinhardt's Hollywood film from 1935; the profoundly discomfiting score by Carl Orff, commissioned to replace the now-banned Mendelssohn score; there is even a score (apparently unpublished) for incidental *Dream* music by British composer Thea Musgrave – from 1960, the year of Britten's opera. For the complete exploration to date of the play's musical treatment, see Ulrike Küpper, *William Shakespeare's A Midsummer Night's Dream in the History of Music Theater* (Frankfurt: Lang Verlag, 2011).

[8] See Noël Goodwin, 'Brannigan, Owen', in *The New Grove Dictionary of Opera*, Grove Music Online, available at http://www.oxfordmusiconline.com/subscriber/article/grove/music/03847, (accessed 8 December 2010).

[9] Harold Bloom, *Shakespeare: The Invention of the Human* (New York: Riverhead Books, 1998), 151.

[10] Charles Knight, 'A Midsummer Night's Dream', in *Studies of Shakspere: Fanning a Companion Volume* (London: 1849), 232–3.

[11] G. K. Chesterton, 'A Midsummer Night's Dream' [1904], reprinted in *The Common Man* (London: Sheed and Ward, 1950), 10–21.

[12] Stephen Pinker, *How the Mind Works* (London: Penguin Books, 1997), 289–90. See also Mark Solms, 'A Psychoanalytic Perspective on Confabulation', *Neuropsychoanalysis* 2 (2000): 133–8, in particular the following account on 135:

> … the female patient mentioned above (Case F) believed that she had done things the night before that she could not possibly have done (e.g., joined an all-night party at home while we knew she had been asleep in her hospital bed). In her analytic sessions it became apparent that these were actually dream events (psychical reality) that she was mistaking for real events (external reality) … I have sometimes observed a possibly related phenomenon in the neuropsychological assessment of such patients. When I ask them to recall a story I have recited to them, their recollection of the story is contaminated by material clearly deriving

from thoughts that had occurred to them while I was reciting the story. The thoughts about the story are then confused with the story itself. For example, a patient said — as if it were part of a story I had read to him — that one of the characters in the story said: 'and how am I ever going to remember that; doesn't the doctor realize I've been dreadfully ill?'

13 See, in particular, Jorge Luis Borges, 'Pierre Menard, Author of the Quixote', trans. Anthony Bonner, in *Ficciones* (New York: Grove Press, 1962), 45–55.

14 See Peter Holland and Adrian Poole, 'Series Introduction', in *Great Shakespeareans,* ed. Holland and Poole (London: Continuum Press, 2009–2012), vii–viii.

15 W. Moelwyn Merchant, '*A Midsummer Night's Dream*: A visual recreation', in *Early Shakespeare, Stratford-upon-Avon Studies III,* ed. John Russell Brown and Bernard Harris (London, Edward Arnold, 1961), 183.

16 Borges, 'Everything and Nothing', in *Labyrinths: Selected Stories and Other Writings,* trans. J. E. Irby (New York: Penguin, 2000), 249.

17 Britten, 'A New Britten Opera', in *Observer Weekend Review* (5 June 1960), 9.

18 Britten, 'A New Britten Opera', 9.

19 See Daniel Albright, *Musicking Shakespeare: A Conflict of Theatres,* Eastman Studies in Music, 45 (Rochester, NY: University of Rochester Press, 2007), particularly 265–96; Philip Brett, 'Britten's Dream', in *Musicology and Difference* (Berkeley, CA: University of California Press, 1993), 259–80; Mervyn Cooke, 'Britten and Shakespeare: *A Midsummer Night's Dream*', in *The Cambridge Companion to Benjamin Britten,* ed. Mervyn Cooke (Cambridge: Cambridge University Press, 1999), 129–46. I would also heartily recommend Wilfrid Mellers, 'The Truth of the *Dream*?' in *The Britten Companion,* ed. Christopher Palmer (London: Faber and Faber, 1984), 181–91. In particular, I find Albright's thesis of a 'conflict of theatres' very telling in light of my attempts to define the intertextual field of Britten's opera as a kind of alternate theatre. 'Shakespeare's favorite dramatic device', writes Albright, 'is to juxtapose two kinds of theatres within a single play ... By abutting different drama-games, Shakespeare calls attention to the inadequacy of anyone taken singly — and perhaps gestures at the world beyond the play, "real life", which isn't a game, or which is a game, but a game played by conflicting and semi-incomprehensible rules ... ' (29)

20 In her virtuosic exploration of sixteenth-century mnemotechnics, *The Art of Memory* (London: Routledge and Kegan Paul, 1966), Francis Yates describes the utopian project of Giulio Camillo Delmino, one of the more celebrated-and-then-forgotten intellectuals of the time; Yates goes so far as to suggest that Shakespeare modelled his Globe Theatre on Camillo's 'theatre of memory'. Without wanting to defend this rather tenuous connection, I would venture that Camillo's alleged theatre offers a quite apt model (and an alternative to the *Wunderblock*) for the intertextual storehouse contained in Britten's opera – or for that matter, the operas of many others. Here is Viglius describing Camillo's theatre in a letter to Erasmus (Yates, 31–2):

> The work is of wood, marked with many images, and full of little boxes; there are various orders and grades in it. He gives a place to each individual figure and ornament, and he showed me such a mass of papers that, though I always heard that Cicero was the fountain of richest eloquence, scarcely would I have that one author could contain so much

or that so many volumes could be pieced together out of his writings. …
He calls this theater of his by many names, saying now that it is a built
or constructed mind and soul, and now that it is a windowed one. He
pretends that all things that the human mind can conceive and which
we cannot see with the corporeal eye, after being collected together by
diligent meditation, may be expressed by certain corporeal signs in such
a way that the beholder may at once perceived with his eyes everything
that is otherwise hidden in the depths of the human mind.

[21] Dorothy Kehler, 'The Critical Backstory and The State of the Art', in *A Midsummer
Night's Dream: A Critical Guide*, ed. Regina Bucola (London: Continuum Press,
2009), 15–43.

[22] See in particular Gilles Deleuze's famous 'letter to a harsh critic' (*Negotiations,
1972–1990*, trans. M. Jouphin (New York: Columbia University Press, 1995), 6)
in which he envisions

the history of philosophy as a sort of buggery or (it comes to the same
thing) immaculate conception. I saw myself as taking an author from
behind and giving him a child that would be his own offspring, yet
monstrous. It was really important for it to be his own child, because
the author had to actually say all I had been saying. But the child was
bound to be monstrous too, because it resulted from all sorts of shifting,
slipping dislocations, and hidden emissions that I really enjoyed.

[23] G. W. Leibniz, *Dissertatio de arte combinatoria* (1666), in *Logical Papers*, ed. and
trans. G. H. R. Parkinson (Oxford: Oxford University Press, 1966). Here is the
extended passage:

A proposition is made up of subject and predicate; hence all propositions are combinations. Hence the logic of inventing [discovering]
propositions involves solving this problem: 1. given a subject, [finding]
the predicates; 2. given a predicate, finding the subjects [to which it
may] apply, whether by way of affirmation or negation.

[24] Albright, *Musicking Shakespeare*, 197.

[25] Ibid., 197. Here is the complete passage:

Of course, all comedies embrace disorder; but not all comedies posit
some mechanism of science or theology that explicitly accounts for
disorder … In the absence of the devil, and God, and human free will,
what mechanisms exist for distributing desirable and undesirable things
at random to the just and to the unjust? The most important mechanism
is Fortuna …

[26] See among other critical and interpretative writings Frank Kermode, 'The
Mature Comedies', in *Early Shakespeare, Stratford-upon-Avon Studies 3*, ed. John
Russell Brown and Bernard Harris (London: Edward Arnold, 1961), 211–27; Jan
Kott, 'The Bottom Translation', trans. Daniela Miedzyrzecka, in *Assays: Critical
Approaches to Medieval and Renaissance Texts*, ed. Peggy A. Knapp and Michael A.
Stugrin (Pittsburgh, PA: University of Pittsburgh Press, 1981), vol. 1: 117–49;
Louis A. Montrose, ' "Shaping Fantasies": Figurations of Gender and Power in
Elizabethan Culture', *Representations* 1.2 (1983): 61–94; 'A Kingdom of Shadows',
in *The Theatrical City: Culture, Theatre, and Politics in London 1596–1649*, ed.
David L. Smith, Richard Strier and David Bevington (Cambridge: Cambridge

University Press, 1995), 68–86; *The Purpose of Playing: Shakespeare and the Cultural Politics of the Elizabethan Theatre* (Chicago, IL: University of Chicago Press, 1996); Alan Sinfield, 'Cultural Materialism and Intertextuality: The Limits of Queer Reading in *A Midsummer Night's Dream* and *The Two Noble*, in *Shakespeare Survey* 56 (2003): 67–78.

27 Humphrey Carpenter, *Benjamin Britten: a Biography* (London: Faber and Faber, 1992), 394.

28 This thought experiment was inspired by a passage from David Selbourne's book *The Making of A Midsummer Night's Dream: an eye-witness account of Peter Brook's production from first rehearsal to first night* (London: Methuen, 1982), 25. The passage follows:

> The session ends with further tentative exploration. Its first subject is the speech 'Over hill, over dale', which begins the Second Act. As an initial step, Brook asks that its lines be spoken in alternation by two actors; then that each *line* be divided in half between actors; then that each *word* of each line be spoken in alternation by two actors. The same exercise is repeated, using four actors, the allocations of lines and parts of lines being made by the actors themselves on quick impulse ... For the third step, Brook says: 'Now bring something extra to the pattern. Listen to the rhythm of whoever is speaking. Complement it by echo and repetition of word or line. Take over the one from the other. Take it like a jazz improvisation.' The effect of the swift susurration (in the creaking studio) is immediate and electric ... 'Be freer still' says Brook ...

29 Doundou Chil, *Classical Iconoclast*, 23 September 2009, available at http://classical-iconoclast.blogspot.com/2009/09/unknown-britten-new-material-nmc.html (accessed 18 January 2011).

30 Benjamin Britten, *Unknown Britten*, Northern Sinfonia conducted by Thomas Zehetmair, NMC D140, compact disc, 2010.

31 Whitney Davis, *Replications: Archaeology, Art History, Psychoanalysis* (University Park, PA: Penn State University Press, 1996), 30.

32 The premise of the unconscious as 'unknown knowledge', as knowledge one doesn't know or understand oneself to 'have', is a widely circulating trope across many schools of psychoanalysis (Freudian, Kleinian, Lacanian). Many have written about this aspect of the unconscious; Christopher Bollas gives a particularly attentive and articulate account of it in his book *The Shadow of the Object: Psychoanalysis of the Unthought Known* (New York: Columbia University Press, 1987).

33 Davis, *Replications*, p. 30.

34 See in particular Donald Mitchell and Hans Keller, *Benjamin Britten: a Commentary on His Works from a Group of Specialists* (London: Rockliff, 1952); Keller, 'The Psychology of Opera' in *Music and Psychology: From Vienna to London, 1939–52*, ed. Christopher Wintle (London: Plumbago Books, 2003), 121–56; Philip Brett, 'Britten and Grimes', *The Musical Times* 118 (December 1977): 995–1000; Humphrey Carpenter, *Benjamin Britten* (1992); Claire Seymour, *The Operas of Benjamin Britten: Expression and Evasion* (Suffolk: Boydell Press, 2004); and J. P. E. Harper-Scott, 'Being-with Grimes: The Problem of the Others in

Britten's First Opera', in *Art and Ideology in European Opera: Essays in Honour of Julian Rushton,* ed. Rachel Cowgill, David Cooper, and Clive Brown (Suffolk: Boydell Press, 2010), 362–81.

[35] Sigmund Freud, 'The Unconscious' (1915), in *SE* 14: 169.

[36] For a fascinating (if slightly biassed) survey of the adaptations of Purcell's stage works (Britten being one of the most ambitious adaptors), see Michael Burden's essay 'Purcell Debauch'd: the dramatick operas in performance', in *Performing the Music of Henry Purcell,* ed. Michael Burden (Oxford: Oxford University Press, 1996), 145–62.

[37] Harold Bloom, *The Anxiety of Influence: A Theory of Poetry,* 2nd ed. (New York: Oxford University Press, 1997), 96.

[38] See Freud, *The Interpretation of Dream,* Ch. 6, 'The Dream Work', in *SE* 5: 277–508. In this, by far the largest chapter of *The Interpretation,* Freud lays out in exhaustive detail the four mechanisms by which dream work operates: *Verdichtung* (condensation), *Verschiebung* (displacement), *Rücksicht auf Darstellbarkeit* (considerations of representability) and *sekundäre Bearbeitung* (secondary revision).

[39] See Jacques-Alain Miller's concluding speech at the 'Rally of the Impossible Professions: Beyond the False Promises of Security', hosted by London Society of the New Lacanian School on 20 September 2008, available at http://www.youtube.com/watch?v=OwrYXfiu1o4, (accessed 22 July 2011).

[40] Eric Roseberry, 'A Note on the Four Chords in Act II of "A Midsummer Night's Dream" ', *Tempo* (New Series) 66/67 (1963): 36–7.

[41] Roseberry, 'A Note': 36.

[42] Roseberry, 'A Note': 37.

[43] These are the opening lines of the Keats's 'sonnet to sleep' with which Britten closes the cycle of songs in his *Serenade for Tenor, Horn, and Strings* of 1942 (the entire work ends, as it began, with an extended call for unaccompanied horn).

[44] Jonathan Culler, 'The Call of the Phoneme', in *On Puns: The Foundation of Letters* (Oxford: Basil Blackwell, 1988), 3–4.

[45] Samuel Johnson, 'Preface to Shakespeare', in *Poetry and Prose,* ed. Mona Wilson (London, 1970), 500, cited in Culler, 'The Call', 6–7.

[46] The original phrase 'a forza di levare' comes from Michelangelo Buonarroti's 1549 letter to Benedetto Varchi ('... io intendo scultura, quella che si fa *per forza di levare*: quella che si fa per via di porre, è simile alla pittura ...'), in Gaetano Milanesi, ed., *Le Lettere di Michelangelo Buonarroti* (Firenze: Le Monnier, 1875), 522.

[47] The 'Interview Chords' in *Billy Budd,* Act 2, scene 2 are, in turns out, a source of remarkable scrutiny in Britten studies. Among the more elaborate engagements are: Arnold Whittall, ' "Twisted Relations": Method and Meaning in Britten's *Billy Budd*', *Cambridge Opera Journal* 2/2 (1990): 145–71; Clifford Hindley, 'Britten's "Billy Budd": The "Interview Chords" Again', *The Musical Quarterly* 78/1 (Spring 1994): 99–126; and Philip Rupprecht, *Britten's Musical Language* (Cambridge: Cambridge University Press, 2001), 130–5.

[48] See Franz Liszt, 'Über Mendelssohns Musik zum Sommernachtstraum', *Neue Zeitschrift für Musik* 40 (26 May 1854): 236. See also Marian Wilson Kimber,

'Reading Shakespeare, Seeing Mendelssohn: Concert Readings of *A Midsummer Night's Dream*, ca. 1850–1920', *The Musical Quarterly* 89 (2006): 199–236.

49 See Cooke, 'Britten and Shakespeare', 138.

50 As an adult Britten lost no great love over Bruckner; but the composer's earliest works were not at all immune to Bruckner's sound, as can be discerned from Britten's Overture in B-flat minor, written in the summer of the composer's thirteenth year. See Christopher Mark, 'Juvenilia (1922–1932)', in *The Cambridge Companion to Benjamin Britten*, 18.

51 The first quote is taken from a postcard sent by Britten to Grace Williams while he was still in Barcelona; all other quotes taken from Britten's personal diary (19 April, 1 May, 30 November, and 9 December, 1943 respectively). All passages are published in *Letters from a Life*, ed. Donald Mitchell and Philip Reed (London: Faber Music, 1998), vol. 1: 425–6.

52 Britten's sonnet setting at the end of the *Nocturne* is widely regarded as one of his finest musical treatments of a text. An unabashed lyrical declaration of love from Britten to his partner Peter Pears (who sang the tenor part at the première), it is also a musical declaration of love to another: Gustav Mahler, two of whose symphonic slow movements are conflated and condensed here (the third movement, 'Ruhevoll (Poco Adagio)' from Symphony No. 4, and, far more directly, the 'Andante moderato' second movement from Symphony No. 6). Again, Shakespeare's presence seems to function less as an end than a means of 'speaking in the high style', and, furthermore, a patriarchal one: in marked contrast to the other songs in this quasi-cycle, 'When I most wink' is forged in a patently nineteenth-century Germanic-Romantic style, with sweeping string lines and slow-rolling timpani. Nonetheless, Shakespeare's poetry is allowed to retain 'a verbal music of its own', existing on a 'quite different level' from Britten's 'musicking' register, which corresponds to Mahler through identical keys (Eb major and C minor in Mahler 6/II), remarkably similar gestural and melodic inflections, uncanny correspondences in orchestration and so on. Numerous commentators have offered fine accounts of the *Nocturne* (see below), but Donald Mitchell (' "Now Sleeps the Crimson Petal": Britten's Other "Serenade" ', *Tempo* 169 (1989): 22–7) is especially insightful on the Shakespeare sonnet's role as an perspectival inverter:

> 'When most I wink, then do mine eyes best see,' lifts the cycle onto an entirely fresh plane of experience: it is the reality offered by a loved one, the work tells us, that is in fact more real than the nocturnal visions of the 'real' world, whether its beauties or its nightmares. The shift in perspective is radical; but in the *Nocturne* it proves to have been elaborately prepared, so that the final avowal of love emerges as an entirely logical and inescapable — though unforeseen — *denouement*.

See also Imogen Holst, 'Britten's *Nocturne*', *Tempo* 5 (1958–9): 14–22; Arnold Whittall, *The Music of Britten and Tippett: Studies in Themes and Techniques* (Cambridge: Cambridge University Press, 1982), 170–5; Christopher Palmer, 'The Orchestral Song-Cycles', in *The Britten Companion*, ed. Christopher Palmer (London: Faber and Faber, 1984), 181–91; Donald Mitchell, 'Violent Climates', in *The Cambridge Companion to Benjamin Britten*, 129–46.

53 Italo Calvino, rehearsing a venerable trope (and paraphrasing Borges and David Hume in particular), writes,

> I read in a book that the objectivity of thought can be expressed using the verb 'to think' in the impersonal third person: saying not 'I think' but 'it thinks' as we say 'it rains' ... Will I ever be able to say, 'Today it writes,' just like 'Today it rains,' 'Today it is windy'? ... And for the verb 'to read'? Will we be able to say 'Today it reads' as we say 'Today it rains'?

See Calvino, *If on a Winter's Night a Traveler*, trans. William Weaver (Orlando, FL: Harcourt, 1981), 176.

54 It's interesting to note that Berg's Concerto has an elaborate programme (which Britten could not have known in 1960), complete with its own complex and ambivalent fantasy of forbidden forest love; among other materials which Berg metabolized into his score is the Carinthian folk tune 'Ein Vogel auf'm Zwetschgenbaum'. See Anthony Pople, *Berg: Violin Concerto* (Cambridge: Cambridge University Press, 1991), particularly 60–4.

55 For an unparalleled analysis of one such set of 'verbariae' see Nicolas Abraham and Maria Torok, *The Wolf Man's Magic Word: A Cryptonomy*, trans. Nicholas Rand (Minneapolis, MN: University of Minnesota Press, 1986). Jacques Derrida's forward to the volume, 'Fors', offer an excellent example of types of constellations found in the Wolf Man's psyche (xl):

> Schematically: the six in the six wolves [*sechs*] ... is translated into Russian (*chiest*: perch, mast, and perhaps sex, close to *chiestero* and *chiesterka*, 'the six,' 'the lot of six people,' close to *siestra*, sister, and its diminutive, *siestorka*, sissy, towards which the influence of the German *Schwester* had oriented the decipherment: thus, within the mother tongue, through an essentially verbal relay this time, the sister is associated with the phobic image of the wolf. But the relay is nevertheless not semantic; it comes from a lexical contiguity or a formal consonance.

56 Freud, 'The Unconscious', in *SE* 14: 187.
57 Freud, *The Interpretation of Dreams*, in *SE* 5: 179.
58 There is something to be said for the notion of a Puck complex as well – one that would work similarly to that of Bottom in its unswerving dedication to misprision, but would replace Bottom's fructifying memory-slips with a willful, perverse literalism. In Act 3, scene 2 of Shakespeare's text (lines omitted by Britten), Oberon castigates Puck for screwing things up royally:

> What hast thou done? Thou hast mistaken quite,
> And laid the love-juice on some true-love's sight.
> Of thy misprision must perforce ensue
> Some true love turn'd, and not a false turn'd true. (3.2.88–91)

Puck, when pressed, is cognizant but not re-cognizant, and would not change a thing about his latest changing:

> Believe me, king of shadows, I mistook.
> Did not you tell me I should know the man
> By the Athenian garment he had on?
> And so far blameless proves my enterprise,
> That I have 'nointed an Athenian's eyes;

And so far am I glad it so did sort
As this their jangling I esteem a sport. (3.2.347–53)

59 These lines have occasioned great enterprise among Shakespeare scholars, and reveal an intertextual chain of considerable complexity in its own right. Kermode (1961), for instance, identifies Bottom's words as an indisputable 'parody of 1 Corinthians 2:9–10' and quotes the original passage thus:

> Eye hath not seen, nor ear heard, neither have entered into the heart of man the things which God hath prepared for them that love him. But God hath revealed *them* unto us by his Spirit: for the Spirit searcheth all things, yea, the deep things of God.

But Jan Kott (1981) points out that Kermode is citing the King James version; in the Tyndale (1534) and Geneva New Testament (1557) versions, the final verse is translated as 'the Spirite searcheth all thinges, ye the botome of Goddes secrettes'. As Kott would have it, then, Shakespeare's Bottom is a meta-misprision-algorithm, working out the kinks in a specific translation of scripture. Kathryn K. Lynch, on the other hand, believes the misprision to extend beyond the obvious presence of Paul; she maintains that Shakespeare's Bottom provides a means of rewriting one of Chaucer's "dream visions" from the *House of Fame*:

> I wote wel I am here
> But whether in body or in goost
> I not ywys but god thou wast
> For more clere entendement
> Nas me never yet ysent. (980–4)

See Kathryn K. Lynch, 'Baring Bottom: Shakespeare and the Chaucerian Dream Vision', in *Reading Dreams: The Interpretation of Dreams from Chaucer to Shakespeare*, ed. Peter Brown (Oxford: Oxford University Press, 1999), 99–124.

60 'Obviously', wrote Freud in a relatively short note on dream-interpretation in 1925, 'one must hold oneself responsible for the evil impulses of one's dreams. What else is one to do with them? Unless the content of the dream (rightly understood) is inspired by alien spirits, it is a part of my own being.' See Freud, 'Some Additional Notes on Dream-Interpretation as a Whole', in *SE* 19: 133.

61 See Jonathan Gil Harris, 'Puck/Robin Goodfellow', in *Fools and Jesters in Literature, Art, and History: a bio-bibliographical sourcebook*, ed. Vicki K. Janik (Westport, CT: Greenwood Press, 1998), 351–62; see especially 353.

62 For an interesting exploration of the intertextualities of Strauss's own tone-poem (in which it is proposed that *Till Eulenspiegel* crafts a complex parody of Wagner's *Siegfried Idyll*, see James Hepokoski, 'Framing *Till Eulenspiegel*', *Nineteenth-Century Music* 30.1 (Spring 2006): 4–43, particularly the last section.

63 See Jonathan Gil Harris, *Shakespeare and Literary Theory* (Oxford Shakespeare Topics) (Oxford: Oxford University Press, 2010), 61:

> Think, for example, of the handkerchief in *Othello*. On the one hand, it is a singular object. On the other, it is a ceaselessly mobile actor in a network that conjoins many people, many narratives, and many times. The handkerchief forms rhizomatic connections with the play's characters: people use it to bandage an aching head (3.3.290–1) and 'wipe [a] beard' (3.3.444), or blow a nose, clean an ear, and dab a

pair of lips. But it enters also into networks that transform the world through which it moves — and in the process, it too is transformed. As the handkerchief is passed from person to person, its meanings keep changing.

[64] See Musica's opening arioso in Act 1 of Alessandro Striggio's libretto for Monteverdi's *L'Orfeo*, in particular the fifth and last stanza: 'Now while I alternate my songs, / now happy, now sad, / let no small bird stir among these trees, / no noisy wave be heard on these river banks, / and let each little breeze halt in its course.'

[65] The connection between Britten's *ritornelli* and the scene between the child and the trees in Ravel's *L'Enfant* has been noted by Cooke in 'Britten and Shakespeare', 137: 'The chords are linked by atmospheric string glissandi, an idea which may have been consciously borrowed from the music for the swaying tees in Ravel's opera …' I would suggest that the associative constellation connecting these two passages is stranger, richer, and more detailed than the conscious connection Cooke identifies, and that the words and images in Colette's libretto are crucial for understanding this connection – in particular the final transformation of Britten's *ritornelli* into the accompaniment for Tytania's coloratura soprano, which finds its parallel in the coloratura dragonfly in Ravel's score. Here is the complete passage from the libretto:

> THE CHILD, *opening his arms*: 'Ah! What a joy to find you again, my garden!'
> THE TREE, *groaning*: 'Ah, my wound … my wound … The wound you inflicted but yesterday in my side with the knife you stole … Alas! It is still bleeding sap …
> THE TREES, *groaning and swaying*: 'Our wounds … our wounds … they are still fresh and continue to bleed sap … Wicked child!'
> *The Child, moved with pity, leans his head against the bark of the big tree. A dragonfly passes, shrivels and disappears. She repasses and repasses again. Others follow her. A rose colored moth imitates her. Other moths, other dragonflies.*

[66] Albright, *Musicking Shakespeare*, Pt. III, in particular 291–6.

[67] Brian Kane was an invaluable partner in conceiving and visualizing the data in this area.

[68] Britten's music for Thisby in the *Pyramus* skit constitutes something of an intertextual tour-de-force in the opera, at least as far as operatic history is concerned. Many have pointed out that Thisby's first aria ('O wall, full often hast thou heard my moans') is a double parody, of both a text and a performance: the text is Lucia's 'mad scene' ('Il dolce suono … Spargi d'amaro pianto') from the last act of Donizetti's 1835 opera *Lucia di Lamermoor*; the performance is none other than Joan Sutherland's rendition of this scene in Franco Zeffirelli's famous Covent Garden production of 1959. (Pears had a fabulous time exaggerating Sutherland's *grande dame* mannerisms in rehearsals and during the première performances, and often left the audience in stitches.) Interestingly, though, Britten's actual Thisby music bears a closer resemblance to other famous nineteenth-century Italian arias for the flute/harp/disconsolate-young-female-lover complex; Thisby's first aria is considerably closer in figuration to 'Perché non ho del vento' in Act 1 of Donizetti's *Rosamonda d'Inghilterra*, and also

Bellini's 'A una fonte afflitto e solo' from Act 3 of *I Puritani.* Interestingly enough, this trope can be traced back to yet another Shakespeare heroine: Desdemona, singing 'Assisa a pie d'un salice' in Act 3 of Rossini's *Otello.* By the end of Act 3 of Britten's *Dream,* however, a listener would have already heard music remarkably resonant with Thisby's: the doting aria Tytania sings Bottom ('Be kind and courteous') upon waking under Oberon's spell in Act 2. What do these two characters have in common, besides their mutual status as marionette-like figures, singing machines built to carry out (with notable hitches!) an alien will? Britten bases both their arias in part on a common musical text, the 'wind-up aria' of an actual marionette, the automaton Olympia in Offenbach's *Les Contes d'Hoffman.* While Thisby's music in Act 3 does not sound very much like Tytania's in Act 2, they stem from a common source – which is itself a rather blistering parody of precisely the Italianate trope Britten and Pears do their best to send up. For more on Offenbach's Olympia, see Carolyn Abbate, *In Search of Opera* (Princeton, NJ: Princeton University Press, 2003), in particular 200–1; and Heather Hadlock, *Mad Loves: Women and Music in Offenbach's 'Les Contes d'Hoffmann'* (Princeton, NJ: Princeton University Press, 2000).

[69] Britten's Quince also re-/mis-writes the 'Western Union Boy' (another awkward messenger trying to hold it together in the shadow of his recipient) in the composer's first work for the musical stage, *Paul Bunyan,* written in collaboration with Auden (who wrote the libretto) and premiered in New York City in 1941.

[70] Verdi did not directly set Shakespeare's text (or a translation of it), but rather had his friend and librettist Francesco Maria Piave adapt it (with some additional 'help' from Andrea Maffei); allegedly, Verdi became acquainted with the entirety of Shakespeare's play only *after* he had completed work on his opera. See Daniel Albright's chapter in this volume.

[71] Interestingly, this results in Britten's *Dream* citing not one but *both* of Stravinsky's works in which a hapless naïf is forced to bargain with the devil (the older composer's *L'Histoire* informs Puck's music).

[72] For an especially penetrating exploration of this topic, see Heather Wiebe's wonderful article 'The Rake's Progress as Opera Museum', *Opera Quarterly* 25/1–2 (Winter–Spring 2009): 6–27.

[73] See Britten's Letter 717 (to George and Marion Harewood), 2 October 1951, in *Letters from a Life,* ed. Donald Mitchell, Philip Reed, and Mervyn Cooke (Berkeley, CA: University of California Press, 2004), vol. 3 (1946–51): 681.

[74] Albright, 295.

[75] See in particular Niall Rudd, 'Pyramus and Thisbe in Shakespeare and Ovid', in *Creative Imitation and Latin Literature,* ed. David West (Cambridge: Cambridge University Press, 1979), 73–93; and Jonathan Bate, *Shakespeare and Ovid* (Oxford: Clarendon Press, 1993).

[76] Carpenter's biography paints a psychologically astute portrait of the tumultuous relationship between Britten and Auden, and identifies it as a key to the formation of Britten's adult psyche; for a far more thorough and detailed account of the actual work the two artists did together, see Donald Mitchell's *Britten and Auden in the Thirties: The Year 1936* (Suffolk: Boydell Press, 1981).

Select Bibliography

Abbate, Carolyn. *In Search of Opera*. Princeton, NJ: Princeton University Press, 2003.

Albright, Daniel. *Berlioz's Semi-Operas*. Rochester, NY: University of Rochester Press, 2001.

—*Musicking Shakespeare: A Conflict of Theatres*. Eastman Studies in Music, 45. Rochester, NY: University of Rochester Press, 2007.

Barzun, Jacques. *Berlioz and the Romantic Century*. 2 vols. Boston: Little, Brown and Company, 1950; 3rd ed., New York: Columbia University Press, 1969.

Berlioz, Hector. *Correspondance générale*. Edited by Pierre Citron et al. 8 vols. Paris: Flammarion, 1972–2003.

—*Critique Musicale*. Edited by H. Robert Cohen, Yves Gérard, Anne Bongrain, Marie-Hélène Coudroy-Saghaï et al. 6 vols [of a projected ten]. Paris: Buchet/ Chastel, 1996–2007.

—*Evenings with the Orchestra*. Translated and edited by Jacques Barzun. Chicago, IL: University of Chicago Press, 1999.

—*Mémoires*. Edited by Pierre Citron. Paris: Flammarion, 1991; English translation by David Cairns, *The Memoirs of Hector Berlioz*, edited by David Cairns. New York: Knopf, 2002.

Bernstein, Jane. '"Bewitched, bothered and bewildered": Lady Macbeth, sleepwalking and the demonic in Verdi's Scottish opera'. *Cambridge Opera Journal* 14, 1 & 2 (2002): 31–46.

Bloom, Harold. *The Anxiety of Influence: A Theory of Poetry*. 2nd ed. New York: Oxford University Press, 1997.

Bloom, Peter. 'Un épisode (politique) de la vie de Berlioz'. In *Musique, esthétique et société en France au XIXᵉ siècle*, edited by Damien Colas, Florence Gétreau, and Malou Haine. Wavre: Margada, 2007.

—ed. *The Cambridge Companion to Berlioz*. Cambridge: Cambridge University Press, 2000.

—ed. *Berlioz: Past, Present, Future*. Rochester, NY: University of Rochester Press, 2003.

—ed. *Berlioz: Scenes from the Life and Work*. Rochester, NY: University of Rochester, 2008.

Brett, Philip. 'Britten and Grimes'. *The Musical Times* 118 (1977): 995–1000.

—'Britten's Dream'. In *Musicology and Difference*. Berkeley, CA: University of California Press, 1993.

Britten, Benjamin. *Letters from a Life*. Edited by Donald Mitchell, Philip Reed, and Mervyn Cooke. 4 vols. London: Faber Music, 1998–2008.

Budden, Julian. *The Operas of Verdi.* 3 vols. New York: Oxford University Press, 1973–81.

Burden, Michael. 'Purcell Debauch'd: the dramatick operas in performance'. In *Performing the Music of Henry Purcell*, edited by Michael Burden. Oxford: Oxford University Press, 1996.

Cairns, David. *Berlioz: The Making of an Artist 1803–1832.* London: Deutsch, 1989.

Carpenter, Humphrey. *Benjamin Britten: a Biography.* London: Faber & Faber, 1992.

Claudon, Francis, 'A propos de *Tristan*: Wagner et Shakespeare: Ja dramaturgie du sublime'. In *D'Eschyle à Genêt: homage à Francis Pruner.* Dijon: Editions universitaires dijonnaises: Diffusion, J.-P. Collinet, 1986.

Conati, Marcello and Mario Medici, (eds) *The Verdi-Boito Correspondence.* Translated by William Weaver. Chicago, IL: University of Chicago Press, 1994.

Cooke, Mervyn. 'Britten and Shakespeare: *A Midsummer Night's Dream*'. In *The Cambridge Companion to Benjamin Britten*, edited by Mervyn Cooke. Cambridge: Cambridge University Press, 1999.

Deathridge, John. *Wagner Beyond Good and Evil.* Berkeley, Los Angeles, CA, and London: University of California Press, 2008.

Folkerth, Wes. *The Sound of Shakespeare.* London: Routledge, 2002.

Foster, Daniel. *Wagner's Ring Cycle and the Greeks.* Cambridge: Cambridge University Press, 2010.

Grey, Thomas. S. 'Richard Wagner and the Legacy of French Grand Opera'. In *The Cambridge Companion to Grand Opera*, edited by David Charlton. Cambridge and New York: Cambridge University Press, 2003.

—'*Meister* Richard's apprenticeship: the early operas (1833–1840)'. In *The Cambridge Companion to Richard* Wagner, edited by Thomas S. Grey. Cambridge: Cambridge University Press, 2008.

Habicht, Werner. 'Shakespeare and the German imagination: cult, controversy, and performance'. In *Shakespeare: World Views*, edited by Heather Kerr, Robin Eaden, and Madge Mitton. Newark, DE: University of Delaware Press, 1996.

Hadlock, Heather. *Mad Loves: Women and Music in Offenbach's 'Les Contes d'Hoffmann'.* Princeton, NJ: Princeton University Press, 2000.

Harper-Scott, J. P. E. 'Being-with Grimes: The Problem of the Others in Britten's First Opera'. In *Art and Ideology in European Opera: Essays in Honour of Julian Rushton*, edited by Rachel Cowgill, David Cooper, and Clive Brown. Suffolk: Boydell Press, 2010.

Hepokoski, James. *Giuseppe Verdi: Falstaff.* Cambridge: Cambridge University Press, 1983.

—*Giuseppe Verdi: Otello.* Cambridge: Cambridge University Press, 1987.

Hindley, Clifford. 'Britten's "Billy Budd": The "Interview Chords" Again'. *The Musical Quarterly* 78.1 (1994): 99–126.

Hoenselaars, Ton. 'Richard Wagner and the great lost Shakespeare play'. *Shakespeare-Jahrbuch* 137 (2001): 38–49.

Inwood, Margaret. *The Influence of Shakespeare on Richard Wagner.* New York: Edwin Mellen Press, 1999.

Istel, Edgar. 'Wagner and Shakespeare'. *Musical Quarterly* 8 (1922): 495–509.

Keller, Hans. 'The Psychology of Opera'. In *Music and Psychology: From Vienna to London, 1939–52*, edited by Christopher Wintle. London: Plumbago Books, 2003.

Kolb, Katherine. 'Hector Berlioz'. In *European Writers: The Romantic Century*. Vol. 6. New York: Scribner's, 1985.

—'Berlioz's *Othello*'. In *The Musical Voyager: Berlioz in Europe*, edited by David Charlton and Katharine Ellis. Frankfurt am Main: Peter Lang, 2007.

—'The Berlioz-Wagner Dialogue'. In *Hector Berlioz: Ein Franzose in Deutschland*, edited by Matthias Brzoska, Hermann Hofer, and Nicole Strohmann. Laaber: Laaber-Verlag, 2005.

Kramer, Lawrence. 'The strange case of Beethoven's "Coriolan": romantic aesthetics, modern subjectivity, and the cult of Shakespeare'. *Musical Quarterly* 79 (1995): 256–80.

Küpper, Ulrike. *William Shakespeare's 'A Midsummer Night's Dream' in the History of Music Theater*. Frankfurt: Lang Verlag, 2011.

Larson, Kenneth. E. 'The origins of the "Schlegel-Tieck" Shakespeare in the 1820s'. *The German Quarterly* 60 (1987): 19–37.

Lippman, Eduard. 'The formation of Wagner's style'. In *Music and Civilization: Essays in Honor of Paul Henry Lang*, edited by Edmond Strainchamps and Maria R. Maniates. New York, 1984.

Macdonald, Hugh. *Berlioz*. London: Dent, 1982.

—'Berlioz's Lost *Roméo et Juliette*'. In *Berlioz: Scenes from the Life and Work*, edited by Peter Bloom. Rochester, NY: University of Rochester, 2008.

Mellers, Wilfrid. 'The Truth of the *Dream*?'. In *The Britten Companion*, edited by Christopher Palmer. London: Faber and Faber, 1984.

Mitchell, Donald. *Britten and Auden in the Thirties: The Year 1936*. Suffolk: Boydell Press, 1981.

—'Violent Climates'. In *The Cambridge Companion to Benjamin Britten*, edited by Mervyn Cooke. Cambridge: Cambridge University Press, 1999.

Mitchell, Donald and Hans Keller. *Benjamin Britten: a Commentary on His Works from a Group of Specialists*. London: Rockliff, 1952.

Nilges, Yvonne. *Richard Wagners Shakespeare*. Würzburg: Königshausen & Neumann, 2007.

Palmer, Christopher. 'The Orchestral Song-Cycles'. In *The Britten Companion*, edited by Christopher Palmer. London: Faber & Faber, 1984.

Pemble, John. *Shakespeare Goes to Paris*. London: Hambledon and London, 2005.

Raby, Peter. 'Shakespeare in Paris, 1827'. In *The Musical Voyager: Berlioz in Europe*, edited by David Charlton and Katharine Ellis. Frankfurt am Main: Peter Lang, 2007.

Rose, Michael. *Berlioz Remembered*. London: Faber & Faber, 2001.

Rosen, David and Andrew Porter, (eds) *Verdi's Macbeth: A Sourcebook*. New York: W. W. Norton & Company, 1984.

Rupprecht, Philip. *Britten's Musical Language*. Cambridge: Cambridge University Press, 2001.

Rushton, Julian. *The Music of Berlioz*. Oxford: Oxford University Press, 2001.

Schmidgall, Gary. *Shakespeare and Opera*. New York: Oxford University Press, 1990.

Seymour, Claire. *The Operas of Benjamin Britten: Expression and Evasion*. Suffolk: Boydell Press, 2004.

Smith, Bruce R. *The Acoustic World of Early Modern England: Attending to the O-Factor*. Chicago, IL: University of Chicago Press, 1999.

Stravinsky, Igor and Robert Craft. *Conversations with Igor Stravinsky*. Berkeley, CA: University of California Press, 1980.

Toye, Francis. *Giuseppe Verdi*. New York: Vintage Books, 1959.

Vazsonyi, Nicholas. *Richard Wagner: Self-Promotion and the Making of a Brand*. Cambridge: Cambridge University Press, 2010.

Wagner, Cosima. *Cosima Wagner: Die Tagebücher*. Edited by Martin Gregor-Dellin and Dietrich Mach, 2 vols. Munich and Zurich: R. Piper & Co. Verlag, 1976–7.

—*Cosima Wagner's Diaries*. Edited by Martin Gregor-Dellin and Dietrich Mack, English trans. by Geoffrey Skelton, 2 vols. London: Collins, 1978.

Wagner, Richard. *Das Liebesverbot*, piano vocal score. Wiesbaden: Breitkopf & Härtel, 1922.

—*My Life*. Translated by Andrew Gray, edited by Mary Whittall. Cambridge, New York, Melbourne: Cambridge University Press, 1983.

—*Richard Wagner: Sämtliche Briefe*. ed. Gertrud Strobel and Werner Wolf (vols. 1–5), Hans-Joachim Bauer and Johannes Forner (vols. 6–8), Klaus Burmeister and Johannes Former (vol. 9), Andreas Mielke (vol 10), Martin Dürrer (vols. 11–13, 16), and Andreas Mielke (vols. 14–15). Leipzig: Deutscher Verlag für Musik, 1967–2000 (vols. 1–9); Wiesbaden, Leipzig and Paris: Breitkopf & Härtel, 2000– (vols. 10–).

—*Richard Wagner: Sämtliche Schriften und Dichtungen*, Volks-Ausgabe. Edited by Richard Sternfeld. 16 vols. Leipizig: Breitkopf & Härtel and C. F. W. Siegel, 1911 (vols. 1–12), 1914 (vols. 13–16).

Wenzel, Peter. 'German Shakespeare Translation: The State of the Art'. In *Images of Shakespeare: Proceedings of the Third Congress of the International Shakespeare Association*, edited by Werner Habicht, D. J. Palmer, and Roger Pringle. Newark, DE: University of Delaware Press, 1988.

Whittall, Arnold. *The Music of Britten and Tippett: Studies in Themes and Techniques*. Cambridge: Cambridge University Press, 1982.

—'"Twisted Relations": Method and Meaning in Britten's *Billy Budd*'. *Cambridge Opera Journal* 2.2 (1990): 145–71.

Williams, Simon. 'Wagner's *Das Liebesverbot*: from Shakespeare to the Well-Made Play'. *Opera Quarterly* 3 (1985): 56–69.

Wilson Kimber, Marian. 'Reading Shakespeare, Seeing Mendelssohn: Concert Readings of *A Midsummer Night's Dream*, ca. 1850–1920'. *Musical Quarterly* 89 (2006): 199–236.

Zaragoza, Georges, (ed.) *Hector Berlioz: Homme de lettres*. Neuilly-lès-Dijon: Éditions du Murmure, 2006.

Index